D1590401

The Story of N

Studies in Modern Science, Technology, and the Environment
Edited by Mark A. Largent

The increasing importance of science over the past 150 years—and with it the increasing social, political, and economic authority vested in scientists and engineers—established both scientific research and technological innovations as vital components of modern culture. Studies in Modern Science, Technology, and the Environment is a collection of books that focuses on humanistic and social science inquiries into the social and political implications of science and technology and their impacts on communities, environments, and cultural movements worldwide.

Matthew N. Eisler, *Overpotential: Fuel Cells, Futurism, and the Making of a Power Panacea*

Mark R. Finlay, *Growing American Rubber: Strategic Plants and the Politics of National Security*

Jill A. Fisher, *Gender and the Science of Difference: Cultural Politics of Contemporary Science and Medicine*

Hugh S. Gorman, *The Story of N: A Social History of the Nitrogen Cycle and the Challenge of Sustainability*

Finn Arne Jørgensen, *More than a Hole in the Wall: The Story of What We Do with Our Bottles and Cans*

Gordon Patterson, *The Mosquito Crusades: A History of the American Anti-Mosquito Movement from the Reed Commission to the First Earth Day*

Thomas Robertson, *The Malthusian Moment: Global Population Growth and the Birth of American Environmentalism*

Jeremy Vetter, *Knowing Global Environments: New Historical Perspectives on the Field Sciences*

The Story of N

A Social History of the Nitrogen Cycle and the Challenge of Sustainability

HUGH S. GORMAN

RUTGERS UNIVERSITY PRESS

NEW BRUNSWICK, NEW JERSEY, AND LONDON

LIBRARY OF CONGRESS CATALOGING-IN-PUBLICATION DATA

Gorman, Hugh S. (Hugh Scott), 1957–

The story of N : a social history of the nitrogen cycle and the challenge of sustainability / Hugh S. Gorman.

p. cm. — (Studies in modern science, technology, and the environment)

Includes bibliographical references and index.

ISBN 978–0–8135–5438–9 (hardcover : alk. paper) — ISBN 978–0–8135–5439–6 (e-book)

I. Nitrogen—Environmental aspects. 2. Nitrogen cycle. 3. Sustainable development. 4. Nature—Effect of human beings on. I. Title.

TD196.N55G67 2013

547'.64—dc23   2012009901

A British Cataloging-in-Publication record for this book is available from the British Library.

Visit our website: http://rutgerspress.rutgers.edu

Manufactured in the United States of America

to Bonnie

CONTENTS

PREFACE

The word *sustainability* has, for good reason, come into common use over the past decade or so. It suggests, among other things, that the planet Earth is finite and that our interactions with the planet should be structured so as to sustain the integrity of Earth systems in a way that is economically viable and socially just. But what will it take to make our interactions with the planet more sustainable? Will a simple nip and tuck of existing environmental policies, along with some clever technological advances and new educational initiatives, do the trick? Or are more fundamental changes needed? These are the questions, framed historically, that lie at the core of this book.

The past, of course, is relevant to these questions. By examining change over time, it is possible to gain a better sense of not only the trajectory that we are on but also the options and possibilities available. With that goal in mind, I examine the history of society's changing interactions with one particular slice of nature: the nitrogen cycle. Anybody familiar with this biogeochemical cycle knows that the history of our interactions with it is rich and complex. Today, flows of nitrogen are intimately entangled with a wide variety of human activities, ranging from growing food and processing sewage to manufacturing explosives and combusting fuels. In many ways, it would be difficult to find a better lens for examining society's changing interactions with the rest of nature.

At the same time, it is important to remember that the main purpose of this book is to examine the notion of sustainability. The nitrogen cycle is simply a powerful organizing device, a stand-in for the rest of nature. One could, of course, focus on any ecological, geophysical, or biogeochemical system. The issue of climate change, for example, has centered attention on how human interactions with the carbon cycle have changed over time. Focusing on the nitrogen cycle serves as an alternative way to examine important changes in the relationship between humans and the rest of nature.

The first half of the story takes place over millennia and involves humans learning to bypass an ecological limit, one associated with the capacity of bacteria to place nitrogen compounds into circulation. By the late nineteenth century, efforts to secure increasingly large quantities of nitrogen for use in fertilizers and explosives stood out as one of the critical challenges facing industrializing societies. Scientists and engineers met that challenge in the years before World War I by developing an inexpensive way to fix atmospheric nitrogen—that is, to transform this inert gas into a chemically active compound. This innovation significantly changed the relationship between humans and the rest of nature. Previously, bacteria (and archaea) had been the only types of organisms capable of fixing nitrogen; industrial fixation gave this ability to humans as well.

The second half of the story takes place mainly in the twentieth century and involves efforts to resolve conflicts associated with too much, rather than too little, nitrogen. In general, as greater amounts of chemically active nitrogen were placed into circulation, some of that material began to accumulate in aquifers, surface water bodies, and even the air, forcing people to wrestle with new concerns. Gradually, those efforts (and efforts to address other environmental concerns) have led to new forms of governance over human interactions with the environment. And at the core of these new forms of governance are human-defined limits replacing the ecological ones previously bypassed. Indeed, one goal of this book is to make this process of establishing and respecting limits, which provides insight into the challenges that lie ahead, more visible.

I refer to this book as a *social history* because I am focusing on human activity, institutions, and learning rather than the dynamics of the nitrogen cycle. The term also suggests that the book is less about heroic individuals than about the social and economic institutions in which they operate. For example, I spend relatively little time discussing the individuals (Fritz Haber and Carl Bosch) who developed the process of industrial fixation that ultimately disseminated throughout the world. To some extent, I limit that discussion simply because much good work has already been written about them. Moreover, what really matter are the economic, political, and social structures that facilitated their innovation. It is safe to say that other engineers and scientists would have stepped up to the challenge if Haber and Bosch had not. Indeed, others had already developed less efficient technologies for industrially fixing nitrogen; from an economic perspective, the Haber-Bosch process simply lowered the costs associated with securing nitrogen from the air. Again, what is essential to examine, especially if one is interested in the notion of sustainability, are the larger social, political, and economic forces that shape such innovations and their dissemination.

As a historian who examines policy choices and technological innovations affecting human interactions with the environment, I have focused most of my previous work on events in the twentieth century. The first half of this book, however, begins well before that period and draws on the work of a wide range of scholars. Integrating this material into an argument about the nature of sustainability without oversimplification and without stepping into specialist territory has been an ongoing challenge, which I have done my best to meet.

My intention from the start has been to keep the book accessible to upper-level undergraduates, regardless of discipline. In the end, by examining, first, how humans learned to bypass an important ecological limit and, second, how societies are now learning to manage the consequences of that action, this book speaks directly to what it means for an industrial society to construct a sustainable relationship with the rest of nature.

ACKNOWLEDGMENTS

The idea for this book took shape while I was on sabbatical as the John Haas Environmental Fellow at the Chemical Heritage Foundation in Philadelphia (2003–4), and the book was finished seven years later while I was on sabbatical as a Fulbright scholar in Panama, hosted by the Centro Internacional para el Desarrollo Sostenible at the Ciudad del Saber (2011). In addition to providing time for research and writing, my institutional home, Michigan Technological University, also provided funds for several research trips. All of this support has been invaluable and greatly appreciated.

It would, of course, be impossible to acknowledge all the colleagues whose scholarly work influenced this book. Here, I want to specifically thank those who reviewed chapters, commented on papers, participated in nitrogen-related paper sessions with me, pointed me to critical material, or simply provided encouragement: Brad Baltensperger, Guillermo Castro, Ed Constant, Tom Crawford, Mary Durfee, Louise Dyble, Mark Finlay, Kathleen Halvorsen, Daniel Holbrook, David Hounshell, Ann Greene, Edward Landa, Adam Levine, Carol MacLennan, Alex Mayer, Audrey Mayer, John McNeill, Edward Melillo, Peter Mickulas, Tom Misa, Robert Nemiroff, Samir Qadir, Fred Quivik, Terry Reynolds, Donna Rilling, Barry Solomon, Genevieve Borg Soule, Joel Tarr, Andrés Tarté, William Toffey, Frank Uekötter, Doreen Valentine, Verena Winiwarter, Lee Vinsel, Mel Visser, Kristoffer Whitney, Audra Wolfe, and Chris Young. In addition, I thank the staffs at the Rockefeller Archive Center; the National Archives and Records Administration in College Park, Maryland, and Atlanta, Georgia; the University Archives at the University of Minnesota; the Michigan State Archives; the Records Center of the Milwaukee Metropolitan Sewerage District; and the Records Center of the Illinois Environmental Protection Agency.

The Story of N

Introduction

On the eastern shore of Mobile Bay in Alabama, they call it a jubilee.[1] When conditions are right, usually in late summer and often at night, crabs and shrimp and fish head for shore and spill onto beaches. There, residents carrying flashlights and coolers arrive at the beach amid calls of "jubilee" and scoop up as much seafood as they can.

For a long time, nobody understood the underlying causes of this phenomenon; many thought it had something to do with the moon.[2] We now know that jubilees are associated with hypoxic conditions in the bay. In essence, the fish and crustaceans are trying to escape pockets of water that do not have enough oxygen. In the case of Mobile Bay, hypoxic conditions—and jubilees—have been occurring for millennia. The bay is shallow, roughly ten feet deep at high tide, and light reaching the bottom of the bay creates a productive environment for crabs and bottom-dwelling fish. On calm summer days, though, the top layer of water can reach unusually high temperatures, sometimes as high as ninety degrees. The result is a stratification of layers, with little mixing between the warmer water above and the cooler water below. If that happens, the bottom layer can become isolated, resulting in oxygen levels dropping below what is needed to support aquatic life. When those conditions push a thriving community of fish and crabs toward the shore, a jubilee—a gift from the bay to the people who inhabit the land—occurs. Conditions return to normal as soon as a stiff breeze stirs the bay and remixes the two layers of water.[3]

Today, in coastal areas around the world, incidents of hypoxia are occurring more frequently and on a larger scale than ever before, but not in ways that direct the bounty of the sea into the arms of jubilant people. In these incidents, a jolt of nutrients, mainly nitrogen-based compounds flowing out of agricultural regions, triggers an explosion of aquatic plant growth. Then, when those organisms die, the decomposition process consumes the available oxygen, turning a portion of the sea into an aquatic desert. What are often referred to as "dead zones" now emerge annually in approximately four hundred different places throughout the world.[4] Each spring, for example, the nutrient-rich water that the Mississippi River discharges into the northern Gulf of Mexico gives rise to a hypoxic dead zone covering about six thousand square miles.[5]

Dead zones are only one of several concerns associated with excessive amounts of chemically active nitrogen compounds cascading through ecological and geophysical systems.[6] Other concerns include red tides, nitrates in groundwater, photochemical smog, acid rain, fine particulates in urban air, climate change, and ozone depletion. The relative importance of these concerns and the impact of nitrogen-related compounds on them vary; but even when the concern or the contribution of nitrogen is minor, it matters. For example, although the concentration of nitrous oxide in the atmosphere is much smaller than that of other greenhouse gases, such as carbon dioxide or methane, nitrous oxide is still a greenhouse gas and any increase in its atmospheric concentration only adds to the problem at hand. Some research suggests that flows of nitrogen play a role in the regulation of carbon dioxide in the atmosphere and that altering those flows complicates the dynamics of climate change (as well as the modeling of those dynamics) in ways that are more subtle than scientists once thought.[7]

The important point is not that nitrogen-related environmental concerns are radically different from other types of environmental concerns. Just the opposite is true. All environmental concerns (and, for that matter, all efforts to address them) involve changes in how people use their environments. In this case, the major change involves humans' learning to manipulate a biogeochemical cycle that lies at the core of nature. For eons, the delivery of nitrogen to plants in ecosystems throughout the world was determined primarily by the activity of nitrogen-fixing, nitrifying, and denitrifying bacteria. Indeed, for most of human history, solar energy-based constraints on the activity of nitrogen-fixing bacteria represented a fundamental ecological limit on the productivity of agricultural systems. Then, humans figured out how to use other energy sources to fix nitrogen without bacteria.[8] Doing so, however, resulted in unexpected consequences. This book is the story, first, of how humans learned to bypass that ecological limit and, second, in response to the conflicts and concerns that emerged, gradually learned to govern their interactions with the environment in new ways. In short, it is a story that uses changes in human interactions with the nitrogen cycle as a way to examine the challenge of sustainability.

Bypassing an Ecological Limit

One of the most significant innovations affecting flows of chemically active nitrogen occurred on the eve of World War I. At the time, agricultural scientists viewed nitrogen as a particularly critical resource. They knew that plants secured the bulk of their elemental material (carbon, oxygen, and hydrogen) directly from air and water. They also realized that plants needed nitrogen in fairly large quantities but that access to the element depended on the presence of nitrogen-rich material in the soil. In particular, for every six pounds of protein harvested from agricultural land, approximately one pound of nitrogen had to be drawn from the soil. In addition, chemical manufacturers, especially those producing gunpowder and high explosives, required large supplies of nitrogenous compounds. The problem was that, over the long term, securing enough nitrogen ultimately depended on how fast nitrogen-fixing bacteria could replace the amount removed from agricultural soil; and in the early twentieth century, those organisms could not keep up with demand. Increasing both the production of explosives and the productivity of agricultural soils depended on finding ways to secure more chemically active nitrogen compounds.

The atmosphere represented a potential source of nitrogen. A century earlier, chemists had learned that air was approximately four-fifths nitrogen. Plants, they knew, could not make direct use of that nitrogen because almost all of it was locked up in an inert tightly bonded molecule (N_2). By the mid-nineteenth century, however, a few scientists suspected that something was fixing atmospheric nitrogen in the soil and making it available to plants, although they were not sure what. Only later, in the 1870s and 1880s, did agricultural scientists verify the existence of microorganisms capable of working symbiotically with plants to convert inert atmospheric nitrogen into chemically active compounds. The activity of these nitrogen-fixing bacteria, they realized, made it possible to harvest crops from the same land year after year without depleting the nitrogen content of the soil.[9]

A thriving market for nitrogen-rich material developed even before scientists reached consensus on the role that microorganisms were playing in fixing nitrogen. In general, nineteenth-century merchants obtained their nitrogen-rich material from distant places, such as from the guano-heavy islands of Peru or from deposits of sodium nitrate discovered in the harsh Chilean desert. Limited amounts of chemically active nitrogen could also be secured from coal in the form of ammonia sulfate, which nineteenth-century manufacturers produced as a byproduct when converting coal into gas for illuminating cities or, later in the century, into coke for iron making. Some nitrogen-rich organic wastes, such as the oil cake left over when manufacturers crushed seeds for their oil content, were available on the market.[10] Animal manure also contained valuable quantities of fixed nitrogen, but all of that material typically went back to the same soil from which it came, simply replacing what had been previously removed.

All of the nitrogen-rich materials available on the market were relatively expensive, in limited supply, or both. In fact, by the end of the nineteenth century, deposits of Peruvian guano had pretty much been mined out. Supplies of ammonia sulfate from coal were also limited; as a byproduct, its availability depended on the demand not for nitrogen but for illuminating gas and iron. Some potential existed for recycling nitrogen from urban sewage, but sanitary engineers in Europe and America had yet to develop systems for accomplishing that.[11] Only supplies of Chilean nitrate could be increased to meet the growing demand for nitrogen; but in the event of a war, shipping channels to Chile were sure to be disrupted.[12]

For these reasons, European leaders desired to see their engineers and scientists develop ways to fix nitrogen directly from the atmosphere. The breakthrough came just before World War I when Fritz Haber and Carl Bosch of Germany developed a catalytic process for mass-producing ammonia from nitrogen in the atmosphere. By that time, other technologies for fixing atmospheric nitrogen had already been developed, but none could do so efficiently enough to compete with imports of Chilean nitrate. Ammonia produced from the Haber-Bosch process, on the other hand, could be priced below all other sources of nitrogen, and the dissemination of this innovation dramatically altered the market for nitrogenous compounds. It also happened to demolish ecological limits on the production of fixed nitrogen that had existed for eons.[13]

Humans, working within this ecological limit, had first started manipulating flows of nitrogen thousands of years earlier, long before anybody knew about bacteria or agricultural chemistry. The first important change in flows of nitrogen came with the emergence of stationary agriculture, when farmers began harvesting crops from the same land year after year. Before stationary agriculture, nitrogen could be removed from the soil in the form of harvested foods with little consequence. After all communities were small and mobile and could shift their activity to new land if need be. With the emergence of stationary agriculture, however, the removal of nitrogen became more significant. Indeed, much of agricultural history revolves around how societies learned, by trial and error, to maintain crop yields by cultivating plants that host nitrogen-fixing bacteria and circulating nitrogen-rich manures back to the soil.[14]

Another important change occurred when nitrogen-related compounds came to be valuable for their use in the production of gunpowder. In the recipe for explosive powder developed by Chinese alchemists in the first millennium, the ingredient required in the largest proportion was the nitrogen compound saltpeter (potassium nitrate). In the fifteenth century, leaders in the emerging nation-states of Europe realized that securing a steady supply of saltpeter, something very difficult to do, was crucial if they hoped to win wars with their neighbors and survive as political entities. By the sixteenth century, state-backed efforts to transform urine-soaked mounds of manure into saltpeter placed the military demand for nitrogen in direct competition with food production.[15]

Efforts to secure saltpeter also produced knowledge important to the development of modern chemistry and agriculture.[16] By the end of the eighteenth century, some of Europe's leading scientists—including Antoine Lavoisier, charged with helping the French secure greater quantities of the elusive material, and Alexander von Humboldt, the scientist-explorer who sent samples of Peruvian guano back to Europe for chemical analysis—were participating in the search for nitrogen-rich material. By the mid-nineteenth century, Europe's scientists knew enough about plant chemistry to realize that the availability of nitrogenous compounds was a main factor limiting the productivity of agricultural soils. In part, this new knowledge encouraged farmers to seek out material containing nitrogen-containing compounds, giving rise to the nineteenth-century markets for guano, Chilean nitrate, and ammonia sulfate from coal.

The existence of these markets initiated a regional change in the relationship between humans and the cycling of nitrogen. By introducing nitrogen fixed by bacteria at other times and places (such as the nitrogen compounds in coal, Peruvian guano, and Chilean nitrates), farmers were able to bypass local ecological limits.[17] The subsequent development of the Haber-Bosch process moved industrial society even further into unknown ecological territory. Like athletes pumping protein-building steroids into their bodies, industrial societies began to pump protein-building chemicals into their agricultural ecosystems, eventually allowing them to reach levels of productivity previously thought impossible. At the same time, with the introduction of automobiles and electric power plants, cities also became a direct source of nitrogen compounds: every new automobile and power plant released additional nitrogen oxides into the atmosphere.

Today, the amount of chemically active nitrogen that humans place into circulation each year—which includes the amount produced by industrial fixation (about 100 million metric tons), the intentional cultivation of nitrogen-fixing hosts such as legumes (about 32 million metric tons), and the unintentional emissions of nitrogen oxides by combustion sources (about 25 million metric tons)—exceeds the amount annually fixed on land by the rest of nature (roughly 110 million metric tons).[18] In many regions of the world, fixed nitrogen is now being added faster than it can be removed by denitrifying bacteria, resulting in an accumulation of chemically active nitrogen compounds in various biogeochemical reservoirs, including aquifers, surface bodies of water, and the atmosphere. And over the past half-century, scientists have linked this accumulation of chemically active nitrogen to a variety of environmental concerns.

Indeed, human activity has come to be a significant component of the biogeochemical cycle we refer to as the nitrogen cycle. Industrial and urban flows of chemically active nitrogen through factories, farms, grocery stores, sewers, treatment facilities, and power plants are now intimately intertwined with flows of nitrogen through streams, seas, the soil, and the atmosphere. As individuals, we now affect some portion of this cycle every time we eat protein, flush our toilets, turn on a light, drive our cars, apply fertilizers, and, in general, participate in the basic activity of an industrial society. Human choices, including technology and policy choices that affect the practices of billions of individuals, have become as important as bacterial activity in the dynamics of this biogeochemical system.

Societies, of course, cannot put the genie of industrially fixed nitrogen back into the bottle. Nor would many people want to. The simple fact is that the world could not feed 7 billion people, half of them living in cities, without supplementing the activity of nitrogen-fixing bacteria—at least not without a radical restructuring of diets and agricultural practices.[19] Societies can, however, learn to reward innovations that make it easier to prevent nitrogen-related environmental concerns and conflicts. Indeed, my main goal in this book is to examine the process by which industrial society is learning (very slowly) to reward this type of innovation.

Establishing Human-Defined Limits

The story told here is not simply a tale of how humans conquer nature and generate environmental concerns in the process. It also examines how societies, in response to various conflicts and concerns, have begun to manage releases of nitrogen in innovative ways. Indeed, many flows of nitrogen are now partially governed by policy tools such as discharge permits, emissions trading programs, ambient air-quality standards, watershed management plans, best management practices for farms, wetland restoration efforts, rules guiding the application of biosolids to agricultural soils, and the regulation of fertilizer use within wellhead management zones. In many ways, these forms of governance can be seen as part of the twenty-first-century nitrogen cycle.

This aspect of the story also provides insight into the notion of sustainability. All changes that disseminate within a society, regardless of whether they are changes in technology and practices or policy and law, involve innovation. Clearly, market societies have been particularly good at encouraging innovation. Indeed, the amount of technological innovation that the world has experienced over the past several centuries staggers the imagination. In less than a half-millennium, the world has gone from supporting 500 million people living in relatively isolated societies dominated by subsistence-level agriculture to one in which billions of people live in cities and interact through a global economy. The flow of capital and information through human networks has become almost as important to survival as is the flow of energy and material (including nitrogen compounds) through farms, factories, cities, and homes. But it would be perilous, of course, to forget that this global economy is intimately tied to the rest of nature and that, at the very least, markets should reflect this reality.

In part, the first societies to embrace market capitalism were also the first to experience industrialization because they rewarded innovation in ways that previous societies had not.[20] In societies that embraced market capitalism, innovators who adopted more efficient ways to produce agricultural and manufactured goods (often through technologies that relied on the division of labor and the application of new forms of energy) acquired more wealth and hence the means to innovate even more. However, with that innovation often came changes that pushed societies into new ethical territory, giving rise to new types of conflicts and new legal questions, including some involving uses of the environment.

In general, industrial societies have sought to govern uses of the environment only when new technologies and practices have led to concerns and conflict. A substantial amount of learning has occurred as a result of such efforts. For example, in the nineteenth century, market capitalism rewarded innovations without any regard to their effect on air quality. Hence, a century ago, smoke laden with particulates, sulfur dioxide, and nitrogen oxides billowed out of countless industrial facilities and residences.[21] By the end of the twentieth century, though, the amount of particulates and gases being emitted into the air had, in most industrial cities, dropped considerably despite significant increases in population and fuel consumption. A parallel story can be told about changes in the amount of pollution-causing wastes that are discharged into water bodies. Over the course of a century, real learning occurred as industrial societies began to govern the release of pollution-causing discharges and, indirectly, the evolution of technological systems.

This learning process involved, of course, more than the development of new technology. It also involved people who valued the same resource in different ways and who learned to articulate their visions of the future as well as a system of governance capable of responding to the resulting conflicts and years of reaching consensus on how to proceed with new air- and water-quality laws. Learning and adaptation continued with the inevitable legal challenges that followed and the gradual emergence of effective forms of governance. In the process, politicians learned a great deal about what various portions of the public were willing to support and, just as important, willing to tolerate. In short, the massive changes that took place depended on the complex co-evolution of public expectations, science and technology, and policy.

Learning to encourage innovations that make our interactions with natural systems more rather than less sustainable is surely a more complex task than managing pollution is. However, the story of society's changing interaction with the nitrogen cycle suggests that the two tasks are not radically different. In both cases, the goal is to construct an economy that recognizes a need for boundaries on how we interact with the rest of nature and rewards innovation that respects those boundaries. Indeed, what follows is an examination, first, of the long-term process by which humans learned to bypass an important ecological limit and, second, are learning to replace it with a new set of boundaries.

This book is organized into four parts. In Part I, two brief chapters explore the emergence of the nitrogen cycle before humans arrived on the scene and the changes that occurred as the first stationary agricultural societies took root. Part II examines the role of science and market capitalism in accelerating the pace of innovation, allowing humans to bypass the activity of nitrogen-fixing bacteria. Part III covers the twentieth-century response to the nitrogen-related concerns that emerged as more nitrogenous compounds flowed into the environment. Finally, a concluding chapter places the entire story into the context of constructing an ecological economy in which innovations that contribute to sustainable practices are rewarded. In the end, this book argues that sustainability is not something that can be achieved without harnessing three powerful, socially constructed systems of knowledge production—engines of innovation—that lie at the core of market societies: (1) market capitalism, which has facilitated technological innovation geared toward the efficient production of goods and services; (2) the process of modern science, which has facilitated the rapid accumulation of positivist, predictive knowledge capable of guiding problem-solving tasks; and (3) the adaptive rule of law, which facilitates the resolution of conflicts in ways in which most members of a society are willing to embrace or at least tolerate without significant resistance and conflict. From this perspective, the challenge of sustainability can be viewed as more of a process than a goal, one in which societies learn to use these systems of knowledge production to develop interactions with the rest of nature that are socially just and economically and ecologically sustainable.

PART I

The Knowledge of Nature

1

The Emergence of a
Biogeochemical Cycle

How did the nitrogen cycle come to be the nitrogen cycle? That is, how has this biogeochemical cycle evolved over time? Strictly speaking, the nitrogen cycle is not an entity capable of evolving. It is not even an entity. After all, when we use the term *nitrogen cycle,* we are imposing a pattern on nature that suits our own interests. What we choose to incorporate into or leave out of the cycle is somewhat arbitrary. That said, what we call the nitrogen cycle depends on the activity of a wide variety of organisms, each carrying evolutionary-acquired knowledge embedded in its genetic material, and these organisms have evolved over time.

If nothing else, asking about the emergence of a biogeochemical cycle reminds us that, when we alter such cycles, we are altering something that took several billion years to reach a dynamic balance. Over the expanse of geological time, as countless species of organisms co-evolved in changing environments, refining their ability to exploit the material available to them, they became part of the cycle through which that material flowed. In the case of nitrogen, different types of bacteria eventually acquired (through evolutionary processes of variation and selection) the ability to fix atmospheric nitrogen, to decompose organic material into ammonia, to convert ammonia into nitrite and nitrate, and to transform those compounds back into gases. The ability of plants to use nitrate as a raw material also involved the evolutionary acquisition of knowledge, as did the ability of certain plants to work symbiotically with nitrogen-fixing bacteria. The notion of sustainability surely has something to do with humans learning to integrate their activities with Earth systems that have been refined by several billions years of evolutionary change.

The Knowledge of Nature

Cosmologists tell us that our entire universe burst into existence approximately 15 billion years ago. In the opening moments of the universe, however, the element we call nitrogen did not exist. No elements existed until
the universe had cooled enough to allow various configurations of mass
and energy to form stable structures. The lightest elements—hydrogen and
helium—formed first. Heavier elements, such as carbon, nitrogen, and oxygen, did not form until much later, when great clusters of matter coalesced
as stars. There, in the center of stars, nuclear fusion converted lighter elements into heavier ones, a process that continued until a star exploded and
dispersed the newly created elements.[1]

To emerge, more complex structures, including molecules that serve as
the basis of life, needed conditions favorable to their formation. One such
set of conditions emerged, cosmologists tell us, after interstellar matter
thrown from the furnace of an exploding star consolidated into a new star
and a handful of orbiting bodies. On one of those bodies, the planet Earth,
something unusual happened: several billion years of evolutionary change
eventually gave rise to a complex web of organisms, ecological relationships,
and geophysical processes.

As it happened, nitrogen atoms turned out to be important in the system
of nature that emerged on Earth. Unlike most elements, nitrogen can bond
in eight different ways—by donating one, two, three, four, or five electrons
or accepting one, two, or three electrons—which makes it exceptionally ver-
satile in joining with other atoms. It is not surprising, then, that nitrogen
came to occupy pivotal positions in two of nature's most crucial building
blocks: amino acids (which are the basic components of all proteins) and
nucleotides (sequences of which serve as the basis of all genetic material).

For the first several hundred million years of Earth's existence, few
complex molecular structures had a chance to form. The young planet was a
hellish place, unrecognizable as the Earth that exists today. Chunks of debris
traveling in the same solar orbit frequently collided with the new planet,
vaporizing on impact and generating tremendous amounts of heat and gas.
Even after the number of collisions dwindled and the surface of the new
planet cooled, countless volcanoes continued to spew forth gases. The planet,
as it turned out, was massive enough to keep most gases from escaping its
gravitational grasp and just far enough from the sun to allow for condensation
and the formation of seas without everything freezing solid. The consensus
among most geologists (but not all) is that this post-cooling atmosphere consisted primarily of carbon dioxide (CO_2), water (H_2O), and molecular nitrogen
(N_2), along with smaller amounts of anything that volcanoes might release,
including hydrogen sulfide (H_2S), methane (CH_4), ammonia (NH_3), sulfur

dioxide (SO_2), and nitric oxide (NO).[2] Electrical storms of mythic proportions, especially those centered around ash-spewing volcanoes, stoked a variety of chemical reactions and served, some theorists suggest, as a source of slightly more complex molecules.[3]

Evolutionary molecular biologists hesitate to discuss the formation of life from lifeless molecules without first discussing a range of different possibilities, including whether the focus should be placed on the first proteins or the first pieces of genetic material. Some suggest, for example, that the critical event occurred when a chain of amino acids happened to form a protein with an important catalytic property: the ability to facilitate the construction of another molecule like itself.[4] Once such a molecule formed, new copies of the structure would be created again and again. Others favor the appearance of a so-called naked gene, a template-like structure constructed from segments of paired nucleotides. If such a structure were to split in two, each half could serve as a template for a new copy of the original structure. If the splitting and rebuilding were to continue, one structure would soon become two, two would become four, then eight, and so on.[5]

Any ability to multiply or replicate, whatever the process and however simple or complex, would have made all the difference in the world: in such cases, a molecular structure could be propagated again and again, at least until the raw material required to form new structures ran out. Furthermore, a crude cycle of variation and selection—the basis of all evolutionary change—would have begun. As new copies of the same structures were created and re-created, variations became inevitable. Differences in environmental conditions—temperature, pressure, pH, the availability of raw material—could easily result in new structures that were slightly different from previous ones. Although most variations might not improve the ability of a molecule to replicate, some variations could. And over millions of years and countless cycles of variation and replication, the most successful replicators would come to dominate.

The continual replication of lifeless molecular structures depends, of course, on a steady supply of raw material and enough energy to keep everything in physical and chemical motion. Otherwise, the process eventually comes to a dead stop. However, as long as some level of variation and replication continues, a scarcity of raw material (such as carbon and nitrogen) can actually accelerate the process of change. After all, any variation that happens to provide some advantage in securing scarce raw material becomes extremely beneficial. For example, any enzyme-like ability to disassemble competing macromolecules and free up their carbon and nitrogen would have spread like wildfire. Of course, any variation that resulted in a replicator becoming resistant to enzymatic attacks would have provided a major advantage and have rapidly disseminated, as would have variations that defeated those defense mechanisms.

The precise evolutionary chain of events is, of course, lost to time. The general consensus, though, is that, over hundreds of millions of years, this crude process of lifeless variation and selection eventually led, about 3.5 billion years ago, to entities that we would recognize as energy-metabolizing living organisms.[6] Evolutionary biologists tell us that the first were probably single-celled organisms capable of surviving in extreme environments and extracting energy from phenomena such as suboceanic thermal vents.[7] In conjunction with those organisms and the cycling of material from one generation to the next came the first biogeochemical flows of material.

Scientists who study the emergence of Earth systems are not in total agreement as to the sequence in which the various components of the current nitrogen cycle emerged. One scenario suggests that the first major nitrogen-manipulating organism to emerge was a denitrifying bacterium, perhaps as early as 3.2 billion years ago, a time when little free oxygen existed in the atmosphere or oceans. In this scenario, these denitrifiers learned—that is, evolved—to "breathe" using nitrogen compounds. In essence, they learned to extract energy from other compounds by oxidizing them with nitrite (NO_2) and nitrate (NO_3). In the process, however, these bacteria were continually removing nitrogen from circulation by reducing it to molecular nitrogen (N_2), an atmospheric gas that is chemically inert. Only lightning, which releases enough energy to break the bonds of that gas, could place chemically active nitrogen compounds back into circulation. Over geological time, therefore, a crude nitrogen cycle would have emerged in which—at least in this scenario—the flow of nitrogen through the biosphere was governed by the intensity and frequency of lightning.[8]

One thing, though, is for sure: the evolution of bacteria capable of photosynthesis—that is, the ability to use the sun's energy to extract carbon from the atmosphere and produce organic material—would have increased the demand for nitrogen. This capacity to fix atmospheric carbon is generally believed to have been acquired by the ancestors of today's cyanobacteria about 2.5 billion years ago. With access to a steady supply of energy and carbon, this new organism would have been able to spread throughout the ancient oceans, at least until supplies of other raw material ran out. Given that 10 percent of a cyanobacterium's dry weight is nitrogen, the availability of nitrogen would have been especially critical. In the long term, increases in the production of biomass would have depended on how fast lightning could supply new quantities of chemically active nitrogen.[9]

Evolutionary biologists suggest that lightning ceased to be a limiting factor in the expansion of microbial life some time after the emergence of photosynthesis. The change came when a strain of cyanobacteria developed the solar-powered ability to convert atmospheric nitrogen into ammonia. After that, with supplies of other critical materials available in the mineral-rich seas of the Archaean Earth, the population of carbon- and nitrogen-fixing organisms would have begun to increase, steadily pumping more and more organic material into the oceans.[10]

Now that solar-powered photosynthesis and nitrogen fixing were being carried out on a large scale, the Earth's oceans and atmosphere also began to change. A major part of this change was due to the oxygen released during photosynthesis. Initially, much of this oxygen was consumed by the oxidation of iron in the ocean. Eventually, however, levels of oxygen in both the ocean and the atmosphere began to rise, contributing to what has been called the Great Oxygenation Event.[11] This increase in oxygen levels not only turned parts of the ocean into an inhospitable environment for many organisms but also significantly changed the chemistry of the atmosphere. At the same time, any lines of organisms that developed ways to tolerate oxygen, or even use it to their benefit, gained an evolutionary advantage. Indeed, a line of bacteria eventually evolved in ways that allowed for the extraction of energy through respiration—that is, by using oxygen to consume carbon-based organic compounds as fuel. In the process, these organisms balanced the action of photosynthesis by cycling carbon and oxygen back into carbon dioxide. Other types of bacteria began to exploit rising oxygen levels in ways that affected flows of nitrogen. For example, nitrifiers learned to secure energy by oxidizing ammonia to nitrite and nitrite to nitrate.[12]

With the emergence of these and other carbon-, oxygen-, and nitrogen-manipulating organisms, the basic components of the Earth's biogeochemical cycles were in place, complete with one set of organisms that was balancing the activity of others.[13] As these organisms pumped critical elements through solar-powered biogeochemical cycles, the process of evolutionary change through variation and selection not only continued but accelerated. Indeed, within a relatively few ticks of the geological clock, the descendants of these organisms—and the biogeochemical cycles in which they were entangled—moved from the sea to land, extending the reach of nature.

The biology-related milestones that evolutionary biologists typically identify as being especially significant include the emergence of cells with organelles (eukaryotes), the development of sexual reproduction, and the emergence of multicelled organisms with the capacity to sense and explore environments. The first change, which laid the foundation for the latter two, involved the emergence of structures (organelles) within cells capable of performing specialized functions. For example, one type of organelle, mitochondria, manages the conversion of energy through respiration; another, the nucleus, manages the duplication of genetic material. In plant cells, photosynthesis is carried out in organelles known as chloroplasts. Among other things, the development of these specialized organelles laid the foundation for sexual reproduction and the emergence of multicelled organisms.[14]

No plants or animals, however, ever developed organelles capable of fix-ing nitrogen.[15] Some evolutionary biologists theorize that the first organelles emerged as the result of the symbiotic evolution of two lines of bacteria. In such a scenario, each line of cells would have been evolving in an environ-ment highly influenced by the other. The ecological relationship between the two organisms would have grown tighter and tighter until, the theory goes, they eventually merged into a single organism with one becoming an organelle of the other. The point here is that the emergence of something as complicated as cells with organelles is not necessarily the result of the isolated evolution of one line of genetic material. Through co-evolutionary relationships, the knowledge embedded in one set of genes can be influenced by the knowledge embedded in a different set of genes, adding another level of complexity to the process of variation and selection.[16] However, given that no nitrogen-fixing organelles emerged, plant and animals continued to rely on organelle-less bacteria for some chemical-processing services.

The emergence of sexual reproduction further accelerated the process of evolutionary change. With sexual reproduction, genetic material from two different lines of cells can be integrated, allowing for desirable traits from each line to collect in a single organism. Sexual reproduction can also facili-tate systematic variability in a population, increasing the probability that some individuals—and the population as a whole—will continue to flourish even in the face of changing environments.[17]

Yet another development that accelerated the pace of evolutionary change was the emergence of multicellular organisms.[18] Among other things, cellular specialization allowed for the development of appendages capable of facilitating motion, organs capable of acquiring sensory information, and mechanisms by which the latter could be used to guide the former. This ability to sense some aspect of the immediate environment and to alter motion based on that information represented a fundamental change in the acquisition of adaptive knowledge. In essence, those organisms were now engaged in a nested cycle of variation and selection. Each direction in which the organism moved served as a type of variation, and each decision to alter that motion served as a form of selection. Any ability to sense and react to the presence of nutrients or toxins was, of course, a significant advantage. Furthermore, any genetic variation that improved the guidance system would quickly spread through a population.[19]

Meanwhile, the harsh ultraviolet radiation that had previously pre-vented organic life from surviving outside the sea dropped in intensity. That radiation was now being absorbed some ten to twenty miles above the earth's surface by the continual production and destruction of ozone in the oxygenated atmosphere. Indeed, by the beginning of what geologists refer to as the Devonian period, which began a little more than 400 million years ago, mosses and insects had begun to colonize the land. By about 300 million years ago, ferns, trees, and other plants were covering many terrestrial surfaces, and the first reptiles had emerged from the oceans. Also involved in this migration were the nitrogen-manipulating bacteria that all forms of life needed to survive, which gave rise to a terrestrial nitrogen cycle quite different from the oceanic cycle that had preceded it.[20]

The Nitrogen Cycle before Humans

When the first humanoids arrived on the scene approximately 15 million years ago, the biogeochemical cycles at the core of the Earth's basic "nature" had been relatively stable for several hundred million years. To be sure, the Earth was still experiencing major changes. If those 300 million years could be squeezed into several minutes, one would see major changes in the position of land masses, dramatic shifts in climatic patterns, and even a noticeable rise in the length of the day. But the basic mechanisms for cycling elements through the biosphere remained constant.[21]

Of all the biogeochemical cycles, the one involving nitrogen emerged as the most complex. Dependent upon the activity of highly specialized organisms distributed through the world's seas and soils, it includes numerous subcycles and pathways through which nitrogen can flow. The nitrogen cycle that occurs on land differs from that in the ocean, but in both environments the activities of nitrifying, denitrifying, and nitrogen-fixing bacteria interact in such a way that each part of the cycle has some balancing influence on another part.

On land, in the absence of humans, the cycling of nitrogen in mature ecosystems tends to be local. When plants die or leaves fall to the ground, decomposers feed on the dead organic material and convert any nitrogen present into ammonia. In moist soils, that ammonia forms ammonium ions, which adhere to soil particles. Nitrogen in this form generally cannot flow into the root zone and be assimilated back into growing plants. However, nitrifying bacteria such as those of the genus *Nitrosomonas* can oxidize ammonium ions into nitrite. Then other nitrifying bacteria, such as those of the genus *Nitrobacter,* convert the nitrite into highly soluble nitrate ions, which water can carry into the root zone.[22]

In mature forests and prairies, relatively little nitrogen has to be secured from the atmosphere. After all, in ecosystems left to themselves, plants grow, shed material, and decompose in roughly the same place, allowing the same nitrogen to be recycled through the ecosystem again and again. All things being equal, growth is balanced by death, and the decomposition of dead material supplies the nitrogen needed for new growth. As long as massive amounts of biomass are not being transported out of the immediate area, most of the available nitrogen stays in circulation.

Of course, not every last bit of nitrogen stays within an ecosystem. Some losses of nitrogenous compounds are inevitable. Fires, for example, can remove nitrogen, as can ammonia vapors released during decomposition. Heavy rains also remove some nitrogen by saturating soil and leaching away any nitrate present. On the surface, runoff can wash soil and nitrogen-rich solids directly into streams. Those streams, in turn, often flow into wetlands, where denitrifying bacteria, which thrive in oxygen-depleted stagnant water, remove the nitrate by converting it into gases.[23]

If losses of nitrogen from an ecosystem were not eventually replaced, the reproductive ability of that ecosystem would slowly but steadily degrade. Precipitation restocks some of the lost nitrogen by washing ammonia vapors and compounds fixed by lightning out of the air. All in all, though, the quantity of fixed nitrogen delivered by precipitation is relatively small and irregularly distributed. For losses to be replaced in a predictable fashion, ecosystems depend on the activity of nitrogen-fixing bacteria.

Fixing nitrogen—that is, breaking atmospheric nitrogen apart and converting it to ammonia—requires relatively large quantities of energy. Free-living nitrogen-fixing bacteria live independently, mainly in the soil but also in places such as leaf surfaces, securing their energy by feeding off bits of organic material. However, they fix only enough for their own needs, and their nitrogen becomes available to other organisms only after they die and decompose. A variety of symbiotic associations with plants, including trees, have also evolved. One of the tightest associations involve nitrogen-fixers such as *Rhizobia*, which work symbiotically with leguminous plants such as alfalfa, clover, peas, beans, lentils, and peanuts. In this relationship, the bacteria occupy nodules on the plant's roots and fix nitrogen in exchange for energy-rich sugars. However, if enough nitrate is available in the soil, the host plant draws first upon that resource. In terms of the plant's use of energy, securing nitrate from the soil is a much less expensive way of obtaining nitrogen.[24]

At the heart of the terrestrial nitrogen cycle, therefore, lie several general types of organisms: (1) decomposers, which convert the nitrogen in dead organic material to ammonia while extracting energy from that material; (2) nitrifiers, which extract energy by oxidizing ammonia to nitrites and nitrates; (3) plants that take in nitrate as a raw material; (4) denitrifiers, which remove nitrate by reducing that material into nitrite and gases such as nitric oxide (NO), nitrous oxide (N_2O), and inert molecular nitrogen (N_2); (5) nitrogen-fixing bacteria, which convert molecular nitrogen (from the atmosphere) into ammonia; (6) plants that have symbiotic relationships with nitrogen-fixing bacteria; and (7) animals that consume plants and release nitrogen-rich wastes. Each category involves a range of organisms, including lines of bacteria adapted to highly specific types of environments, which makes efforts to adequately characterize soil ecology—and the terrestrial nitrogen cycle—quite difficult.

The cycling of nitrogen in the world's oceans is even more variable and less understood. For one thing, ocean currents can transport nitrogenous compounds long distances. Another difference is that marine plants, including microscopic photoplankton, can make more direct use of ammonium ions. After all, no soil particles are present to capture that material. Patterns of nitrogen-fixing activity in marine environments also differ, as do the mechanisms by which nitrogen is removed. For example, one denitrifying organism active in marine environments is not present in soils. In a process known as anaerobic ammonium oxidation, this organism obtains energy for fixing carbon dioxide by converting nitrite and ammonia into atmospheric nitrogen. As a result, under certain conditions, losses of nitrogen from ocean environments can be quite high.[25] Finally, ocean sediments can accumulate nitrogen through the settling of organic material. In shallower portions of the oceans, when currents are right, some of that nitrogen—along with other nutrients—can be carried back toward the surface and help fuel the production of biomass.[26]

On a global scale, the marine nitrogen cycle is only loosely coupled to the terrestrial nitrogen cycle. Rivers, of course, carry some nitrogen to the ocean, but in prehuman times wetlands and floodplains removed much of that nitrogen before it reached the sea. The bodies of spawning fish also carry small amounts of nitrogen in the other direction. In any case, the largest connection between the marine and terrestrial cycle was and is the atmosphere, from which all nitrogen fixers obtain their nitrogen and into which all denitrifiers release their gases. Indeed, some geochemists suggest that the marine nitrogen cycle may be oscillating between periods of large nitrogen losses and periods of net nitrogen increases, possibly playing a role in the regulation of atmospheric carbon dioxide levels.[27]

The atmosphere is also an important part of the nitrogen cycle because of the trace gases that cycle through it, which are eventually converted to inert molecular nitrogen or washed back to the surface. Nitrogen-manipulating bacteria release chemically active compounds such as nitrous oxide and nitric oxide, with much of the latter being converted to nitrogen dioxide (NO_2). Lightning introduces some nitric oxide and nitrogen dioxide as well. All of these gases, present in trace concentrations, are a natural component of the atmosphere and influence its dynamics. Nitrogen dioxide and nitric oxide, for example, play a role in the dynamic process of ozone creation and destruction in the lower atmosphere. In addition, nitrogen dioxide can be washed out of the atmosphere as nitric acid, altering the acidity of precipitation and the amount of fixed nitrogen that reaches certain ecosystems. Nitrous oxide, on the other hand, is a greenhouse gas. It also has the potential to reach the upper atmosphere and affect the protective ozone layer.

Given that the atmospheric concentrations of these chemically active gases are naturally quite low, relatively small increases can have a significant effect. At concentrations greater than that found in the atmosphere, these gases also have biological effects. For example, at levels greater than one hundred parts per million, nitrogen dioxide is potentially fatal to humans. Nitrous oxide, known as laughing gas, is often used as an anesthetic in dentistry. Inside the body, nitric oxide serves as an important chemical for regulating the cardiovascular system; minuscule amounts of the gas are capable of dilating blood vessels and stimulating muscles. It is also produced by the immune system to kill bacteria.

Putting precise numbers on where all the nitrogen is and how much gets fixed and denitrified each year is difficult because of the complexity of the processes involved. Ecologists and earth scientists have made a detailed accounting of what is known and unknown, at many different scales and for a variety of purposes. One thing they know is that the amount of fixed nitrogen that human activity is now adding to the world is on the same order of magnitude as that contributed by nature. If one does the accounting just for terrestrial systems, human activity has already surpassed natural systems (see table 1.1). If we focus only on regions that include large amounts of industrial agriculture, the numbers shift further toward the anthropogenic side.

TABLE 1.1

Nitrogen Fixation, Natural and Anthropogenic

Activity	Millions of Metric Tons
Natural	
Terrestrial N-fixing (nonagricultural)	89
Ocean N-fixing	140
Lightning	5
Total	234
Anthropogenic	
Cultivation of legumes	33
Industrial N-fixing	85
Emissions of NOx from combustion	21
Total	139

Source: James N. Galloway and Ellis B. Cowling, "Reactive Nitrogen and the World: 200 Years of Change," Ambio 31 (2002): 64–71. Estimate is for 1990.

Scientists are much less certain about the amount of fixed nitrogen that is being returned to the atmosphere each year by denitrification. Most assume that before humans began cultivating nitrogen-fixing hosts, fixing nitrogen industrially, and altering wetlands and floodplains (where terrestrial denitrification occurs), the amount being fixed was roughly equal to the amount being denitrified. Have denitrifiers kept up with human activity? If not, where is all the extra nitrogen going, and what effect is it having as it cascades through ecosystems? If denitrification has increased, what are the effects of greater emissions of nitric oxide and nitrous oxide?[28]

The amount of nitrogen being fixed each year (about 400 million metric tons) pales in comparison to the amount of inert molecular nitrogen that is stored in the atmosphere (about 4,000 trillion metric tons). It is also much smaller than the amount of fixed nitrogen that is stored in biomass, dead organic matter, and inorganic compounds in the ocean (about 1.5 trillion metric tons).[29] However, the relatively small amount of nitrogen fixing that takes place belies its significance. Manipulating this quantity may be akin to manipulating a small control signal that drives a much larger and more complex process.

Basic logic suggests that any complex Earth system that has lasted for hundreds of millions of years must be self-regulating within the boundaries of small disturbances. However, the Earth did not come with a user's guide, and nobody knows what size disturbance can be tolerated without significant change. One way to discover such things is by trial and error, as humans are currently doing, albeit unintentionally. Indeed, scientists' suggestion that the planet has entered a new geological age—the Anthropocene, one in which the activity, knowledge, and choices of humans matter on a geological scale—is surely appropriate.[30]

2

From Adaptation to Innovation

By the time *Homo sapiens* migrated out of Africa 100,000 years ago, nitrogen had been cycling through the biosphere for hundreds of millions of years. As with earlier migrations of fire-wielding hominids, such as *Homo neanderthalensis* and *Homo erectus,* the arrival of anatomically modern humans caused barely a ripple in the gentle flow of nitrogen from the soil into plants and back again. The bacteria that fixed, nitrified, and denitrified nitrogenous material continued on, unaffected by the occasional human foot that passed by.[1]

Homo sapiens proved to be even more highly skilled at adapting to new environments than their ancestors were. Indeed, they soon came to occupy every corner of the Earth. In particular, about 50,000 years ago, the population of *Homo sapiens,* after hovering for millennia at a few tens of thousands, steadily began to increase. Even in face of retreating temperatures, groups of *Homo sapiens* flourished, reaching a population of about 6 million by the end of the Ice Age, roughly 12,000 years ago. At the core of this expansion lay an explosive capacity to adapt to new environments and an ability to pass knowledge directly from person to person and from one generation to the next, independent of genetic material.[2]

Humans Learning by Variation and Selection

Describing the ability of early humans to adapt as "explosive" is, of course, relative. Compared to industrial societies, early groups of humans rarely made changes to their practices. Indeed, too much change could be dangerous. Any group that deviated too far from what had proven to be successful in the past put the reproduction of its community at risk. Moreover, much of the knowledge that communities acquired came to be embedded in rituals and stories. Altering those stories and rituals too quickly could result in the loss of valuable knowledge.[3]

Variations, though, were bound to occur. As groups told their stories, enforced their rules, and reproduced their practices, those stories, rules, and practices inevitably evolved through gradual processes of variation and selection. A major source of variation lay in the sheer number of different groups struggling to survive. Over tens of thousands of years, as groups of *Homo sapiens* spread across the Earth, some groups flourished while others disappeared. Groups that flourished often split to survive, disseminating their languages, stories, and practices. And when they split, their cultures gradually diverged, generating another layer of variation as each new group continued to accumulate knowledge that came to be embedded in practices, stories, rituals, laws, and ethics.[4]

This description of societal change as evolutionary, as being rooted in processes of variation and selection, is not unusual. Indeed, some scholars see the process of variation and selection as a general phenomenon that includes but is not limited to the natural selection of biological traits. Various terms denote this generalized process of variation and selection, including *evolutionary epistemology, universal selection theory, multiprocess selection theory,* and *memetics*.[5] All of the theories behind these terms emphasize that anything subject to cycles of variation and selection evolves, whether it be ideas, behaviors, technologies, laws, ethics, or organisms. Note that these theories are not simply a rehash of older ideas involving social Darwinism, which were often used to suggest that the competition for survival in nature justified laissez faire capitalism. Humans, unlike the rest of nature, can make choices, including ethical choices that place boundaries on how individuals are allowed to treat each other or, for that matter, to interact with natural systems or make use of natural resources. The ethical boundaries that societies establish, whether on economic and social activity or on interactions with the environment, influence the direction in which societies evolve.

The theorist who introduced the term *evolutionary epistemology* also introduced the powerful concept of nested variation and selection.[6] This concept is important to any discussion of innovation and societal change, including an examination of how societies learned to fix nitrogen industrially (chapters 4–8) and how they are now slowly learning to manage their nitrogen-related interactions with the rest of nature in a more sophisticated way (chapters 9–12). In general, nested variation and selection occurs whenever a simpler and faster process of variation and selection guides a slower and more complex one by using knowledge acquired in the past. The process lies at the heart of what it means to learn.

Nested variation and selection can occur at a biological level. Consider the example discussed in the previous chapter, that of a simple self-propelled organism capable of sensing its environment and altering its direction based on what it senses. Without a guidance system, the organism's exploration would be blind and random, a process of pure trial and error. The guidance system, however, improves the organism's chances of survival. It lies at the center of a nested process of variation and selection in which the guidance system selects one variation, one direction, among many possibilities. That choice of direction, though, eventually gets tested for real. A guidance system that directs an organism toward toxic conditions, for example, is not likely to be around for long. The notion of nested variation and selection also implies that the guidance system continues to evolve as well. Indeed, genetic variations that alter a guidance system in ways that prove beneficial are likely to disseminate through a population.

Nested systems of variation and selection always contain knowledge about the larger environment in which variations are ultimately tested. The guidance system of a simple organism, for example, contains knowledge about the environment through which that organism moves. That knowledge may be something as simple as registering the advantage of avoiding a certain chemical. Furthermore, in the case of a simple organism, the knowledge is encoded in genetic material; each new generation does not have to rediscover the same knowledge again and again. If the guidance system evolves further, addition knowledge about how to exploit resources or avoid trouble in the surrounding environment would also come to be encoded in the organism's genetic material.

Systems of nested variation and selection grow even more powerful when multiple cycles of nested variation and selection come to be hierarchically embedded in each other, with simpler systems filtering out variations for more complex ones. A cat's instinct, for example, surely involves many layers of nested variation and selection. The systems guiding humans are, of course, even more complex, with countless systems of nested variation and selection interacting in ways too complex to comprehend. Humans, for example, including those who migrated out of Africa 100,000 years ago, have the capacity to construct mental models of the world. Hence, individuals can test a variety of choices in their minds before committing time and resources to a particular plan of action. Ideally, before a human acts, the most risky and least promising alternatives have already been filtered out. Through the use of these mental models, human efforts to exploit resources and manipulate the environment have come to be so well guided that it is difficult to think of these efforts as being nested processes of blind variation and selection.

Mental models also evolve—that is, people learn—through processes of variation and selection. A person, of course, can never completely predict the full consequences of her actions. Ultimately, each human act is a test of one person's mental model of the world. When people compare what they expect to happen with what actually happens and then, consciously or otherwise, adjust their mental models to compensate for the difference, learning occurs. There is no guarantee that those adjustments will actually help, but this process of adjusting and retesting allows mental models to evolve. Scientists have barely begun to understand how the human brain operates. But one can be sure that an unbelievably tangled system of nested pretesting, filtering, and screening is at work, transforming trial-and-error exploration into actions guided by not only immediate goals and desires but also abstract values and ethical codes.[7]

In one sense, with the emergence of *Homo sapiens,* adaptation became more Lamarckian than Darwinian. Jean-Baptiste Lamarck, wrestling with the origin of species some fifty years before Charles Darwin did, suggested that animals acquired biological traits by striving. For example, he proposed a mechanism by which a species of swimming birds gradually acquired webbed feet by constantly stretching their toes in water and, more famously, by which giraffes acquired long necks by stretching to reach higher fruit.[8] Although this sort of theory fails miserably in explaining how animals acquired biological traits (and my summary is an oversimplification of Lamarck's theory), it does describe some aspects of adaptation by cultural variation and selection. Humans envision the future in their minds and then, by stretching to reach that vision, gradually acquire the knowledge needed to move in that direction.[9]

What do nested systems of variation and selection have to with societies learning to be environmentally sustainable, whether in their interactions with the slice of nature we refer to as the nitrogen cycle or with any other aspect of nature? Everything. The knowledge that eventually allowed industrial societies to bypass ecological limits such as those associated with limits on the production of fixed nitrogen were facilitated by the emergence of the three powerful socially constructed systems of nested variation and selection: the adaptive rule of law, market capitalism, and the process of science. Harnessing these systems of knowledge production in a way that rewards innovators for reinforcing rather than undermining efforts to sustain the integrity of Earth systems is surely linked to the concept of sustainability.

Early Humans' Acquisition of
Nitrogen-Related Knowledge

The importance of socially constructed cycles of nested variation and selection emerged long before complex agricultural and industrial societies did. A nomadic tribe of hunters and gatherers could, for example, embrace stories about the importance of testing new foods when entering unfamiliar land. Any tribal encounter with unknown plants or animals would trigger a guided process of trial and error, a powerful cultural strategy for producing knowledge about what might be safe to eat in new environments. Once such a system is in place, adapting to new environments becomes much more systematic.

As long as groups of early humans remained mobile, however, they did not have to acquire knowledge about how to sustain the fertility of soils. Whatever challenges mobile groups faced had little to do with exhausting the nutrient content of soil. If a group stressed a certain piece of land beyond its ability to supply nutrients, the group could shift its activities elsewhere, using fire to clear a new swath of land and leaving the previous land to recover. As long as societies kept their populations low enough to be mobile, their interactions with the nitrogen cycle placed few constraints on their way of life.[10]

When societies ceased to be mobile and started harvesting food from the same land year after year, their effect on local flows of nitrogen increased. Given that stationary agriculture emerged before the development of writing did, our understanding of this transition comes mainly from archeological evidence. According to that evidence, a handful of stationary agricultural societies emerged independently throughout the world. Scholars have different explanations for why those first transitions occurred, but they generally focus on changes that pressured communities to obtain subsistence from smaller or increasingly resource-poor environments over time. For example, an increase in the number of people who were drawing resources from a given region, perhaps due to the migration of new groups into the area, would certainly have encouraged some communities to experiment with ways in which to extract more resources from the available land. Whether that involved taking advantage of domesticatable animals, manipulating environments to grow desirable plants, or both, communities that succeeded in such efforts increased their chances of survival. If a community continued to acquire knowledge of how to cultivate plants and manage animals, significant but gradual changes to that community would occur.[11]

In areas in which stationary agriculture emerged, the transition occurred over many generations, without any one generation explicitly choosing to make the shift. Indeed, the changes that occurred were probably self-reinforcing. That is, changes in practice that allowed groups to make more efficient use of local resources could also make future mobility more difficult and hence increase dependence on local resources. For example, when a group is mobile, women cannot care for several young children at once, so most mobile groups develop strategies to control birth rates. In addition, mobile groups tend not to build permanent structures, manufacture containers, or store large quantities of food. But several generations of low mobility could easily lead to increases in the size of families, the construction of semi-permanent homes, and the production of containers to store surplus food. The adoption of such practices could also result in a further rise in population density, well above a level that could be supported without the intensive use of resources that stationary agriculture makes possible.[12]

Wherever population densities rose and villages became larger and more sedentary, the value placed on various types of knowledge also shifted. Knowledge associated with stalking and killing animals gave way to knowledge associated with managing and regenerating animal populations under human control. Knowledge about where to find plants slowly gave way to knowledge about how to cultivate plants. Furthermore, the practice of land ownership, the building of structures, and the accumulation of wealth led to new concepts of property, inheritance, and kinship. Over time, more complex social structures emerged, and eventually a small segment of the population began devoting time to something other than securing food while a larger segment produced the food that everybody consumed. In short, the shift to stationary agriculture was accompanied by profound changes in social relations and the types of knowledge that people valued and rewarded.[13]

To flourish over the long term, stationary agricultural societies had to acquire ways to keep land fertile with a minimum of human ingenuity. In particular, land cultivated generation after generation could not support a growing network of towns and villages without some way of resupplying the soil with nitrogen. Otherwise, as peasants harvested protein-containing crops from the same land year after year, they would remove nitrogen faster than free-living nitrogen-fixing soil bacteria could replace it. Over time, stores of organic nitrogen in the soil—and hence the productivity of the land—would drop, and producing enough protein to sustain the population would become increasingly difficult.

Although nutrients other than nitrogen are also important for crops, nitrogen tends to be the one that limits growth if enough sunlight and water are available. Supplies of carbon, for example, never pose a problem. Although plants need about thirty times more carbon than they do nitrogen, a plant's source of carbon from the air is never in short supply. Minerals such as phosphorus and potassium are also needed but in smaller amounts than nitrogen. Tiny rocks integral to good soil contain these minerals; and the weathering of these rocks, along with the deposition of particles carried by the wind, usually provide enough of these nutrients for low-intensity agriculture. Inputs of nitrogen from nitrogen-fixing bacteria, however, are generally too small to replace the amount removed from land farmed year after year.[14]

Some land, however, has a nitrogen-replacing mechanism already built in: river valleys routinely flood and resupply alluvial land with nutrient-rich silt. Most archaeologists agree that large, long-term, stationary agriculture societies were rooted in such soils, giving rise to civilizations capable of supporting extended networks of villages and small cities over millennia. Examples include land in the fertile crescent of the Tigris and Euphrates (emerging about 10,000 years ago), along the Huang He (Yellow River) in China (about 8,000 years ago), and along floodplains in Mesoamerica (4,500 years ago) and sub-Saharan Africa (4,000 years ago).[15] A large agricultural society also emerged independently along the Andean coast of South America, but in that case the Humboldt current—churning up nutrients in shallow coastal waters and funneling in nitrogen-rich fish from a broad expanse of the Pacific Ocean—rather than a floodplain could have been the reason. In the words of archeologist Richard Burger, "anchovy schools alone could have supported more than 6,500,000 people at only sixty percent of the carrying capacity."[16] Large stationary agricultural societies also emerged along other floodplains, such as along the Nile River in Egypt and the Indus River in India, but not necessarily independently of the other areas.[17]

The people of river valley societies who attempted to cultivate higher land surely discovered and rediscovered, time and time again, that the productivity of that land could decline over time, even if plenty of sun and water were available. For example, forests and grasses cleared by fire would initially provide access to fertile soil, with stores of nitrogen capable of keeping production high for a generation of harvests or more. Eventually though, if that land were farmed continuously, bountiful harvests could not be sustained without some method of replacing the nitrogen they removed.

How did peasants and farmers who cultivated upland soils learn to maintain the fertility of their fields? The sheer number of people working the land inevitably introduced variations that came to be integrated into local practices. Obviously, nobody knew anything about nitrogen or nitrogen-fixing bacteria, at least not in ways that science makes possible. Perhaps, though, observant farmers noticed that soil abandoned for being infertile eventually recovered its power to support plant growth and concluded that letting land rest from time to time was a good idea. They may even have observed that certain plants, such as beans, did well in tired soil. Whatever the source of their insights and reasons for varying practices, a gradual process of variation and selection surely occurred, leading farmers to cultivate legumes, recycle manures, leave fields fallow, and embrace strategies that, unknown to them, sustained the nitrogen content of soils.[18]

Not surprisingly, different practices—and different ways of getting enough nitrogen back into the soil—emerged in different parts of the world. Variations in climate, plants and animals, soils, and population densities all influenced the outcome, as did differences in social structures and cultural beliefs. In any case, these nitrogen-sustaining practices, wherever they developed, freed ancient agricultural societies from the grasp of river valleys, allowing them to maintain crop production on higher ground and to become even larger and more complex.

Agricultural societies also proved to be capable of creating socially constructed cycles of variation and selection that were more complex that those created by small groups of hunters and gatherers. For example, a very powerful socially constructed system of variation and selection is one in which law is written down and allowed to be challenged, reinterpreted, and altered to fit new circumstances. Among other things, adaptive systems of law can help produce knowledge about how to resolve conflicts when a society, perhaps due to innovation, finds itself in new ethical territory. Indeed, it is safe to say that any society that embraces innovation or undergoes fairly rapid change without a system of law for resolving conflicts places itself at risk, with the potential for conflicts to grow rather than be resolved and eventually blow a society apart.[19]

Not all systems of law, though, are equally adaptive. About 4,000 years ago, in ancient Mesopotamia, Hammurabi's code established a clear set of rules for resolving conflicts, but that code, metaphorically written in stone, was not particularly adaptive. The Ten Commandments that the tribes of Israel produced several centuries later were less specific and more adaptive, with much of the adaptation occurring through layers of rabbinic interpretation. Even more adaptive were legal systems constructed by the ancient Greeks, who established systems of litigation and legislation backed by written records. In particular, under the Athenian rule of law, different visions of the future and different ideas of how to achieve those visions were constantly being tested, contributing to the gradual accumulation of knowledge about what the members of that polis were willing to embrace as ethical and fair.[20]

The rule of law, of course, was not particularly useful in producing the kind of nitrogen-related knowledge that farmers valued. It did, however, lay the foundation for two other socially constructed systems of nested variation and selection that were capable of producing that type of knowledge: market capitalism (which facilitates technological innovation) and the process of science (which facilitates the production of predictive models). Although each of these systems were centuries, if not millennia, in the making, once they were constructed, they accelerated the production of knowledge to levels never before experienced.

PART II

Learning to Bypass an Ecological Limit

3

Innovation within an
Ecological Limit

All ancient societies had to live within the limits of an important ecological constraint: the capacity of nitrogen-fixing bacteria to resupply agricultural soil with nitrogen. Even the great river valley civilizations, blessed by floods that routinely delivered nutrient-rich silt to agricultural soils, depended on the services of these single-celled creatures. The fertile alluvial soil along the Nile River, for example, depended upon the activity of nitrogen-fixing bacteria scattered throughout the entire 3.2 million square kilometers drained by the river, one-tenth of the entire African continent.

Ancient societies did not greatly alter the quantity of nitrogen moving through regional ecosystems. For one thing, rivers collected and deposited silt whether people downstream made use of that material or not. For another, the Earth was home to a lot fewer people then. Today, about 120 million people live in the Nile River basin, nearly 80 million in Egypt alone. In contrast, 3,500 years ago, at the height of ancient Egypt's power, the Nile River valley and delta, one of the most densely populated areas of the ancient world, supported 4 to 5 million people. At the time, the population of the entire world stood at about 50 million people, less than 1 percent of the global population today.[1]

The largest effect that ancient societies had on flows of nitrogen was due to landscape-scale changes in support of agriculture. These changes, such as the clearing of forests, the construction of irrigation systems and levees, and the elimination of wetlands, altered patterns associated with denitrification and the distribution of nitrogen-rich silt. Even where humans were bumping up the production of fixed nitrogen by cultivating plants that worked symbiotically with nitrogen-fixing bacteria, the landscape-scale changes mattered more. For example, 3,000 years ago, as the ancient Zhou dynasty emerged along the Huang He in northern China, many peasants in the watershed grew soybeans, an important nitrogen-fixing host. The land supported up to fifty people to the square kilometer, and most of the harvest was consumed locally.[2] Even if we assume that all of the protein in a peasant's diet came from what he grew and that no nitrogen-rich waste was recycled, the amount of fixed nitrogen that the cultivation of soybeans added to the Huang He would have amounted to something less than ten kilograms per hectare each year.[3] The amount is on the same order of magnitude as that which escapes from minimally disturbed landscapes.[4] In terms of regional environmental changes, physical alteration of the land, especially actions that increased erosion or eliminated wetlands, mattered more.

On the other hand, the cultivation of crops that worked symbiotically with nitrogen-fixing bacteria mattered greatly to the peasants of the Huang He basin. The nitrogen secured by growing a legume such as soybeans ensured that a steady supply of protein could be obtained from the land; and 13 to 19 percent of protein consists of nitrogen, which must be available while plants are growing. If nitrogen compounds are unavailable to growing plants, their ability to produce green matter is also compromised, reducing their ability to capture the sun's energy and hence to grow at all.

Higher yields made possible by the cultivation of legumes had consequences that went far beyond simply putting more protein on the table. All ancient societies hovered near subsistence, and only a relatively small amount of nutrition was available to keep people who were not engaged in agriculture alive. As a result, relatively small increases in agricultural productivity could translate into an opportunity for substantially more people to devote their labor to something other than agriculture. And over the long term, the amount of labor that ancient societies could devote to something other than agriculture mattered greatly.

N and the Large Consequences of Small Increases

No ancient society could maintain a population of soldiers, miners, artisans, judges, accountants, and administrators unless peasants were able to produce enough food to feed them. And generating that surplus presented a significant challenge. A rough rule of thumb is that, in a traditional agricultural society, about 90 percent of the population was needed to produce, process, and transport enough food to feed the entire society. In other words, it took about nine people engaged in agriculture to support one nonagricultural worker. Slight differences in that ratio translated into big differences in how much labor a society could devote to something other than subsistence-related tasks. A society that could devote 20 percent of its population to something other than food production, for example, was quite different from one that could only free up 5 percent.[5]

A large harvest by itself did not necessarily guarantee a large surplus. The number of people required to produce that harvest also mattered. Traditional wet rice cultivation, for example, produced more protein per hectare than other grains, but producing that crop required lots of labor. Growing wheat, on the other hand, required less labor but also produced less protein per hectare, especially when one accounts for the unavailability of land during fallow rotations. Intercropping, which involves planting a mix of complementary crops—such as a legume, a cereal, and perhaps a leafy weed-suppressing crop—also tended to be labor-intensive. In the end, what mattered most, at least in terms of how many people a society could devote to nonagricultural tasks, was how much more food farmers could produce above and beyond what they and their families needed to survive: the higher the productivity of the rural population, the greater the percentage of people who could be engaged in other types of activities.[6]

Getting peasants to produce the surplus needed to feed the nonagricultural portion of a society required incentives. Social structures for collecting and distributing that surplus also were needed. Without such incentives and social structures—whether in the form of slavery, a tax or tithe, a thriving market, or some mix of all of these—rural populations were not likely to produce more food than they needed. In Japan during the Tokugawa shogunate, for example, taxes had to be paid in rice, and the tax was so steep that few peasants actually ate much rice, turning instead to inferior grains such as millet. The tax, in effect, was calibrated—or, rather, had evolved—to capture as much of the peasant's labor as possible.[7]

The productivity of the land also influenced how much surplus food a society could produce. In dry areas poorly suited for agriculture, no amount of taxes or forced labor could make things grow. In such areas, a group of people could secure nutrition by grazing livestock over a large area, but such groups tended to be semi-nomadic and have relatively small populations.[8] If a nomadic tribe grew too large for its resource base, it eventually had to move into land more suitable for agriculture, which created a problem if that land were already occupied. Indeed, time and again, the rapid expansion of nomadic tribes during bountiful times presented significant challenges to the stationary agricultural societies with which they interacted.[9]

A reasonably complex society also needed enough storage to protect against fluctuations in food production. Lower-than-average levels of annual rainfall or years with far more clouds than normal could affect crop growth, as could the activity of pests or the availability of seed. Indeed, poor harvests were a constant threat. Pestilence or drought could even result in the complete failure of a crop. But multiple years of good harvests could be disastrous as well. After all, large surpluses for several years in a row could swell the nonagricultural population to a level beyond what could be supported in lean years. Storage—at the household, village, and regional levels—buffered societies from the effects of such fluctuations. At one site in Egypt, for example, archeologists have found the remains of more than twenty granaries, some more than three stories tall and with a footprint of two hundred square meters. Such levels of storage reduced the impact of annual fluctuations and made the average harvest as important as the peaks and valleys.[10]

In any society, then, a mix of many factors, including the productivity of peasants, a region's specific agricultural practices, the richness of soils, the availability of water and sun, and social structures for encouraging the production and distribution of surplus food, determined the number of people who could be engaged in nonagricultural tasks. What those nonagricultural tasks were—building pyramids, conducting wars, forging metal tools, building cities, or trading for luxury goods—was another matter altogether.[11]

Societies could increase their surplus by increasing the quantity of food being grown without proportionally increasing the number of people needed to produce and process that food. In general, two types of surplus-increasing innovations were possible: those that increased the productivity of rural populations and those that increased the productivity of the land. The first category included any labor-saving innovations that made it easier to prepare and irrigate fields, harvest a crop, or transport and mill grains. Labor saved by powering these technologies with nonhuman sources of energy—such as draft animals, wind, or water power—could raise a society's agricultural productivity even further. In the second category were innovations that resulted in higher yields. For example, any change that reduced the percentage of a crop lost to pests, delivered more fixed nitrogen to the soil, or resulted in seeds' being planted more effectively could boost the productivity of the land.

To what extent did ancient farmers experiment with new practices and learn, by trial and error, to secure larger harvests with fewer people? One important source of variation involved the diffusion of practices and cultivars from one area to another, such as that which occurred when migrants moved into a new region. After all, reproducing farming practices exactly would have been difficult even if the new area had had the same climate, geography, and soils as the old one. Furthermore, migrations made possible an exchange of knowledge among groups that employed different agricultural practices. Over time, whenever and wherever different groups of people came into long-term contact, each could adopt (and adapt) what they saw as the benefits associated with the other set of practices.[12]

Innovations that required significant changes in land use and social practices were unlikely to disseminate in the absence of societal upheaval. In China, such a change began in the third century after the collapse of the Han Dynasty and the migration of northern populations into the Yangtze River valley. The cultivation of rice had been practiced for millennia in much of Asia, though usually not as the dominant crop. In the centuries following the collapse of the Han Dynasty, however, a form of wet cultivation involving the use of paddies emerged and diffused widely in the Yangtze valley. Indeed, the success of agricultural systems based on intensive wet rice cultivation—and on the surpluses associated with them—played an important role in the economic achievements of both the Tang Dynasty (618–907) and the Song Dynasty (960–1279).[13]

Farmers in the Song Dynasty further increased yields through innovations associated with double cropping. An early-ripening form of rice obtained from Champa (Vietnam) allowed farmers to grow two crops each year.[14] However, the long-term benefits of double cropping, at least in terms of yields, would have been minimal without enough nitrogen to support a higher level of production. But the system of wet rice cultivation that emerged did supply enough nitrogen. Among other things, paddies created an aquatic environment in which nitrogen-fixing cyanobacteria worked symbiotically with the water fern *Azolla*. Upon decomposition of these organisms, their fixed nitrogen became available to the rice plants.[15]

Population densities supported by wet rice cultivation also facilitated the spread of another practice: storing animal manure and night soil (human wastes) and using that material in preparing rice fields. In effect, peasants began recycling nitrogen and other nutrients, such as phosphorus, that otherwise would have escaped from the agricultural system. Some farmers also made use of green manure in the form of nitrogen-rich leguminous plants that were plowed under or cut and used as mulch on seedbeds. Exactly when and how these practices emerged is uncertain, but over time they came to be well integrated into the cultural, social, and physical ecology of societies dependent on wet rice cultivation. Other aspects of flooded rice paddies, notably the ability of the water to suppress weeds and support pest-eating frogs, fish, and birds, also led to increased yields.[16]

Along with securing higher yields through double cropping and weed-suppressing and pest-reducing paddies, the Chinese also employed some labor-saving technologies. One such device, the water-powered trip hammer for milling grain, had been introduced many years earlier during the Han Dynasty. Numerous types of irrigation systems were also in place by the time double cropping emerged. In addition, the Grand Canal, a 1,770-kilometer-long transportation channel completed in the early seventh century, facilitated the transport of food. Together, these technologies increased the percentage of people who could live in villages and cities and devote their labor to something other than agriculture.[17]

Song Dynasty rulers explicitly recognized the value of many agricultural innovations and facilitated their dissemination by printing and distributing agricultural manuals. By 1100, the population of China had reached 100 million, up from about 50 million in 750. Urban centers thrived, and government-backed paper money supported a substantial cash economy. Hence, landowners could sell their surplus in markets and use the profits to purchase goods such as tea, oil, and wine. Iron production reached 125,000 tons per year, and ships with up to ten sails carried goods from one port to another, each vessel capable of carrying hundreds of people and large loads of marketable products. During the Song Dynasty, the Chinese and their neighbors also developed many technologies unrelated to agriculture, including movable type, gunpowder, and various types of navigational tools.[18]

By the end of the eleventh century, a system of agriculture capable of delivering reliable surpluses also emerged in Europe, albeit on a more modest scale. One agricultural change involved a shift from a two- to a three-course system of crop rotation. In the Roman-dominated Mediterranean world, landowners had practiced a two-course system in which they left half of their wheat fields fallow each year. Roman writers appreciated the fertilizing value of legumes and recommended planting them if the soil appeared to be exhausted, but typically farmers simply let half the land lie fallow.[19] In such cases, additional inputs of nitrogen depended on any leguminous weeds that happened to grow during the fallow period. Nitrogen produced by free-living nitrogen-fixing bacteria and any nitrogen deposited by precipitation also represented an input, but all land received that contribution, whether fallow or not.[20] Similar farming techniques spread to western Europe with the expansion of the Roman Empire. However, in the fifth- and sixth century, control of the land passed on to the Franks after the collapse of Roman institutions, and a new set of agricultural practices, revolving around a three-course system of crop rotation, emerged.[21]

To speak of a medieval three-course system of crop rotation as if it were a well-defined form of agriculture is problematic. After all, even within the Frankish kingdoms, factors such as the mix of crops and the organization of fields varied widely. Still, despite the variations that existed, we can identify a set of agricultural practices in villages and manors centered around a three-course system. In one variation, peasants planted a third of the land in autumn with winter wheat, which meant that the crop would already be in the ground for spring. In the spring, they planted another third of the land with oats or barley or a legume. The remaining third of the land would be plowed and left fallow, subject to whatever weeds—potentially leguminous— happened to grow. Each year, they rotated the various land uses.[22]

The shift from a two- to a three-course system increased by one-sixth the amount of land being cultivated each year. However, on manors that did not introduce leguminous plants into the rotation, the advantage of the shift depended on other benefits, such as reducing the risk of losing an entire crop and more evenly dividing the labor over the year. Even where manors introduced legumes, fallow fields remained part of the rotation; legumes were planted in the extra rotation.[23]

Draft animals also came to be an important part of the medieval economy, which made a difference in yields. Initially, the farmers of Europe used the labor provided by those draft animals to tap into a rich source of natural capital, the thick fertile soils made accessible by clearing ancient forests. The heavy plows used to break that soil, first introduced during Roman times, required more animal power than other types of plows did and hence encouraged the integration of draft animals into the rural economy. Such animals, through their manure, moved nitrogen from meadows to agricultural soil. Perhaps even more important was the fact that the labor performed by oxen and horses was inexpensive in terms of nitrogen, at least when the fields they plowed received their manure. Although horses and oxen had to be fed, which reduced the amount of nutrition available for humans, much of their manure—and therefore nitrogen—remained in the field, allowing greater levels of protein to be produced overall.[24]

According to historian Lynn White, Jr., those plows also had another effect: they ended up saving human labor by eliminating the need for cross plowing, which had been necessary with the lighter scratch plows. In addition, when fields were plowed in the same direction year after year, a sequence of low ridges and valleys formed on the land. In the wettest years, the ridges helped to ensure a better crop, as did the valleys in the driest years. The dissemination of technologies such as the horse collar, which allowed a horse to pull without putting pressure on its windpipe, and the horseshoe, which increased traction and protected hooves, further facilitated the use of animal power in medieval fields.[25]

By the eleventh century, despite periodic invasions and social upheaval, the manorial estates of feudal Europe proved to be capable of freeing up a relatively large amount of labor for nonagricultural tasks. Europe, however, remained a cultural backwater compared to its trans-Eurasian contemporary, the Song Dynasty. For that matter, it was also a backwater compared to the Byzantine and Islamic empires that lay between the two. Greater cities and wealth could also be found in India and southeast Asia. Yet by the eleventh century, an important piece of nitrogen-related knowledge, unrelated to agriculture, was diffusing east to west—an innovation that would have a substantial effect on the institutions of Europe: the recipe for explosive powder.

A Long Line of Empires and the Dissemination of Technology

The capacity of the Song Dynasty to support a thriving urban population and the capacity of feudal Europe to produce a reliable surplus were both part of a much larger dynamic, one that encompassed the whole of Eurasia. Within 7,000 years of agriculture's roots along the Tigris and Euphrates and 4,000 to 5,000 years after its emergence in other major river valleys, sedentary societies could be found throughout the Eurasian land mass, each with its own forms of social organization, guiding myths, and patterns of trade and governance. On no other continent did such a large area of land come to be occupied by a contiguous line of agricultural societies.

The development of this network of kingdoms, empires, and civilizations along what Jared Diamond has called the long "east-west axis of Eurasia" did not occur in a tidy fashion.[26] Over the course of several thousand years, environmental disasters—such as the slow buildup of salts in the soils of ancient Mesopotamia and a volcanic event that hastened the slow decline of the Minoans—sometimes led to the collapse of entire civilizations.[27] Also, in more than a few cases, nomadic societies exploded out of the territory that nurtured them, conquering populations and creating powerful empires, only to have those empires collapse, leaving the land they had temporarily ruled in chaos. At other times and in other places, empires came and went without much effect on local practices; the only thing that changed was the direction in which tribute flowed. Amid the rise and fall of individual societies, empires, and civilizations, though, a vast network of agricultural societies remained.

This line of agricultural societies, stretching 6,000 miles from the Pacific to the Atlantic, gave rise to a phenomenon with important implications for the dissemination and adaptation of knowledge. An innovation originating in one society could now disseminate along this line of civilizations, slowing evolving as various societies adapted it to their benefit. Over the long term, an innovation anywhere along this line could potentially affect all societies, slowly disseminating from civilization to civilization, from one side of Eurasia to the other and, in some cases, back again. Furthermore, if one society, empire, or civilization collapsed, its knowledge and technology did not necessarily die with it. Whatever had already been disseminated to neighboring societies remained, eventually flowing back into whatever societies replaced those that had collapsed. Neither the Song Dynasty nor feudal Europe—nor the civilizations between the two—would have experienced the same pattern of development if they had emerged in geographical isolation.[28]

Compared to today, however, few innovations disseminated quickly. The spread of agricultural innovations, for example, tended to be fairly slow. After all, agricultural systems that are suited for a particular set of soils and climate gradually co-evolve with local patterns of land use and governance, local religious practices and rituals, and other local aspects of culture and social structure. Over time, therefore, agricultural practices come to be deeply embedded in the daily and seasonal flow of rural life, highly specific to the political, cultural, and social systems with which they have co-evolved. Knowledge associated with how to prepare paddies, for instance, was not likely to spread to regions in which life revolved around an entirely different agricultural system.

Even the diffusion of recipes for making medicines, dyes, inks, and solvents posed challenges. Although some knowledge, such as how to separate two liquids by distillation, was fairly portable, other knowledge was not, especially if it depended on the availability of specific types of plants and minerals. The diffusion of knowledge associated with smelting and working iron posed similar difficulties due to variations in things such as the content of ores. However, those who acquired and manipulated this type of knowledge tended to be far more willing to experiment than were peasants engaged in agriculture. If nothing else, a failed experiment posed much less risk than a failed crop did. In the end, diffusion of this type of knowledge—although slow, passing from master to apprentice and traded among masters with caution—occurred regularly and was accompanied by substantial trial-and-error learning.

Nobody knows who mixed the first batch of explosive black powder—a mixture of saltpeter (the nitrogenous compound potassium nitrate), charcoal, and sulfur—or when and where he or she did it. Most likely, the mixture has its roots in the alchemical networks of the Tang Dynasty, a period in which practitioners made flares and weapons out of powders that burned with intensity. What is known is that, by the eleventh century, military handbooks in the Song Dynasty were describing how to produce black powder for use in incendiary weapons. Diffusion of knowledge related to explosive black powder also required diffusion of methods for obtaining saltpeter, which, of the three ingredients, was necessary in the largest quantity and the most difficult to obtain.[29]

In Europe, efforts to secure large supplies of gunpowder (and hence saltpeter) for cannon and firearms eventually became entangled with the emergence of two powerful systems of knowledge production—that is, two powerful socially constructed systems of nested trial and error: first, the process of science, which facilitated the production of explanatory or predictive knowledge; and second, market capitalism, which facilitated the production of technological knowledge. These two systems eventually allowed Europeans to bypass the ecological limit associated with the production of fixed nitrogen in agricultural systems dependent on nitrogen-fixing bacteria. Over the course of the millennium, western Europe first reached that limit and then pushed beyond.

4

N and the Emergence of Market Capitalism

Europeans' exposure to black powder is inextricably linked to a wide range of societal changes, many of which were well under way before the arrival of this explosive material. However, subsequent efforts to secure its main ingredient, nitrogen-rich saltpeter, serve as a good lens for viewing these changes. Of special importance is the emergence of market capitalism in Europe, a socially constructed cycle of variation and selection that facilitates the production of technological knowledge. Among other things, this new system of knowledge production rewarded innovators for developing more efficient methods of production, including those associated with the production of saltpeter. Furthermore, given that the search for saltpeter placed merchants in competition with farmers for access to chemically active nitrogen, it also shows that nitrogen-related changes in the agricultural sector accompanied the rise of capitalism.

An Explosive Mix

At the end of the eleventh century, before the arrival of explosive black powder, feudal Europe faced a significant challenge. Some of its surplus was being used to train armed fighters who fought petty battles among themselves and terrorized those around them, contributing to a general atmosphere of lawlessness. In short, a portion of the wealth of medieval society was being used to increase, rather than reduce, the general level of violence and chaos in that society.

Leaders recognized that a problem existed. Indeed, in 1095, when Pope Urban II convened a meeting of three hundred French lords and bishops in Clermont, a cathedral city situated on a tributary of the Loire River, about four hundred kilometers south of Orléans, he declared: "It is so bad in some of your provinces, I am told, and you are so weak in the administration of justice, that one can hardly go along the road by day or night without being attacked by robbers; and whether at home or abroad one is in danger of being despoiled either by force or fraud."[1] He sought the group's council on a range of issues, but one stood out among all others: a request from the Byzantine emperor for military support against the Seljuq Turks, who were pushing into Byzantine territory. This request, for which Urban II passionately argued, represented an opportunity to dedicate the knights of Europe to something other than petty squabbles.

Urban painted his call for support as a holy war for the liberation of Jerusalem, which the Seljuqs had closed to Christian pilgrims some two decades earlier. He knew that his words would resonate with the assembled leaders. After all, his predecessor, Pope Gregory VII, had made a similar proposal twenty years earlier. At that time, a major dispute between the pope and the Holy Roman Emperor had complicated matters. Since then, however, a variety of other voices had begun to call for the kingdoms of Europe to support their fellow Christians. What Urban II did not anticipate, though, was the magnitude of the response. Soon after the council disbanded, tens of thousands of untrained peasants, emboldened by a charismatic monk and led by a handful of minor knights, mobilized, departing months before the date sanctioned by Urban II. Streams of better-trained fighters soon followed, albeit with little more coordination of strategy than those who had preceded them.[2]

Neither did Urban II anticipate that, during the next two hundred years, waves of knights and assorted adventurers would make the journey eastward, with each successive crusade becoming a more and more transparent exercise in organized plundering. Furthermore, each returning wave of crusaders brought back intriguing artifacts and stories of cities larger and more sophisticated than any found in feudal Europe. Gradually, these crusades morphed into trade between Europeans and distant merchants, with the Mediterranean Sea serving as their economic highway.[3]

The exposure of crusaders and medieval traders to other cultures reinforced several trends. Even before the crusades, Greek and Arab scholarship had been trickling into Europe from Moor-occupied portions of the Iberian Peninsula, and a body of Christian scholars had become acquainted with the philosophical systems of Aristotle and other ancients. Some of these scholars hoped to use Greek approaches to reason and logic to explain the teachings of the Roman church, and increased contact through trade channels simply reinforced scholars' interest in using eastern knowledge to benefit European society.

By the thirteenth century, scholastics such as the Franciscan Roger Bacon were working directly with Arab texts and beginning to ask sophisticated questions about the nature of knowledge and how to determine whether something was true. Bacon came to the conclusion that arguments based on logic alone had limits. He emphasized the value of rooting logical arguments in empirical evidence obtained through measurement, mathematics, and observation. In the end, Bacon did not have much direct influence on the development of an empirically based system of inquiry in Europe, but his emphasis on the empirical did affect something just as dramatic: the art of making explosive powder from European ingredients.[4]

Although Bacon is often credited with testing and disseminating one of the first written recipes for explosive powder within the alchemical networks of Europe, historians familiar with the period note that he probably played a relatively small role.[5] Bacon did have an interest in the alchemical arts and, like others of his time, probably did come into contact with explosive powder in the form of firecrackers that traders had brought back from the Arab world. Perhaps he also sought out more information about this novelty and even experimented with the powder himself, but it is unlikely that he played a central role. In any case, the dissemination of explosive power from east to west did not depend on the actions of a single pivotal individual. What is more important is that a network of practitioners capable of experimenting with and disseminating information about explosive powder and its ingredients existed. Early European knowledge about explosive powder flowed within this network from one practitioner to another, each experimenting with the recipe in his or her own way. Much effort was devoted to securing the necessary ingredients—saltpeter, sulfur, and charcoal—and learning, through trial and error, how to mix them in a proportion that produced the desired result.

Of the three ingredients in explosive powder, the one needed in the greatest quantity, saltpeter, was also the most difficult to acquire. The challenge lay in obtaining enough of the salt to produce more than a small amount of powder. Generally, saltpeter can be found wherever moist soil containing decaying matter dries out, resulting in the crystallization of nitrate salts. While moist, soil supports the activity of nitrifying bacteria, which convert the ammonia released from decaying matter into nitrate. When that soil dries—or if nitrate-rich water leaches onto a dry surface, as might happen if the soil lay in contact with a porous wall—the nitrate crystallizes into several different kinds of salts, forming a white powder that can be scraped off and collected. In some places, such as parts of India, the climate and sequence of rainy and dry periods mean that these salts form naturally. In most parts of Europe, though, conditions are less favorable, and in the thirteenth century the most reliable source was the efflorescence found on interior walls below ground level.[6]

At first, the properties of European explosive powder varied widely from batch to batch due to differences in the size of granules and the quality of ingredients. Securing pure saltpeter posed a special challenge. When salt-peter (potassium nitrate) crystallizes out of soil, it appears as part of a mixture of several nitrate salts, including sodium nitrate and calcium nitrate. Because the other salts readily absorb water, any explosive powder containing those compounds deteriorates rapidly when exposed to dampness. In China and elsewhere, alchemists had learned how to convert a mixture of salts into pure saltpeter before using it as an ingredient in explosive powder. To remove the unwanted salts, they dissolved the crude mixture in a solution of wood ash (sometimes called pot ash or potash). The potassium in the wood ash replaced the unwanted material, leaving only potassium nitrate upon recrystallization. Europeans initially obtained most of their refined saltpeter from India through trade that passed through cities such as Milan and Venice.[7]

Over the course of the fourteenth century, as Europeans experimented with many different mixtures and uses, they learned to manufacture an explosive powder with fairly consistent properties. To Europeans, the main value of explosive powder lay in its ability to propel projectiles out of weapons. With the technology associated with casting church bells readily available (and with regular warfare encouraging experimentation), Europeans soon learned to build cannons as effective as those developed elsewhere, even in China. In the process, knowledge of how to produce explosive powder gradually flowed from the hands of alchemists into new craft networks capable of obtaining, processing, and mixing all the necessary ingredients into a consistent product.[8]

Being able to secure steady supplies of gunpowder (and saltpeter) became very serious business in the latter half of the fifteenth century, when warring states' use of cannons became less experimental. In the Battle of Castillon (1453), the last battle of the Hundred Years' War, French cannons breached English strongholds with relative ease. In the same year, the Ottoman Turks successfully used artillery to pound the walled city of Constantinople into submission. Less than a half-century later, the armies of Castile broke Moorish strongholds on the Iberian Peninsula with a siege train of 180 cannons. The demand for gunpowder further increased when ships carrying cannons proved to be an especially effective weapon against other ships and land-based defenses. As a result, the lightly armed caravels used by early European explorers soon gave way to the heavily armed galleons that would dominate the oceans for almost two centuries. The development of reliable muskets, which by the seventeenth century became the main infantry weapon in European armies, further increased the demand for gunpowder with consistent properties.[9]

As the craft of producing gunpowder advanced in Europe, officials in emerging nation-states began sending out saltpeter collectors to gather the valuable material wherever they could find it, giving them authority to scrape powder off walls and to dig around as necessary. By the late fourteenth century, saltpeter collectors knew that soils around stables were particularly rich in whatever it was that gave rise to saltpeter's special qualities, a material that English speakers came to call *nitre*. They also learned that they could dig up this soil, filter water through it, and capture and refine whatever nitre-rich liquid drained out.[10]

As the need for gunpowder continued to grow, saltpeter collectors using these methods found that they could not keep up with demand. Eventually, they turned to a more systematic method of generating the desired material: the construction of nitre beds. This technology, first used by the Chinese sometime before the mid-twelfth century, generated saltpeter by imitating nature. In this system of production, urine and dung were routinely added to heaps of decomposing organic matter. Then, as salts formed on the heap, they were removed and refined. In essence, people were colonizing nitrifying bacteria and using them to convert decaying matter into nitrates.[11]

In Europe, the first nitre beds were in operation by the early fifteenth century, but their widespread dissemination did not occur until the sixteenth. By then, different systems for operating nitre beds had emerged in different regions. In seventeenth-century Sweden, for example, each homestead was required to deliver some portion of the material needed for nitre beds—soil, sheep dung, ashes, wood, and straw—to saltpeter works operated by the Crown. Between 1630 and 1700, thousands of such Swedish saltpeter works sprang into operation.[12] In England, *petermen,* who were as feared as tax collectors, hauled the desired material away themselves. Landowners complained that petermen routinely commandeered carts, tore up floors without replacing them, and generally acted without respect for property. But so valuable was saltpeter to the state that, in 1626, King Charles I ordered his subjects to save their urine so that petermen could collect it and pour it on their nitre beds.[13]

Even with nitre beds, saltpeter collectors could not supply enough material to meet the demands of the military, so states with large militaries began to explore alternatives. The simplest alternative involved turning to imports. In 1694, for example, the British House of Commons required that the East India Company annually supply the state (for a price) with five hundred tons of saltpeter from India.[14] Not all states could increase their imports as easily. By 1750, the French were consuming almost 2,000 tons of the material each year and relied on private companies to deliver what they needed. However, those suppliers failed to keep the military adequately supplied during the Seven Years' War (1756–63). In response, the French created a Royal Gunpowder and Saltpeter Administration to develop a method for efficiently producing the material. This organization, led by commissioners such as the former salt tax collector and pioneering chemist Antoine Lavoisier, was among the first to turn to science for answers. However, another shift, just as fundamental—the emergence of market capitalism—was already well under way.[15]

N and the Shift to Market Capitalism

While ocean-going explorers seeking new trade routes streamed out of western Europe in the fifteenth and sixteenth centuries, the population of the world stood at 400 to 500 million people.[16] Relatively few lived in cities and towns. Even in the largest and most powerful societies, most people were peasants, working the land to produce the food that kept everyone alive. Unless a society could increase the productivity of its agricultural base, the proportion of people tied to the land was not likely to change much. Yet in western Europe new social institutions were emerging, facilitating change that would, during the next several hundred years, dramatically alter agricultural practices. An important part of this change had to do with the system of political economy we refer to as *market capitalism,* a societal-level cycle of variation and selection that rewards innovators who develop and adopt methods for producing food and other goods more efficiently.

The emergence of a decentralized system of rural production for the collection and processing of saltpeter exemplifies the transition to market capitalism. Among other things, it reflects the increasing capacity of European merchants to coordinate the production of goods using rural labor. As the emerging states of Europe were empowering commercial agents to produce saltpeter through rural resources, merchants were also beginning to use rural workers to perform a variety of other nonagricultural tasks— everything from the production of charcoal and iron to the manufacture of textiles. Indeed, over time, in what has come to be known as the "putting-out" system of manufacturing, individuals and even entire villages came to specialize in jobs such as the combing or spinning of wool while merchants moved flows of material from village to village and ultimately through the entire production process.[17]

These systems of rural production allowed societies to tap into the surplus labor available in the countryside and laid the foundation for a new set of social relations, gradually disintegrating the bonds that tied peasants to the land and agriculture. Over the course of several centuries, the peasants of feudal Europe shifted from being integrally linked to the land to a more portable commodity, one whose labor could be bought for cash and released at will. Simultaneously, land shifted from being primarily dedicated to peasant subsistence (any surplus was merely skimmed off the top) to something that could be owned and organized as landowners saw fit—for example, supplying merchants with wheat, wool, and meat in exchange for cash.[18]

This shift from the rules governing feudal society to those we associ-ate with market capitalism gave rise to an entirely new dynamic. Among other things, the new rules encouraged constant innovation. People who succeeded in producing food or other goods more efficiently than others did acquired great wealth, which many used to foster further innovation. For example, the first merchants to provide rural workers with spinning machines or, in a later generation, to gather those machines under one roof and power them with belts driven by steam engines, steadily accumulated wealth and, with wealth, power. Those who shied away from innovation lost both. In effect, market capitalism gave rise to a continuous cycle of variation and selection that resulted in the generation and dissemination of technological knowledge associated with efficiently producing goods for a market.

Market capitalism also set the stage for innovation—and changes in flows of nitrogen—within the agricultural sector. When agricultural land was viewed as part of a manorial commons, with peasants working strips of land according to tradition, relatively few changes in practice could occur. How-ever, as traditional practices disintegrated and feudal obligations eroded, landowners increasingly became free to experiment with new agricultural practices. Indeed, by the early eighteenth century, many English landown-ers were systematically experimenting with different agricultural schemes, searching for ways to produce more of what merchants—that is, the mar-ket—valued. Gradually, over many generations, much of the land that peas-ants had previously depended on for subsistence came to be dominated by herds of livestock and fields dedicated to growing crops for urban markets. In the process, many peasants had no choice but to engage in rural, proto-industrial activities, reinforcing the change that was already taking place. Furthermore, the kings and leaders of fledgling states—interested in access-ing more wealth, which they needed to maintain a well-equipped military force capable of winning wars and suppressing rebellion—encouraged the ongoing transformation of manorial commons into private property, first passively and later by laws that explicitly allowed for their enclosure.[19]

This transition to market capitalism did not happen everywhere in western Europe at the same pace or even in the same way. But over the course of several centuries, roughly from 1500 to 1800, more and more of western Europe's productive capacity flowed into markets. Various types of markets, of course, had previously existed, not only in medieval Europe but in all societies and civilizations. But most had involved the movement of a society's surplus and little else. In western Europe, however, even food nor-mally associated with subsistence began to move through these channels. Indeed, urban populations began to exert as much claim on the food supply as did the peasants who labored in the fields.[20]

New patterns of agriculture also emerged, altering flows of nitrogen and increasing the amount of protein that could be produced per hectare of land. For example, by the eighteenth century, English landowners, who had been systematically experimenting with new agricultural practices for several generations, had converged upon a four-course scheme of crop rotation, replacing fallow fields with fields that grew legumes for grazing and adding a field for fodder crops. By using nitrogen-fixing leguminous plants such as clover to maintain stocks of animals, farmers could produce relatively large quantities of meat, wool, and other marketable products while capturing most of the animal's nutrient-rich manure for future rotations of nitrogen-hungry grains. In addition, systematic trial-and-error experimentation also led to improved seed varieties, more efficient methods of sowing seed, more intensive weeding, and the practice of adding lime (which can be beneficial when soils are too acidic). Once proven useful, such practices spread rapidly through the rural areas of England and further increased the nation's agricultural productivity. As a result, average yields of wheat rose from roughly twelve bushels per acre in medieval England to about twenty bushels per acre in 1800. Other crops experienced a similar increase in yield, and increased levels of nitrogen fixing were critical to the change.[21]

This rise in agricultural productivity was accompanied by a steady rise in England's urban-rural ratio. In 1500, for example, England's population—still rebounding from a plague-related collapse—hovered at about 2.5 million, with fewer than 10 percent of all people living in cities and towns. By 1700, the total population had climbed to about 5 million, with approximately 20 percent living in cities and towns. A century later, with a total population of about 9 million, close to 30 percent of the people lived in cities and towns, an urban-rural ratio that had rarely been achieved anywhere before and certainly not on the same scale. If nonagricultural rural laborers caught in the proto-industrial netherworld had also been taken into account, England's urban-rural ratio would have been even larger.[22]

A growing urban-rural population ratio also meant that a greater proportion of the nitrogen removed from agricultural soils was now being transported longer distances and concentrated in cities. Very roughly, the flow of nitrogen into English cities by way of food supplies increased from about 800 tons in 1500 to about 9,000 tons in 1800. Most of this nitrogen ended up in cesspools and privies, embedded in urine and feces. The manure produced by urban horses only added to total. In any case, in English cities, little of the nitrogen in the food and feed that entered cities made it back to agricultural soil.[23]

Along with this steady increase in England's urban-to-rural ratio came an increase in the size of English cities. In societies dependent primarily on muscle power—that is, pre-industrial agricultural societies—few cities ever reached populations greater than 100,000 residents. After all, large cities require a large rural base to supply it with food. With rural-urban ratios hovering at about nine to one, a city of 5,000 people implied a hinterland of about 45,000 peasants who were raising food. Doubling the size of a city from 5,000 to 10,000 people meant doubling the rural base as well, from about 45,000 to 90,000 people. Furthermore, the amount of land that was being worked also had to double. After all, increasing the rural population without a proportional increase in agricultural land did nothing in the way of securing more food for urban centers. If anything, increases in the rural population without a corresponding increase in land reduced the food available to feed cities.

Still, with empires, relatively large cities were possible. In 600 B.C.E., the population of ancient Babylon reached about 200,000 people, which suggests that it rested on the surplus produced by another 1,800,000 people or so. Four hundred years later, the center of the Han Dynasty, Chang'an, achieved a population of about 400,000 people. Several hundred years after that, the city of Rome, with a long straw into Egypt's rich granaries, peaked at about 800,000 people. In 800 C.E., several hundred years after the collapse of Rome, the population of Chang'an—this time as the center of the Tang Dynasty—hovered at about 1 million people. At the same time, Baghdad, as the center of an Islamic empire that stretched from North Africa to northern India, sustained a similar population. In 1800, Beijing, home to about 1,100,000 residents, stood out as the largest city in the world.[24]

Even great empires had trouble feeding cities much larger than 1 million people. For one thing, maintaining armies to extract food from distant societies and transporting that food back to urban centers presented a major challenge. Furthermore, when an empire collapsed, the food flowing into its large cities dwindled. Large cities also faced challenges in trying to effectively dispose of sewage. Given that the physical size of cities did not expand in proportion to population increases, significant crowding often occurred and gave rise to sewage-filled and rat-infested slums. Few cities managed the disposal of sewage well, and poor sanitary conditions eventually turned most cities into death machines that consumed rural migrants. Even cities that developed mechanisms for managing waste, such as Beijing, which used scavengers to return the city's night soil to agricultural land, faced sanitary challenges.[25]

In 1800, London, with a population of about 850,000 people, was rapidly approaching the size of history's largest and greatest cities. Increased yields made possible by four-field systems of crop rotation certainly contributed to this growth. After all, every increase in what each acre of land yielded translated into more food for cities. But English cities were also importing food from other nations. Indeed, in 1800, England imported roughly 30 percent of what was needed to feed its cities, leading observers such as Thomas Malthus to argue that continued population increases would eventually outstrip the available food supply.[26] However, England did not have to use its armies to secure that food. By trading with other nations through markets, mainly by exchanging manufactured goods for grains, the nation was able to support a portion of its urban population using the agricultural labor (and nitrogen) of other countries. In effect, markets had come to replace armies as a tool for securing the surplus wealth of other societies, especially trade with societies in which a small group of ruling elites—such as the nobility of eastern Europe—benefited from that trade.[27] Furthermore, innovations facilitated by market capitalism, such as those associated with steam engines and the construction of transportation canals, resulted in much more efficient flows of resources.

Meanwhile, the importance of gunpowder to military operations continued to rise. As a result, the production of saltpeter from manure- and urine-rich nitre beds, which removed nitrogen compounds from agricultural soils, competed directly with hungry cities. Eventually, industrializing nations began importing saltpeter, which allowed them to secure the scare material without stripping their own soils of nutrients. For example, by 1800, England had turned almost completely to the nitre beds of India for its supply of saltpeter. In that year, about 3,000 tons of saltpeter flowed out of India to England. In effect, England had shifted its loss of soil nutrients to foreign lands.[28]

Taken as a whole, the world still had to depend on nitrogen-fixing bacteria to fix new supplies of nitrogen. At the same time, industrializing nations were beginning, on a small scale and with no discernable consequences, to bypass that limit regionally through imports of food and saltpeter. However, urban populations and the demand for food continued to grow, as did manufacturers' demand for the nitrogen compounds needed for explosive powder. In the coming century, therefore, efforts to secure enough nitrogen to maintain this growth became even more important.

5

N and the Rise of Science

In the nineteenth century, technological change, fueled by the engine of market capitalism, dramatically altered the ability of industrializing nations to extract, process, and transport the material that flowed through growing economies. Just as important was another type of change, one that accelerated the pace of innovation in directions rewarded by markets. That change involved using the positivist predictive knowledge generated by the process of science to guide the trial-and-error development of new technologies.

Before the nineteenth century, scientific theories played a relatively small role in the process of technological change. Those who worked to make the production of saltpeter more efficient, for example, generally did so without the benefit of chemical theories to test their ideas and to filter out paths not worth exploring. Instead, equipped with the skills of their craft and guided by tacit knowledge accumulated over years of experience, they relied on brute processes of trial and error. Similarly, the English agriculturalists who converged on four-field systems of crop rotation by systematically varying their practices did so without the aid of sophisticated theories of soil ecology. Even the inventors who developed and improved early steam engines did not use scientific theories to guide their experimentation.[1]

In the nineteenth century, however, innovators increasingly began to use science-based predictive models to guide their experimentation, an approach that allowed them to filter out ideas unlikely to be successful and to dedicate resources to the most promising paths of exploration. Using one cycle of variation and selection (science) to guide the trial-and-error exploration encouraged by another (market capitalism), they pushed the pace of technological development into high gear. In short, innovators were learning how to be more efficient in acquiring the types of technological knowledge that markets and states rewarded. Some of that knowledge—such as how to increase the production of fixed nitrogen—eventually allowed industrial societies to bypass ecological constraints that limited growth, fundamentally altering the relationship between humans and the rest of nature.

From the Technology of Alchemy
to the Science of Chemistry

Five hundred years ago, before what historians have called the *scientific revolution,* most knowledge about medicines, salts, solvents, and other chemicals rested in the practices and procedures of alchemists. In China, India, Persia, and the Arab and European worlds, practical matters such as preparing medicines and assaying metals were generally attended to by loosely networked groups of individuals who had mastered the alchemical arts. Some sought to discover the secret of how to convert lead into gold or to prepare life-extending elixirs, but all knew quite a bit about practical matters as well, such as how to produce a range of interesting compounds from material at their disposal. Most knew, for example, how to make acidum salis (hydrochloric acid) and aqua fortis (nitric acid) as well as how to combine the two in a special mixture, aqua regia (nitrohydrochloric acid), capable of dissolving gold. Although they tended to be highly empirical, constantly trying out new materials and processes, their experimentation focused on improving chemical technology—that is, the processes and procedures for manipulating material—rather than chemical theory.[2]

In the world of alchemy, theories as to why materials reacted as they did tended to be static (and not all that useful) due to a culture of secrecy that decoupled theory from practice. Those who possessed alchemical knowledge worked to protect themselves and their art. Being secretive, for example, helped one to avoid being persecuted for pursuing what others might consider to be the black arts or from being pressed into the service of a powerful prince. Alchemists also saw their activities as having a spiritual component, so they sought to protect their body of knowledge. One alchemist warned that, if alchemy were not kept secret, those less skilled would attempt to repeat what the alchemists had learned but would do so with error.[3]

As a result, alchemists often wrapped explanations of their procedures in metaphysical musings that obscured more than they revealed.[4] Even relatively straightforward explanations, such as the Aristotelian notion that everything consisted of four basic elements (fire, water, earth, and air), offered little guidance to experimenters. Thus, alchemists had no tradition of altering explanatory theories to better predict what they might learn through experimentation. While their recipes and procedures (technological knowledge) steadily evolved, their explanatory theories (predictive or scientific knowledge) did not.

This focus on technological knowledge rather than theory is evident in the writings of alchemists. In describing their procedures, they refer to processes such as sublimation, coagulation, fixation, and distillation in precise terms, much like a practical manual for a chemistry lab. But their theoretical explanations appear to be a half-hearted afterthought. For example, in material ascribed to the early Islamic alchemist Jabir ibn Hayyan (known as Gerber in Europe), one text describes the process of calcination—that is, heating something up until it is reduced to ashes—in a straightforward manner. However, the author's explanation of why different materials respond to calcination in different ways is obtuse, revolving around their similarities and differences to Venus, Mars, Jupiter, and Saturn.[5]

This gap between alchemical technique, which was highly refined, and theory, which was not, is hardly surprising. After all, only the technological knowledge of alchemists was under significant evolutionary pressure: procedures had to work, or they did not get passed on. Theoretical explanations, on the other hand, were under little selective pressure for their predictive power. For example, the ability of alchemists to predict the behavior of materials based on their resemblance to planets was limited, yet that explanation was accepted without question. The theoretical explanations that alchemists disseminated were not judged on their predictive power.

Therefore, while alchemy was empirical in the sense that individuals performed trial-and-error experiments to test and improve recipes and procedures, it was not scientific in the sense of testing and improving predictive theories. The only knowledge that could reliably be passed on was the technological knowledge embedded in successful recipes and procedures. Knowledge about failed experiments never got captured. If an individual alchemist learned from his or her mistakes and accumulated significant amounts of tacit knowledge about what worked and what didn't, disseminating that knowledge was difficult. As a result, alchemists often had no choice but to repeat failed experiments that alchemists from previous generations had already performed.[6]

The evolution of theories with predictive power first emerged in an entirely different field of endeavor: efforts to understand the mechanics of motion. Stimulated by the success of oceangoing adventurers such as Columbus and Magellan, who had provided direct evidence that the Earth was round, a community of interested mathematicians, astronomers, and philosophers began asking practical questions about the implications of navigating the ocean on a globe floating in space. Hence, in 1543, when Nicholas Copernicus published his treatise *On the Revolutions of the Celestial Spheres,* the idea that the Earth revolved around the sun attracted the attention of a wider audience than it would have otherwise.[7]

The idea of a sun-centered universe was not new. Almost 1,700 years earlier, a Greek mathematician, Aristarchus of Samos, had proposed a similar idea, but Aristotle had dismissed the theory. Why did things not fly off the Earth as it moved through space? How did objects stick to a moving Earth? Why didn't the Earth move from under people's feet when they jumped into the air? Now global ocean exploration had transformed what had been an abstract debate between philosophers into something far more important.[8] Not surprisingly, those who embraced the church-approved notion that the Earth lay at the center of the universe dismissed the idea of a sun-centered universe by raising questions similar to Aristotle's. This time, however, philosophers—and, just as important, seagoing navigators—knew without a doubt that the Earth was a globe floating in space. In addition, global navigation made theories predicting the movement of stars more valuable.

A century earlier, Church officials might have been able to contain the heretical notion of a sun-centered universe without much effort. For one thing, in the years before long-distance ocean exploration, fewer people would have been interested. Only a handful of scholars had sufficient knowledge to evaluate Copernicus's treatise, and their pedantic interest was not likely to be seen as a threat. But circumnavigation of the globe and technological innovation in general had changed matters. For example, the printing press, the same innovation that had allowed oceangoing travelers to disseminate what they had learned, provided, albeit indirectly, a safe haven for people who embraced heretical ideas. After all, easy access to printed Bibles (and exposure of the not-so-biblical practices of the Roman Church) had facilitated a Protestant rebellion that placed some areas of Europe beyond the reach of the Roman Church. As a result, in those areas, the idea of a sun-centered universe was disseminated and discussed freely. Printing also gave a larger body of younger scholars access to not only the treatise itself but also the material they needed to evaluate it.[9]

In an effort to understand why people sensed no motion as the Earth revolved around the sun, natural philosophers began to examine the nature of motion in more complex ways. Over time, some devised experiments to see if what they thought should happen actually did happen. For example, when Galileo Galilei, born a generation after Copernicus, experimented with rolling objects down inclined planes, neither he nor those who read his work were interested in improving the ability of objects to roll. Instead, they were interested in how well explanatory theories predicted what they had observed. In effect, they began to experiment for the purpose of testing theories rather than improving technology.[10]

Not surprisingly, the emergence of a community of natural philosophers interested in improving the predictive power of theories generated speculation on the nature of knowledge. For example, Francis Bacon, a lawyer turned philosopher and a contemporary of Galileo, attempted to describe the method by which natural philosophers acquired knowledge. In *New Atlantis*, which envisioned science as a means for acquiring the knowledge to conquer nature, he depicted a utopian society in which "interpreters of nature" had the job of creating theories based on observation and experimentation.[11]

Bacon and his contemporaries certainly believed that general laws of nature rooted in observation could be used to improve practices and technologies. Among the most successful of such theories were the laws of motion proposed by Isaac Newton in 1687, a half-century after Bacon's death. Newton's mathematics predicted the motion of bodies so elegantly that one could now experiment using mathematical equations as a stand-in (that is, as a nested process of variation and selection) for the physical world. For example, using Newton's equations, one could test the angle at which to aim a cannon without even firing a shot. One might have to make small adjustments for wind and the like, but the entire process of aiming and designing cannon suddenly became much more predictable and efficient.[12]

While natural philosophers were making remarkable advances in understanding motion, theories explaining why various chemicals reacted as they did remained relatively static. Technical skills associated with manipulating materials—refining metals, dyeing fabrics, manufacturing gunpowder—were certainly improving. After all, entrepreneurial craftspeople producing goods for a market were continually experimenting with new techniques and processes. But like the alchemists from whom they had inherited much of their knowledge, they did not put much effort into refining theories as to why things happened as they did.[13]

Gradually, however, natural philosophers began to question the explanatory assumptions underlying alchemy; and many of them, including Bacon and Newton, were also familiar with language and methods of alchemy.[14] So was Robert Boyle, a founder of the Royal Society for the Improvement of Natural Knowledge (1660), one of the first organizations explicitly dedicated to the free flow of information describing new explanatory theories and the experiments that supported them. The Royal Society, along with parallel organizations such as the French Academy of Sciences (founded in 1666), gave natural philosophers an institutional venue for presenting their theories along with any supporting evidence to interested and capable audiences.

In *The Sceptical Chymist* (1661), Boyle noted that he could not find, after studying the combustion-related behavior of gases in sealed vessels, any evidence supporting the Aristotelian view that some combination of air, water, fire, and earth formed the basis of all materials.[15] People were also beginning to visualize a substance—nitre—that circulated between the air and the soil, playing a role in both fertility and the explosive power of saltpeter and gunpowder. Boyle himself explicitly discussed "earth pregnant with nitre" as being linked to the formation of "salt-petre."[16] In that same year, the English diplomat and natural philosopher, Sir Kenelm Digby, described saltpeter as akin to a magnet that drew nitre out of the air.[17] Similar observations had already been made by Johann Rudolph Glauber, an alchemist who produced salts for therapeutic purposes. Through his experiments, Glauber had established a chemical connection between ammonia, saltpeter, and vegetation, leading him to identify nitre as the common substance.[18] In 1675, the diarist John Evelyn, whose family had acquired its wealth through the manufacture of gunpowder, noted that "were Salt-Peter (I mean fictitious Nitre) to be obtained in plenty, we should need but little other composts to meliorate our ground." He also described rain as being "impregnated . . . with celestial Nitre."[19] Not long after, in 1676, Edme Mariotte, a member of the French Academy of Sciences, speculated that a material critical to plants was volatilizing into the air, mixing with water vapor, and eventually falling back down to earth and seeping into the ground toward the roots of plants.[20] All of these speculations meshed with observation. After all, nitre beds consumed manure that could otherwise be used to fertilize fields, and the saltpeter that came from those beds could also be used to fertilize fields. Hence, saltpeter must contain the essence of something that plants needed. Finally, saltpeter clearly disappeared after being ignited in gunpowder, suggesting the ability of air to absorb it.

Nevertheless, seventeenth-century chemistry still lacked a body of theory to help explain what was happening. In the 1660s, soon after Boyle's critique of the Aristotelian framework for understanding chemistry, the alchemist Johann Joachim Becher took a step in the direction of a more predictive theory when he proposed that all materials contained an invisible substance called phlogiston that was given up during combustion. He came to this conclusion based on the observation that materials, when burned, lost mass. His theory encouraged others to seek explanations of chemical reactions in terms of flows of phlogiston. If nothing else, embrace of this theory reflected the willingness of chemists trained as natural philosophers to replace older theories with newer ones that had more explanatory power.[21]

The phlogiston theory remained in circulation for almost a century, and it was embraced by most of the eighteenth-century scientists whose work resulted in the identification of important gases such as nitrogen, oxygen, carbon dioxide, and hydrogen. Guided by the phlogiston theory and working both competitively and cooperatively, these early chemists learned how to identify gases by measuring their solubility in various solutions, their ability to support combustion and respiration, and their reaction with other materials. Everything, though, was interpreted in terms of phlogiston. For example, Joseph Priestley called oxygen "dephlogisticated air," reasoning that it had been stripped of all phlogiston and had thus increased its ability to receive phlogiston and to support combustion. Daniel Rutherford, on the other hand, called atmospheric nitrogen "phlogisticated air," reasoning that nitrogen did not support combustion because it already contained enough phlogiston and had no ability to absorb more.[22]

Careful measurements of weights, volumes, and densities eventually led scientists to reject the phlogiston theory in favor of a new one. Antoine Lavoisier, the French chemist who developed more efficient methods for preparing saltpeter while serving in France's Royal Gunpowder and Saltpeter Administration, made the critical leap. As a former tax collector, he had developed the habits of an accountant and was always checking to see if flows of goods were balanced. In his new position, he wondered what was happening to the ingredients of gunpowder after detonation. While wrestling with that question, Lavoisier came to the conclusion that the weight of the rapidly expanding gases had to equal the weight of starting materials. Hence, after Lavoisier's contemporaries had demonstrated that inflammable air (hydrogen) burned in the presence of dephlogisticated air (oxygen) and formed an amount of water equal to the mass of the gases consumed, he theorized that water, long considered a fundamental substance, actually consisted of two different substances that could be separated and recombined. Lavoisier then set out to identify the set of all inseparable substances by applying a new theoretical model, the conservation of mass, to the data collected by other chemists. In his final list, he identified thirty-three materials, with all but two (heat and light) now recognized as elements. Nitrogen, not surprisingly, acquired a spot on his list. Although Lavoisier ended up being beheaded during the French Revolution, his theory on the conservation of mass disseminated rapidly and, as much as any other development, marked the start of modern chemistry.[23]

Learning about N

Lavoisier's peers recognized that a theoretical tool such as the conservation of mass opened the door to an entirely new approach to chemistry. By keeping track of masses, one could figure out a great deal about chemical reactions. In the years after Lavoisier's death in 1794, others began to do exactly that, and nitrogenous compounds received their share of attention.

The speed at which the next generation of chemists moved toward constructing a new body of chemical theory is breathtaking, especially after centuries of so little change. By 1805, John Dalton, who made his living as a teacher of natural philosophy, had developed the law of multiple proportions. He showed that elements combined as ratios of whole numbers, such as one unit of nitrogen to two of oxygen, never in ratios of 1.3 to 1 or the like. Among other things, this fact suggested that elements existed as irreducible atoms of different weights and that their relative weights could be calculated.[24] Meanwhile, chemists such as Humphry Davy set about using new technologies, such as electrolysis and equipment for generating electric arcs, to separate and recombine the constituents of various solutions and gases.

Davy, who often demonstrated the findings of chemists in entertaining and well attended public lectures, specifically experimented with a variety of nitrogenous gases. For instance, he demonstrated the effect of nitrous oxide (N_2O), or laughing gas, on the human body and, through public demonstrations backed by a five-hundred-page treatise, helped to popularize its recreational use. He also demonstrated how to use an electric arc to recombine atmospheric oxygen and nitrogen to form nitrogen dioxide (NO_2). From nitrogen dioxide, Davy could produce a number of other nitrogenous compounds, including nitric acid. In effect, chemists had learned to fix nitrogen in small amounts.[25]

Between 1802 and 1812, Davy gave a series of lectures on agricultural chemistry in which he summarized what was currently known in the field. Interest in agricultural chemistry had received a boost from the publication of Thomas Malthus's *An Essay on the Principle of Population* (1798) in which Malthus had argued that Europe's rapidly growing population would soon outstrip its food supply. Periodic food shortages throughout Europe made Malthus's argument far more than just an abstract thesis, and Davy himself recommended Malthus for membership in the Royal Society.[26] In his agricultural lectures, Davy identified vegetable matter as consisting mainly of carbon, oxygen, hydrogen, and nitrogen, with smaller amounts of phosphorus, sulfur, and other "undecompounded" substances. Reporting on the work of chemists such as Nicolas-Théodore de Saussure and Jan Ingenhousz, Davy also noted that, while most nutrients entered through the roots, plants obtained their carbon from the air and, in the process, exhaled oxygen. In addition, he noted that agricultural chemists were just beginning to analyze the content of soils and the various manures that farmers added to their soils.[27]

One notable soil additive was Peruvian guano, which German naturalist and explorer Alexander von Humboldt had encountered in 1804, near the end of a five-year expedition to South America. The first descriptions of Peruvian guano had actually reached Europe two centuries earlier, with accounts of local inhabitants who were mining deposits of bird droppings and applying the material to their fields while also taking steps not to disturb the birds and the creation of more material. Humboldt's observations corroborated those reports. He noted that the material had transformed what appeared to be sandy soil into productive land and that large deposits of the material were available. When chemists in Europe tested samples provided by Humboldt, they determined that the material contained high concentrations of nitrate and phosphorus compounds, suggesting that these chemicals might be an especially important component of good manures.[28]

The deposits of guano that Humboldt encountered, some more than 150 feet deep, were the result of a hyperactive ecological system along the arid South American coast. A northward flowing ocean current (now known as the Humboldt current) creates upwellings in the shallow coastal areas, which carry nutrient-rich waters to the surface and sustain a food chain that supports prodigious amounts of fish. At the top of this food chain fly countless birds that gather in island and coastal rookeries, where they continually drop their waste. At the time of Humboldt's visit to the area, this nitrogen- and phosphorus-rich material, untouched by significant rainfall due to the rain-suppressing effect of cool waters being carried north, had been accumulating for centuries.[29]

Humboldt's glowing reports encouraged small-scale experimentation with the material, which prompted further endorsement. After Edward Lloyd, the governor of Maryland, applied a small amount of Peruvian guano to a patch of soil, he pronounced it to be the most powerful manure he had ever seen. However, the lack of a good explanation as to why it worked made some farmers uneasy. Although they recognized its fertilizing powers, they feared that it might negatively affect the long-term productivity of their soil. Germany's leading agricultural scientist, Justus von Liebig, addressed those concerns and reinvigorated interest in soil additives by noting that, while plants needed a variety of nutrients, the one nutrient least available in the appropriate proportions would limit production. This "law of the minimum," expanded on in his 1840 publication *Organic Chemistry in Its Applications to Agriculture and Physiology,* played an important role in encouraging farmers in Europe and the United States to apply material such as guano to their soils. As a result, exports of guano from South America soon began a steady climb, going from a few tons per year in 1840 to 650,000 tons by 1850.[30]

The practice of using guano as a fertilizer was also helped by chemists who developed tools for testing whether a particular batch of the material was genuine. Given that unscrupulous merchants were not above marketing lower-quality products as pure Peruvian guano, farmers who purchased the material initially had to wait a season before determining if they had been swindled. So agricultural chemists came up with a chemical test to determine whether a particular batch of material contained what one would expect to find in Peruvian guano.[31] In essence, farmers and the middlemen they trusted could avoid a season-long, resource-intensive cycle of trial-and-error testing by replacing it with a simple chemical test. Only samples that passed the chemical test—that met a standard set of specifications—were applied to the soil. Use of such tests represented a form of nested variation and selection in which one cycle of trial and error (testing samples) guided another (applying material to the soil and seeing if it had an effect). Among other things, the development of these chemical tests and product standards reduced the ability of unscrupulous merchants to take advantage of farmers and facilitated the rapid dissemination of Peruvian guano.

Even as imports of guano to Europe and North America increased, scientists continued to debate the role that nitrogen played in agricultural productivity. Liebig, for example, did not see nitrogen as a limiting nutrient. Instead, he believed that plants received most of their nitrogen from ammonia released by decomposing organic matter. That ammonia, according to Liebig, rose into the air as vapors and then eventually fell back to earth dissolved in rainwater.[32] Davy had already made it clear that nitrogen could be fixed by an electric arc, suggesting that lightning could routinely place more chemically active nitrogenous compounds into the air. Here, then, was the basis of a crude nitrogen cycle, complete with a role for ammonia vapors and lightning. Only the details needed to be worked out. Nonetheless, Liebig's version of the nitrogen cycle had an important consequence: it discouraged people from making the connection between the restorative power of leguminous crop rotations and a plant's demand for fixed nitrogen.

The person most responsible for challenging Liebig's theory and pursuing the connection between nitrogen and legumes was the French agricultural chemist Jean-Baptiste Boussingault (1802–82). In 1822, South American general Simon Bolivar put out a call for technically trained personnel to staff a scientific station in Bogotá, and the young Boussingault, trained as a mining engineer, expressed interest. Before his departure, he was introduced to the famous Humboldt, who adopted him as a protégé. Boussingault ended up exploring South America for more than ten years and publishing, with Humboldt's help, information about much of what he discovered.

In 1832, toward the end of his stay, Boussingault visited the guano-laden Peruvian coast and, like Humboldt, noted in amazement how the material had transformed sandy soil into productive farmland. Having experienced food shortages as a child, he decided to study the fertilizing power of guano when he returned to France.[33] From the start, he guessed that the critical ingredients in guano were the same ingredients that made leguminous crop rotations important to agriculture. Furthermore, he suspected that legumes could somehow fix atmospheric nitrogen, akin to the fixing of carbon dioxide that all plants were known to perform. Therefore, he initiated a research program that involved growing plants in a controlled environment and comparing the amount of nitrogen being added to soils with that being removed by plants. Clover, he observed, appeared to be fixing nitrogen from the air, something that Liebig declared to be impossible.[34]

At first there was resistance to Boussingault's challenge of Liebig's theory. Liebig himself continued to maintain that the decay of organic material along with ammonia-rich rainwater supplied enough fixed nitrogen for crops to grow and suggested that Boussingault's results had been skewed by ammonia vapors that were serving as a source of nitrogen. Boussingault eventually repeated his exhaustive experiments on flows of nitrogen. Again he painstakingly measured the quantity of nitrogenous material in soils, plants, gases, animal tissue, and waste products, piecing together the basic accounting of where and how much nitrogen flowed as it moved through agricultural systems. This time, however, he sterilized everything before starting his experiments, including soils, unknowingly eliminating any nitrogen-fixing bacteria present. In any case, his experiments no longer showed any increase in the quantity of nitrogen after legumes were grown. He did show, however, that the amount of nitrogenous compounds in rainwater was not enough to provide what crops needed.[35]

Meanwhile, other researchers performed experiments that backed up Boussingault's previous conclusions. In England, for example, the entrepreneurial and innovative landowner John Bennett Lawes had a direct interest in understanding what helped plants to grow better. He recently had launched a company to manufacture a soluble phosphate fertilizer and desired to know how plants responded to this and other fertilizers under different conditions. Therefore, in 1843, he established an experimental farm and hired a chemist trained by Liebig, Joseph Henry Gilbert, to direct his agricultural experiments. After a decade of controlled experiments (and peppery exchanges with Liebig), Lawes and Gilbert came to the same conclusion as Boussingault: plants were getting most of their nitrogen from sources other than ammonia or nitric acid in rainwater. Data gathered at the Rothamsted Experimental Station (which still remains in operation) also pointed toward the ability of legumes to fix nitrogen and to something in the soil capable of converting ammonia to nitrate.[36]

Debates over the details of how nitrogen cycled continued into the 1870s. As it turned out, fully explaining the process required knowledge of microorganisms that simply did not exist before the discoveries of Louis Pasteur and others in the 1860s. As agricultural chemists became aware of the extent to which microorganisms inhabited all soils, they began to investigate their nitrogen-manipulating activities. In particular, in the late 1870s, Jean Jacques Théophile Schloesing and Charles Archille Muntz observed that sterilizing soil with chloroform vapors inhibited the conversion of ammonia to nitrate, suggesting that microorganisms were involved in the process. They also showed that denitrification—that is, the removal of nitrogenous compounds by their conversion into gases—involved organisms. Less than a decade later, two researchers at an experimental station in Prussia,

Hermann Wilfarth and Hermann Hellriegel, identified root nodules as the site of leguminous nitrogen fixation and established the need for organisms to infect legumes before any nitrogen fixing could take place. By 1888, Martinus Beijerinck, a Dutch botanist, had isolated the bacteria involved.[37]

Further knowledge about the movement of nitrogen through soils was acquired in 1895 when Sergius Winogradsky, a Russian soil scientist and pioneer microbiologist, succeeded in growing cultures of bacteria capable of converting ammonia into nitrate. Winogradsky's work revealed the full complexity of the process by which the nitrogen in decaying organic material was made accessible to plants, complete with one set of bacteria oxidizing ammonia to nitrite and another oxidizing nitrite to nitrate. These bacteria, he showed, assimilated carbon dioxide from the air without photosynthesis, using instead the energy made available through the oxidation process.[38]

Therefore, barely a century after Lavoisier and his contemporaries had replaced the phlogiston theory with the principles of modern chemistry, the basic structure of how nitrogen cycled through the natural world had been established. Now scientists had a powerful new tool at their disposal without having to repeat forty years' worth of tedious experimentation performed by Liebig, Boussingault, and their contemporaries. What had been learned was now embedded in an emerging model of the nitrogen cycle, which could be used to predict the likely outcome of experiments involving nitrogen compounds in the soil. In essence, by serving as a stand-in for the real world, this model of how nitrogen cycled accelerated the testing of ideas. Only questions that could not be answered by the model now had to be explored through expensive trial-and-error experimentation in the real world. The same, of course, was now true in many other fields of knowledge. Given that this knowledge also could be used to eliminate much of the trial and error associated with the development of technology, the pace of change in market societies was unlikely to slow down.

6

Bypassing an Ecological Limit

Over the course of a century, England's population more than tripled, rising from about 9.1 million people in 1800 to 32 million people in 1900. Just as important was the increasing percentage of people who lived in cities: the urban-rural ratio climbed from 28 percent to an unprecedented 77 percent. To be sure, not all of the food flowing into English cities came from the nation's own farms. Imports now accounted for more than half of the total food supply; but that food still had to come from somewhere, and urban-rural ratios were on the rise in all industrializing nations. Major changes in flows of food and nitrogen were clearly under way.[1]

Malthus's warning that food supplies would be unable to keep up with an exponentially growing population lingered ominously over the continent. Indeed, in the first two-thirds of the nineteenth century, agricultural chemists such as Liebig and Boussingault explicitly hoped to avoid Malthusian scenarios by finding ways to increase crop yields. Social critics such as Karl Marx and Friedrich Engels chided Malthusians for directing attention away from what they saw as capitalism's tendency to fuel population growth, which they identified as the more important problem; but a few others raised questions that went beyond the issue of population. The American George Perkins Marsh, for example, noted that humans were changing the physical environment in potentially unwise ways. Large-scale projects such as the Erie Canal, he suggested, could have unforeseen consequences on natural systems and should not be undertaken lightly. He expressed special concern about the increasing availability of steam power to those who desired to make such changes.[2]

Such concerns were no match for the engine of innovation that market capitalism had set in motion. In the latter third of the nineteenth century, that engine kicked into high gear, leaving those who advocated caution in the dust. By the end of the century, a network of coal-fired steamships and locomotives connected city to city in ways previously unimaginable. Now bulk material, including food and fertilizers, could be transported over long distances with much less labor, giving rise to regional and even global markets capable of supporting ever-greater economies of scale. The cost of shipping wheat from New York City to Liverpool dropped from twenty-one cents per bushel in 1872 to three cents in 1901.[3] By that time, however, access to nitrogen compounds, constrained by the pace at which bacteria could produce more, hovered as a potential limit on the production of food and the manufacture of industrial chemicals, especially explosives. Recycling the nitrogen that flowed into cities and exited in urban sewage appeared to be a wise strategy.

Then, in the early twentieth century, an important innovation allowed industrial society to bypass bacterial constraints on the production of fixed nitrogen. The Haber-Bosch process for fixing nitrogen industrially in the form of ammonia relieved fears of a nitrogen shortage and made ongoing efforts to recycle nitrogen from urban sewage economically unattractive. It also changed the relationship between humans and the rest of nature by injecting human goals and choices into the dynamics of a biogeochemical cycle that lies at the core of nature.

Pushing an Ecological Constraint to Its Limit

As agricultural chemists such as Boussingault and Gilbert wrestled to understand the ways in which nitrogen flowed through agricultural systems, farmers continued to learn about the value of fertilizers more directly: by using them. Between 1840 and 1880, approximately 20 million tons of guano flowed out of Peru and into the agricultural soil (and eventually the sewers and streams) of Europe and the United States. Although this quantity of material was not large enough to dramatically change national levels of crop production, many farmers learned that they could use it to revive worn-out land, bump up yields, or even skip a rotation of legumes.[4]

Farms received inputs of nitrogen from other sources as well. For example, when they purchased feed for livestock, they were also purchasing nitrogen for their soil. One particularly rich source of feed-based nitrogen was oilseed cake, a waste byproduct produced when seeds were crushed for their oils. By 1856, British farmers were importing 190,000 tons of this material per year. Of course, the urine and manure from livestock had to reach agricultural soil if the nutrients in the feed were to have an effect on crop production. Still, the end result was simply a shift of nitrogen from one farm to another. After all, the nitrogen in all feed, including oilseed cake, still had to come from somebody's soil. One farm's gain was another's loss.

Guano had no such downside, at least not for farmers in Europe and the United States.[5] Indeed, in 1856 the U.S. Congress passed the Guano Islands Act, which empowered ship captains to claim for the United States any guano-rich island not already claimed by another sovereign state. More than sixty islands, most quite remote, were claimed before the act's suspension in 1863, and nine are still U.S. appurtenances.[6]

Meanwhile, scientists continued to wrestle with the question of exactly how nitrogen was fixed. By the time they discovered the role that bacteria played in the production of fixed nitrogen, the guano trade had already peaked and supplies of the material were beginning to dwindle. However, merchants in Europe and the United States still had access to two other sources of fixed nitrogen: mineral deposits of sodium nitrate located along the arid South American coast and coal byproducts. Companies already had been exploiting both sources of nitrogen for about a half-century, but the rising price of guano in the 1870s shifted attention more fully to these alternatives.[7]

Coal's potential to replace the nitrogen previously supplied by guano was limited. The nitrogen content of coal is low, usually less than 2 percent. Therefore, obtaining this nitrogen made economic sense only when companies mined and processed the coal for other reasons. Essentially, when coal was used to manufacture gas for illumination, one could extract the nitrogen, mainly in the form of ammonia sulfate, relatively inexpensively. But in the long term, supplies of coal-based nitrogen were determined by the demand for illuminating gas (and later coke for steel making), not by the demand for fertilizer or industrial chemicals. Indeed, the 95,000 tons of nitrogen extracted in 1898 as a coal byproduct could not be expected to increase too quickly, especially because the invention of the light bulb had dampened the demand for coal-based illuminating gas.[8]

Mineral deposits of sodium nitrate in Chile's bone-dry Atacama Desert had more potential to supply the world's growing demand for fixed nitrogen. In the nineteenth century, nobody knew how the nitrate-rich caliche had come to be deposited in the desert, but experts surmised it to be of organic origin. Only much later did scientists determine that the nitrate had probably come from eons of nitrogen-rich sea spray blowing over the desert. As the spray evaporated in the desert air, its nonaqueous contents fell to the ground.[9] Anywhere else in the world, the salts that accumulated would have been washed away by the first rainstorm, but the Atacama Desert, often touted as the driest place on Earth, saw little rain. Not only does it lie in the rain shadow of the Andes Mountains, but temperature inversions created by the cool waters of the Humboldt Current further reduce the chance of precipitation.[10] Hence, over geological stretches of time, deposits of this nitrogen-rich resource had gradually accumulated.

Reserves of the material, which came to be known as Chilean saltpeter (even though it consists of sodium nitrate, not potassium nitrate), promised to last well into the future. Early twentieth-century estimates placed the existing amount at about 240 million tons.[11] Furthermore, by the time imports of guano had begun to decline, companies had already demonstrated that they could economically mine and transport Chilean nitrate using imported labor and a fleet of ships traveling between South America and ports in North America and Europe. Given the potential value of these deposits, disputes over their ownership eventually led to a war between Chile, on one side, and Peru and Bolivia as allies on the other. In 1866, Chile and Bolivia, both claiming sovereignty over the desolate Atacama Desert, signed a treaty to share taxes imposed on mining operations in the region. By 1879, companies aligned with Chile had come to dominate mining operations. Leaders in Bolivia then attempted to increase their revenue by raising their portion of the taxes. When one large mining company refused to pay, Bolivia (backed by a secret agreement with Peru) seized its assets. Chile then declared the original treaty void and sent in troops to gain control of the area. After several years of naval battles and Chilean forces' invasion of Peru, the warring nations signed an 1883 treaty that left Chile in sole control of the nitrate deposits. By 1890, exports of sodium nitrate had risen to 927,000 tons per year, 642,000 tons of which flowed to Great Britain.[12]

Although the bulk of the sodium nitrate shipped from Chile was directed toward fertilizer use, manufacturers also needed nitrogen to produce an important industrial chemical: nitric acid. Demand for this chemical, used in the production of goods ranging from dyes and photographic films to metals and explosives, was rising quickly. In 1840, manufacturers produced approximately 4,500 tons of black powder, which still represented the state of the art in explosives. By 1890, with the development of dynamite and other high explosives, production of nitrogen-based explosives had climbed to 45,000 tons. Ten years later, in 1900, manufacturers produced almost 115,000 tons of explosives.[13]

The initial demand for better explosives came from mining and railroad companies. In the 1830s, after the French chemist Jules Pelouze discovered that dipping cotton in nitric acid produced a material that burned as energetically as gunpowder, others experimented with various forms of "gun cotton" to use as a mining explosive. Then one of Pelouze's students, Ascanio Sobrero, created an oily liquid with novel properties. Unlike gunpowder and gun cotton, nitroglycerin combined all the necessary ingredients for an explosion in each molecule of the material. In the blink of an eye, nitroglycerin could decompose into a set of gases and expand ten thousand–fold, producing a shock wave far greater than what was possible with black powder. However, as users of this new material soon learned, it was highly unstable.

Because compression-causing jolts were capable of triggering an unwanted explosion, even transporting the material was dangerous. Indeed, soon after its initial use in mining applications and constructing tunnels, serious accidents led to various bans on its use.[14]

Another of Pelouze's students, Alfred Nobel, made the explosive safer by inventing a way to prevent the mixture from exploding until purposely set off. Nobel, whose father manufactured nitroglycerin, discovered that pouring the oily liquid into an absorbent created a material that could be safely handled. He called the invention *dynamite* and received a patent for it in 1867. By 1874, annual sales of this new material had reached 3,120 metric tons. Meanwhile, pushed by competitors, Nobel continued to experiment with other combinations of nitrogenous compounds, carbon, and absorbents. These experiments led to a variety of specialized explosives, including a nitroglycerin-based product he called "Ballistite," which militaries began purchasing as a powerful smokeless propellant for projectiles.[15]

Militaries also began packing high explosives inside projectiles and in casings that served as floating mines. Trinitrotoluene (TNT) emerged as the packing of choice because of its low melting point and ability to be safely poured into a container such as a military shell. First synthesized in 1863 by a German chemist who was experimenting with dyes, the mixture initially received little attention as an explosive because of the high temperatures required to trigger a blast. However, when Russia and Japan went to war in 1904, techniques for detonating the material had been developed, and naval mines containing TNT proved to be effective and deadly. The next large-scale war was sure to involve the use of TNT and other explosives on an unprecedented scale.[16]

Indeed, the specter of war spurred European leaders and scientists to raise questions about what would happen if supplies of sodium nitrate from Chile were cut off. The most famous articulation of this concern came in 1898, one hundred years after Malthus had first published his thesis on food supplies. While presenting a paper titled "The World's Wheat Supply" to a gathering of English scientists, chemist-physicist William Crookes asked what would happen to food supplies if Chilean nitrate were to stop flowing into England, perhaps due to hostile forces' interception of merchant ships. He also pointed to the value of nitrogenous compounds in the manufacture of weapons, noting that to fix "the nitrogen with which a light heart we liberate with a battleship broadside" required "millions of minute organisms patiently working for centuries." He then pointed to the "treasure locked up in the sewage and drainage of our towns" and expressed hope that sanitary engineers would find a way to unlock it. Primarily, though, Crookes encouraged chemists to find an inexpensive way to fix atmospheric nitrogen industrially.[17]

The growing realization that supplies of fixed nitrogen were limited spurred discussions about the value of nitrogen-rich materials. In the first half of the nineteenth century, few people were concerned about selling nitrogen-rich oilseed cake as animal feed, but after Crookes's speech cotton producers began to see this nitrogen loss in new terms. Indeed, in the United States, at a 1901 meeting of the Cotton States Association of the Commissioners of Agriculture, one presenter noted that the seed from a bale of cotton contained thirty-five pounds of nitrogen and that selling this seed inexpensively made no sense because "we are by degrees selling our farms to dairymen and stockmen."[18]

From one perspective, by 1900 industrial society had already bypassed bacterial constraints on the production of nitrogen. Although coal and Chilean nitrate both contained nitrogen that had been fixed by bacteria, the fixing process had been spread out over long stretches of geological time. The resulting deposits were now being mined and placed into circulation at what could only be described, in geological terms, as blindingly fast. Still, on a global scale, in the years before World War I, the half-million tons of nitrogen being pulled out of storage in the form of Chilean nitrates and coal-based ammonia added relatively little to the approximately 120 million metric tons that bacteria fixed and denitrified on land each year.[19]

Only at a local level, in bodies of water that were receiving large doses of urban sewage, did inputs of nitrogen cause any concerns. Even in the case of urban sewage, however, the main problem was not the release of nitrogen but the sheer amount of organic material that was being discharged into urban rivers and harbors. Most people familiar with the sewage-disposal problem saw the situation as temporary. After all, a growing army of sanitary engineers was already hard at work developing ways to treat sewage more effectively. In addition, by the time Crookes gave his famous speech, these engineers were also experimenting with ways to cycle the nutrients in sewage back to agricultural soils.

The development of sewage-treatment technology in the late nineteenth and early twentieth centuries, including aspects of the technology aimed at facilitating the recycling of nutrients, is nothing short of impressive. However, the nutrient-recycling aspect of this technology failed to disseminate. Instead, an equally impressive technology, one that could fix nitrogen from the air, proved to be more attractive.

The Technological Path Not Chosen: The Recycling of Urban N

By the beginning of the twentieth century, the flow of food, energy, water, and other resources into and out of the world's largest cities reached a new level of intensity. Telephone poles and power lines, sewer pipes and water mains, layers of concrete and rails of steel enmeshed urban dwellers in a growing matrix of technology that buffered their interactions with the rest of nature. Only when conflicts emerged, such as those associated with emissions of soot-filled smoke into the air or the release of pollution-causing wastes into water bodies, did urban interactions with the natural environment come to the fore.[20]

One of the first issues to receive serious attention in the rapidly growing cities of the nineteenth century involved a basic task: getting rid of the nitrogen-rich, bacteria-laden organic material that exited the bodies of urban dwellers. Dealing with urban sewage has always required a substantial amount of human ingenuity, but in the nineteenth century the challenge increased.

In terms of human health, nitrogen compounds in urine and the mass of bacteria and bits of undigested food that form the bulk of feces are not the central problem. Pathogenic bacteria pose the main threat. However, in terms of the action required to direct basic material (carbon, oxygen, hydrogen, nitrogen, and smaller amounts of phosphorus, sulfur, and other elements) back to a biogeochemical reservoir capable of absorbing the flow, nitrogen poses the greatest challenge. Most of the carbon that enters a city as food combines with the oxygen we breathe to form carbon dioxide, which is then exhaled to the atmosphere. And most of the hydrogen and oxygen exits as harmless water, whether exhaled as vapor or released in sweat, urine, and feces. However, all of the reactive nitrogen that enters a city eventually leaves in its sewage, potentially cascading through a number of ecosystems before being removed by denitrifying bacteria or taken up by plants.[21] The exact amount of nitrogen flowing into a city depends on the mix of food that residents eat: nitrogen makes up more than 10 percent of protein-rich foods but under 1 percent of foods such as fruits. Nonetheless, all cities have to supply their residents with enough protein (and hence nitrogen) to survive.[22]

In the first half of the nineteenth century, the population of many cities increased rapidly—as did the problem of removing sewage. In 1800, London's population stood at about 850,000, less than the population of Beijing, which hovered at about 1,100,000. By 1850, however, London's population reached 2 million, making it (at the time) the largest city in world history. Another 7 million people lived in other English cities, many of which competed for the same sources of clean water and places for waste disposal. Paris and New York, both home to more than a million people by 1850, were also expanding rapidly, as were slightly smaller cities such as Vienna, Berlin, and Philadelphia. All faced major challenges in securing clean water and disposing of sewage.[23]

Officials in London were forced to address sewage-related problems sooner than officials in most other cities were. Early in the nineteenth century, Londoners received their water from a patchwork of sources, including the Thames River. Some wastes from nearby homes reached the Thames; but most people, living further away, used privies, and their wastes generally did not contaminate the river. The relatively small amounts of liquids exiting privies generally flowed into cesspools before seeping into the ground. As for the solid material, an army of night-soil men routinely emptied the city's privies and carted away the waste to open land on the outskirts of the city. But serious problems emerged after residents gained access to running water and flush toilets, which overwhelmed the capacity of cesspools. Sewage began to spill into surface drainage systems, giving rise to a number of problems—including a major cholera epidemic that rocked the city in 1832, with the hardest-hit areas being the dirty, ill-drained neighborhoods where the poorest residents lived.[24]

Following a theory commonly accepted at the time, health officials attributed the epidemics to noxious miasmas emanating from sewage that lay stagnant in drainage ditches. Moving that sewage and its miasmas away from homes appeared to be the best way of fighting epidemics. Therefore, in 1848, spurred by additional outbreaks of cholera, the city established a sewer commission to address the problem. This body promptly created plans to construct sewers that would replace more than 200,000 cesspools scattered throughout London. Yet as they executed this plan, more and more pathogen-ridden wastes reached the Thames River, turning it into an open sewer.[25] Outbreaks of cholera continued to occur, but faith in the miasma theory prevented most officials from linking those outbreaks to water contaminated by sewage. At the time, little was known about the role of microscopic organisms in the spread of waterborne diseases. Only in 1854 did John Snow, a physician supportive of new ideas that linked diseases to germs, trace a particularly deadly outbreak back to a neighborhood pump that drew water from a contaminated source. Keeping water supplies separate from sewage, he argued, was more important than removing miasmas.[26]

The miasma theory took another hit several years later. In 1858, during a prolonged heat spell that came to be known as the Great Stink, smells emanating from the Thames virtually shut down the center city. Although no miasma-induced epidemic materialized, the incident jolted leaders into action once again.[27] Their search for a solution led, in the 1860s, to the construction of a major new sewer system that intercepted existing flows and pumped everything to a discharge point further downstream. Over the next three decades, as scientists such as Louis Pasteur and Robert Koch demonstrated that specific cultures of bacteria could cause specific types of disease, the germ theory steadily gained broader support.[28] Furthermore, germ theory proved useful in guiding decisions about how to address sewage-related problems. After all, when cities with cholera or typhoid epidemics succeeded in keeping contaminated sewage away from supplies of drinking water, the frequency and lethalness of such epidemics dropped.[29]

By the 1880s, a professional group of engineers charged with developing and managing a body of knowledge specific to the design of water-supply and sewerage systems had emerged in Europe and, to a lesser extent, the United States.[30] Although their main mission was to remove sewage from cities without contaminating drinking water, they were also aware that the flow of raw sewage represented the loss of valuable nutrients. Many hoped to find some way of directing nitrogen-rich sewage back to agricultural land. Indeed, even when London's first sewerage system was designed in the 1840s, before serious concerns had emerged about the availability of fixed nitrogen, planners were discussing the potential fertilizing value of the city's sewage.[31]

By the mid-1880s, interest in cycling nitrogen back to agricultural soils had grown considerably. Sanitary engineers now recognized that any nitrogenous compounds that urban dwellers flushed into the ocean had to be replaced by soil bacteria, extracted from coal, or imported from South America. J. W. Slater, author of an 1888 treatise on "sewage treatment, purification, and utilization," noted that any nation that diverted its nitrogenous material into the sea was wasting a precious resource. In London, he observed, such waste occurred every time someone flushed a toilet. He also placed the issue in a global perspective: "Suppose that London is fed on Indian wheat, Australian mutton, and Argentine beef. . . . Be it so: we are then sterilising India, Australia, etc., and let this game be carried on long enough, and generally enough, and the whole world will become comparatively barren." Slater argued that the most sensible course of action would be to direct the nitrogenous material flowing out of cities back to agricultural land. Through engineering, he and others hoped to use sewers to duplicate the work of scavengers who, in cities such as Beijing, carted away night soil and dried it for sale as fertilizer.[32]

One potential strategy involved applying urban wastewater directly to land, possibly agricultural land, with the soil (and the bacteria in the soil) serving as a natural form of sewage treatment. But direct application of urban sewage to fields never proved to be practical. First, the presence of pathogenic bacteria in untreated sewage generated health concerns. At the very least, some form of pretreatment seemed to be necessary. Second, cities needed a lot of land to receive their sewage; otherwise, every rainfall turned the sewage-irrigated land into a swampy mess, especially since storm water and sewage usually ran through the same pipe. In addition, the availability of inexpensive land near urban centers that was capable of receiving sewage was limited. Third, when land-disposal systems were attempted, operators learned that they continually had to make informed decisions about when to work the sewage into the soil and how to adjust the rate of application based on changing conditions. What initially appeared to be an easy solution actually needed to be managed as an engineered system. Fourth, much of the highly soluble nitrate in the effluent drained away before plants could assimilate it, undermining one of the main motivations for land irrigation. Finally, in cities with industrial facilities connected to the sewer system, a practice that was becoming more common, wastes containing chemicals rendered the sewage and the receiving soil unusable for agricultural purposes.[33]

Officials in most large cities soon concluded that sewage farming was impractical. However, smaller cities with less sewage, less storm water, and more access to land continued to experiment. In the first decade of the twentieth century, approximately thirty cities in France and fifty in Germany were applying some portion of their sewage to agricultural fields. In Germany, a few cities also attempted to use their effluent as a nutrient source for fish farms, with the goal being to increase the production of biomass at the bottom of the aquatic food chain. In the United States, the most successful experiments were in the arid west, where water rather than nitrogen proved to be the more valuable component of sewage.[34]

Meanwhile, the size of cities continued to climb. By 1900, the populations of the largest cities reached what people a century earlier would have considered staggering levels: London, 4.5 million; New York, 3.4 million; Paris, 2.7 million; and Berlin, 1.9 million. Chicago, a city that did not even exist in 1800, had 1.7 million inhabitants by 1900, roughly the same number as Vienna and Tokyo. Changes were also happening on a global scale. It had taken millennia for the population of the world to reach 500,000 million people, which occurred in about 1500. Then the world added another 500,000 million people within three hundred years, reaching 1 billion in 1800. By 1900, the world's population was well on its way to 2 billion, a milestone reached in the late 1920s.[35]

One question that sanitary engineers had to ask involved the extent to which the sewage flowing out of large cities should be treated. For that matter, they also had to determine what it even meant to treat sewage. Clearly, they would need to remove as much organic matter as possible before releasing effluent into a water body, but exactly how much material to remove and how to do it required investigation and choices. Toward this end, they soon developed a way to measure one of the key characteristics they wished to manage: the oxygen demand of the effluent. They knew that, when a water body received too much organic material, the microscopic organisms that digested this material consumed much of the oxygen dissolved in surrounding water. If too much oxygen were consumed, fish and other living things dependent on that oxygen died and added to the amount of decaying material in the water. Furthermore, in the absence of oxygen, the decomposition process continued through the action of anaerobic bacteria, which emit methane and putrid-smelling sulfur compounds. Thus, a main challenge lay in determining how much organic material could be discharged into a particular water body without consuming too much of the available oxygen.[36]

Sanitary engineers also learned that other quantities, such as the pH of the effluent and the amount of suspended solids, were also useful to know when predicting the effect of sewage on a body of water.[37] Nitrogen, too, received special attention. Sanitary engineers knew, for example, that, while nitrogen generally afforded "nourishment to microbia," ammonia was toxic in relatively low concentrations. They also learned quickly that measuring the amount of nitrogen in sewage presented complications because microorganisms could convert nitrogen compounds from one form to another. In the words of J. W. Slater, these compounds were "constantly passing and repassing in to each other."[38]

Slater also opposed specifying discharge standards in terms of concentrations because that simply invited the operators of treatment facilities to dilute their effluent with additional water. Hence, in 1885, when the English Parliament considered a bill that would have made it illegal to discharge effluent containing concentrations greater than ".3 part by weight of organic nitrogen in 100,000 parts by weight of the liquid," Slater agreed with the intent but opposed the bill on the grounds that it might not have the effect that lawmakers wanted. If a town were to dilute its water to meet that standard, he pointed out, the same amount of nitrogen would still be released into stream.[39]

In general, though, by the turn of the century, sanitary engineers had reached consensus on a body of metrics to use in assessing and managing the characteristics of sewage. Given that the bodies of water receiving this sewage differed widely in terms of size, flow, and uses, decisions about specific standards that particular flows of sewage should meet were left to local planners. Sanitary engineers hired by a city or town saw their job as, first, determining how much sewage the local body of water could tolerate and, second, designing an efficient way to adequately treat the sewage.

Methods for actually removing impurities were still being developed. The simplest method involved running wastewater into tanks and allowing as many of the organic solids to settle out as possible. However, sanitary engineers realized that most solids were too small or soluble to settle out. Certain chemicals, they discovered, such as mixtures of iron salts and aluminum oxide, facilitated the precipitation of those solids. The sludge that settled out, if allowed to dry, could then be disposed of on land more easily than raw sewage could. Other disposal strategies, such as mixing the sludge with coal and burning it, were also developed.[40] But some early sanitary engineers explicitly opposed any practices that failed to deliver the nutrients in sewage back to agricultural land. Slater, for one, specifically argued against a method for using sewage in the production of concrete: "The supply of phosphoric acid and of combined nitrogen in the world are not unlimited, and as these substances are the scarcest items of plant-food, their destruction or misapplication is a serious crime against humanity in general, and ought in every way to be discountenanced."[41]

By the mid-1890s, the most promising method of disposal, one with potential for being much less expensive and far more effective than chemical precipitation was, involved re-creating natural processes inside settlement tanks. While experimenting with methods of disposal, engineers had determined that sludge continued to be digested by bacteria even after it settled out, and they looked for ways to take advantage of this ongoing digestion. The city surveyor of Exeter, England, secured patents for what he called a "septic tank system of sewage disposal." Others patented similar ideas, with one of the most successful being the two-story Imhoff tank designed by the director of the Emscher Sewerage District in Germany.[42]

Meanwhile, other sanitary engineers began experimenting with ways to increase the digestion of organic material that remained in suspension. In one of the more promising schemes, engineers directed wastewater over a bed of rocks, which provided sites for sewage-digesting microbes to flourish. Those well-fed microbes could then be removed by gravity in settling tanks.[43] By 1908, one leading engineer was convinced "that it would be cheaper for many towns to abandon irrigation and replace it by artificial biological processes, especially after they grew beyond a certain size."[44] Over the next several years, several sets of researchers—one working for the Metropolitan Sewage Commission of New York, another at an experimental station operated by the Massachusetts Department of Public Health, and a third in Manchester, England—contributed to an even more effective method of encouraging bacteria to digest sewage. In this process, mechanical arms kept a mass of bacteria (referred to as "activated sludge") suspended in an aerated sewage tank. This mass of living organisms, constantly reproducing itself, digested the small particles of organic material many times faster than would have been possible otherwise.[45]

Gilbert J. Fowler, an expert on how to measure the impurities in sewage, saw activated sludge technology as an opportunity to recover the costs of sewage treatment by selling dried sludge as a fertilizer. He had first learned about the activated sludge process while visiting the research laboratory operated by the Massachusetts Department of Public Health. After returning home to Manchester, England, he and others continued to experiment with the new technology. They learned that it produced a sludge with a greater nitrogen content than that produced by trickling filters, where much of the nitrogen ended up being discharged as nitrate and the dried sludge contained only about 1 percent nitrogen. The activated sludge process, on the other hand, produced a sludge containing about 4 percent nitrogen.[46] Therefore, in 1914, when the chief engineer of the Milwaukee Sewerage Commission contacted Fowler about the possibility of designing an activated sludge facility for the Wisconsin city, Fowler recommended that it also consider drying and marketing its sludge as a fertilizer.[47]

In terms of its need for sewage treatment, Milwaukee was unusual for two reasons. First, in 1910, members of the Socialist party had won most of the seats on the city council and, in 1912, the city had elected a Socialist as mayor. Unlike leaders in most other U.S. cities, these officials, who came to be known as "sewer Socialists," were prepared to make large public investments in sewer systems and wastewater treatment plants. Second, more than any other city in the United States, Milwaukee needed sewage treatment.[48]

All U.S. cities had to make some investment in managing wastewater, but the specifics depended on the particular city. Officials generally sought to invest as little as possible in sewage treatment, which often meant that they discharged raw sewage into a bay or fast-moving river. Typically, only when conflicts occurred and some authority stepped in—whether it be a health department, the courts, or a state or national government—did city officials make a serious investment in waste treatment. City officials on the East Coast, for example, did not see a pressing need to treat their sewage. After all, they could pipe in clean water from higher ground and then discharge the city's wastewater into bays and harbors.[49] Similarly, cities on interior rivers, such as Saint Louis and Pittsburgh, could flush their untreated wastes downstream, albeit at the expense of turning long stretches of rivers into open sewers. The knowledge that drinking water could be made safe by disinfecting it with chlorine further complicated matters. After all, some officials questioned the need for investing in expensive wastewater treatment if drinking water could be kept safe by chlorination. Indeed, as long as downstream communities could obtain safe drinking water by chlorination, the legal pressure on upstream communities remained low.[50]

Some cities, such as Chicago, faced a more serious problem: its sewage flowed into the same water body, Lake Michigan, from which the city pumped its drinking water. Civic leaders in Chicago famously solved their problem by digging a canal that connected the Chicago River to the Mississippi River watershed and by then flushing all of its wastes in that direction. The Chicago Sanitary and Ship Canal, one of the largest engineering projects of its time, carried its first flow of sewage away from Lake Michigan in 1900.[51]

Milwaukee faced a situation similar to Chicago's. The city emptied its sewage into two slow-moving rivers, both of which flowed into Lake

Michigan. But the geography of Milwaukee gave it no opportunity to flush its sewage away from Lake Michigan and into another watershed. Typhoid outbreaks in 1909 triggered a high-profile investigation, resulting in a recommendation that the city construct both a water-filtration plant and a sewage-treatment facility. Hence, at a time when most other U.S. cities, even much larger ones, had managed to avoid investing in sewage treatment, city officials in Milwaukee recognized that they had to take some action.[52]

The city's engineers already had been innovative in their efforts to address the problem of two stagnant rivers flowing through the middle of the city. In 1880, putrid smells emanating from the rivers, partly caused by organic-rich brewery wastes, prompted the Milwaukee health commissioner to demand action. City officials responded with a unique solution. In 1888, the city began pumping 450 million gallons of lake water each day to the upstream portion of the Milwaukee River, which helped to flush wastes down the otherwise stagnant river and into Lake Michigan. In 1907, a flushing system for the Kinnickinnic River was also constructed.

However, as the subsequent outbreak of typhoid indicated, neither system did much for the quality of drinking water drawn from Lake Michigan. State and federal health inspectors then began exerting pressure on civic leaders to construct a system for collecting and treating the sewage for this still-growing city of 400,000 people. By 1913, after some bickering between the city's sewer Socialists and their opponents on the city council, the council approved the creation of an independent sewerage commission to manage the design and construction of a sewage-collection system and wastewater-treatment facility.[53]

In 1914, T. Chalkley Hatton, a no-nonsense civil engineer whom Milwaukee had hired to oversee the design and construction of the entire system, began his job by assessing the various treatment strategies available. He first turned to the Electro-Chemical Company of New York, which promoted a system for precipitating out solids using an electric current. Supposedly, the current sterilized the effluent at the same time. When negotiations over the construction of a pilot plant to demonstrate the technology broke down, Hatton turned his full attention to the activated sludge process.[54]

Hatton contacted Fowler to design a pilot-scale activated sludge plant because he wanted to verify that the process would work in a city that experienced bone-chilling winters. When Fowler suggested that Hatton also experiment with dewatering the sludge and marketing it as a nitrogen-rich fertilizer, Hatton pursued the suggestion as a good engineering solution to a waste-disposal problem. To Fowler, however, the recycling of nitrogen was more than a good engineering solution. Indeed, he would later move to India to serve as an agricultural advisor, where he performed soil research that resulted in a treatise on nitrogen conservation. That research informed the work of another British scientist who served as an agricultural advisor in India: Sir Albert Howard, the pioneering champion of organic farming.[55]

Hatton, though, approached the matter only in terms of dollars and cents. After receiving Fowler's design, he constructed the pilot plant on a large strip of land (Jones Island, actually a peninsula) that separates the city's harbor from Lake Michigan. Up and running by the start of 1916, this pilot facility could process 1.6 million gallons of wastewater per day, making it one of the first large treatment plants employing activated sludge technology.[56] Over the next decade, as Hatton oversaw the construction of the city's sewage collection system, he also experimented with new designs for almost all of the components needed for the treatment plant, including the blowers for pushing air through the tanks and the equipment needed for dewatering and drying the sludge. In addition, he redesigned the process to allow sewage to flow continuously through the facility rather than in batches.

In 1925, after almost a decade of experimentation, Hatton completed the Jones Island Wastewater Treatment Plant and the sewer system feeding it. Capable of processing a maximum of 128 million gallons of wastewater per day, it was larger than any of the other sixty or so activated sludge facilities in operation by that time.[57] Hatton also implemented Fowler's suggestion to market the waste sludge as a fertilizer. The new facility included equipment for drying and packaging approximately one hundred tons of fertilizer per day, all with a nitrogen content of about 6 percent. Furthermore, the concentration of valuable phosphates in the fertilizer stood at about 2.5 percent. Hence, the Jones Island sewage treatment facility placed Milwaukee on the cutting edge of urban technology, both in terms of treating wastewater and converting sludge to fertilizers. The dissemination of this technology for circulating fixed nitrogen from cities back to agricultural land appeared to be imminent.[58]

As it happened, however, the Milwaukee Sewerage Commission entered the nitrogen-based fertilizer market just as another technological innovation was radically restructuring that market: the industrial fixation of nitrogen through the Haber-Bosch process. In 1914, when Fowler first suggested that Milwaukee package its sludge as fertilizer, most fixed nitrogen was still being imported from deposits in Chile at roughly three hundred dollars per ton. Meanwhile, a year earlier, a team of German engineers and scientists led by Fritz Haber and Carl Bosch had constructed the world's first production-scale facility for inexpensively fixing atmospheric nitrogen. After World War I, nitrogen-fixing facilities constructed during the war, mainly to provide the nitrogen required for explosives, began supplying commercial markets.[59]

By the mid-1920s, the technological path that Milwaukee had pioneered in terms of recycling nitrogen from sewage had become economically unattractive. Inexpensive nitrogen in the form of ammonia, not tainted by any association with sewage, was now available. Milwaukee, which had already invested in facilities to process and package its sludge as fertilizer, continued to market it; but cities constructing sewage treatment plants after Milwaukee had little incentive to make that same investment.

The Path Pursued: Bypassing Dependence on Nitrogen-Fixing Bacteria

The development of the Haber-Bosch process for manufacturing ammonia by fixing atmospheric nitrogen industrially is recognized as one of the great technological achievements of the twentieth century. Its social and economic implications were obvious to those involved in its development: industrial societies would now be able to produce as much chemically active nitrogen as farmers, chemical manufacturers, and states were willing to purchase. In the process, though, the seeds of a major change in human interactions with the rest of nature were sown.

The development of the Haber-Bosch process certainly represented a tremendous technical feat. In essence, these facilities transform molecular nitrogen (N_2) and hydrogen (H_2) into ammonia (NH_3) by passing the two gases over a catalyst at high temperatures and pressures. In terms of raw material, all that is needed is a steady supply of hydrocarbons, such as coal or natural gas, either of which can serve as a source of energy and hydrogen. All of the nitrogen comes from the atmosphere. New ground, however, had to be broken on a variety of technological fronts before this catalytic process could be placed into full-scale operation. Specifically, significant advances in process control, the design and use of catalysts, and the manufacture of vessels capable of operating at high temperatures and extreme pressures (up to 1,200 degrees and 400 atmospheres) were necessary.[60]

BASF, the chemical company that developed the process, secured these advances by placing science at the service of engineering goals, facilitating the design of a technology that would have been almost impossible to develop through unguided trial and error. Indeed, this relationship between science and engineering is reflected in the disciplinary training of the process's two famous architects, Fritz Haber and Carl Bosch. The first was a leading German chemist who had developed a bench model of the process; the second was a chemist trained in metallurgical engineering who then transformed the bench model into a production facility. Both steps involved plenty of trial-and-error experimentation. After all, only by testing could one determine whether a particular type of material might serve as a useful catalyst or whether a particular design for a pressure vessel would work at high temperatures and pressures. Scientific models and pilot-scale tests filtered out materials and designs that were the least promising and allowed engineers to devote their resources to testing those with a better chance of succeeding. In 1913, after approximately five years of experimentation and development, the first full-scale facility capable of producing inexpensive ammonia began operations in Oppau, Germany.[61]

Strictly speaking, the Haber-Bosch process was not the first technology for fixing nitrogen industrially. Other nitrogen-fixing facilities using different technologies were already in operation before 1913. However, none proved profitable; that is, none could compete with Chilean nitrates without some form of subsidy. For example, chemists since the time of Davy had known that the intense heat of an electric arc could break the bonds of atmospheric nitrogen and, in the presence of oxygen, create nitrogen dioxide. This gas, when combined with water, could be converted into nitric acid. In 1902, the patent holders for an industrial-scale arc process constructed an experimental facility in Niagara Falls, New York, but even with an inexpensive source of electricity available to them, the company failed to make a profit. Other facilities employing the arc process were later constructed in the hydroelectric-rich areas of Norway, and in 1908 these facilities started producing 7,800 tons of fixed nitrogen each year.[62]

Another approach for fixing nitrogen was discovered in the 1890s by industrial chemists who were experimenting with ways to produce inexpensive cyanide for use in processing gold-bearing ores. They found that passing N_2 over hot calcium carbide (CaC_2) produced calcium cyanamide ($CaCN_2$), which could be further processed into other nitrogen compounds. By 1910, calcium cyanamide plants were producing about 12,000 tons of fixed nitrogen each year, but this process was also inefficient and required large inputs of electricity. In practice, the 350,000 tons of fixed nitrogen flowing out of Chile and the 200,000 tons being produced from coal dwarfed the quantity of nitrogen being produced by calcium cyanamide facilities and those using the arc process. In the long term, any successful process for fixing nitrogen from the air had to do so at a price competitive with Chilean nitrate, which the Haber-Bosch process proved capable of doing.[63]

The development of the Haber-Bosch process also changed the relationship between humans and the rest of nature. No longer were bacteria and bolts of lightning the only entities capable of fixing nitrogen; now humans had nitrogen-fixing technology and an economic system that encouraged its use. What once had been a fundamental ecological constraint—limits on the production of fixed nitrogen by bacteria ultimately fueled by solar power—had been bypassed. Regionally, nineteenth-century industrial societies had begun to push beyond this constraint by drawing on reserves of fixed nitrogen in coal, guano, and Chilean nitrate. The development of the Haber-Bosch process raised industrial societies' capacity to secure nitrogen to a new level.

Aside from the writer who, in 1901, responded to Crookes's call to develop industrial methods for fixing nitrogen by publishing a short story about the dangers of sucking too much nitrogen out of the atmosphere, a tale in which he declared that "nitrogen factories must be destroyed," the development of large-scale processes for industrially fixing nitrogen raised little concern.[64] This is hardly surprising. First, the greater availability of fixed nitrogen solved a resource problem that governmental leaders had explicitly been trying to solve. Why question greater access to inexpensive supplies of a valuable resource? The benefits were obvious. Second, at an institutional level, industrial society had not yet learned to raise questions about the consequences of technological innovation. After all, to most people, social progress and technological change appeared to go hand in hand. In addition, the rules of market capitalism framed innovation as something close to a fundamental right. Relatively few societal checks and balances on innovation existed beyond market forces.[65]

The engineers and scientists associated with the new nitrogen-fixing industry certainly had few incentives or reasons to raise questions about the long-term fate of the nitrogenous compounds in the environment. Based on their remarks in treatises written in the 1920s and early 1930s, some did frame the production of industrially fixed nitrogen as an alteration of the nitrogen cycle, but they raised no concerns about the effects of putting more nitrogen into circulation. Harry Curtis, an industrial chemist who conducted a survey of the nitrogen industry for the U.S. government in the 1920s, observed that "there has been added to the natural cycle of nitrogen transformation a second one wherein the chain of events is more or less determined by human agency," but neither his research nor that of his colleagues was directed toward understanding that change.[66] Nobody, for example, asked whether denitrifying bacteria were capable of keeping up with the additional nitrogen that was being added to the environment through industrial fixation. To a large extent, they perceived industrially fixed nitrogen as simply a replacement for existing imports of sodium nitrate; hence, there was no great change or cause for concern. Furthermore, because scientists had spent many years trying to prevent a nitrogen shortage, the notion that there could be too much chemically active nitrogen in circulation probably did not occur to anyone.

More noticeable were the landscape-scale changes that had taken place in the United States over the course of the nineteenth century. Within sixty-five years, from the opening of the Erie Canal in 1825 to the U.S. Census Bureau's 1890 declaration that no frontier now remained, market-minded and technologically enthralled citizens had woven vast expanses of land into the industrial fabric of a rapidly urbanizing nation. The exponential growth of cities and the rapid transformation of prairies and forests into agricultural land stunned anybody who attempted to make sense of what was happening. By the turn of the century, reformers were wrestling with many immediate concerns, including the rapid disappearance of the nation's forests, deteriorating social conditions in large cities, the rise of dangerously unhealthy work environments, conflicts over the use of urban streams as pollution sinks, and choking emissions of gases into the air.[67] Few could conceive of the notion that industrial society might want to manage its interaction with something as abstract as a biogeochemical cycle.

To some extent, industrial society's capacity to respond to change was lagging behind its ability to innovate. The pace of innovation, on the other hand, was accelerating. No longer did one have to build an entire steam engine to see if a particular change might improve its efficiency. By the 1870s, the laws of thermodynamics and knowledge about the properties of water and steam allowed engineers (or applied scientists, as they were sometimes called) to test their ideas on paper and hone in on the most promising variations before constructing anything. Scientifically trained engineers could easily weed out ideas that, say, violated the laws of thermodynamics or failed to consider the strength of materials. Only after engineers and scientists had filtered out the weakest ideas and reached unexplored territory did trial-and-error experimentation have to take place. The development of sewage treatment technology and the Haber-Bosch process both illustrated this new dynamic.

The exigency of war also accelerated the pace of certain types of innovation. War, of course, represents a societal-level process of variation and selection of the rawest form. As a result, military competition has always served as an engine of technological change, with weapons evolving as combatants desperately attempt to improve their offensive and defensive strategies. Wars, however, were now being fought between large industrialized societies capable of mobilizing millions of soldiers and hundreds of large firms. The latter were themselves capable of mobilizing huge numbers of people to develop and produce better weapons. In the case of the Haber-Bosch process, markets may have set the minimum level of performance the technology had to achieve if it were to succeed in the long term—that is, it had to be cheaper than Chilean nitrates—but military concerns as much than consumer demand drove its creation and dissemination.[68]

In short, while the pace of innovation was accelerating, the institutional mechanisms for anticipating concerns potentially caused by those innovations was not. In the absence of significant conflict, firms and individuals were free to innovate in the manner they chose. Unless one person's actions directly interfered with somebody else's property rights, caused economic harm to another person, or could be identified as a nuisance, there was little reason to question the desirability of an innovation. A guiding ethic that encouraged people to raise questions about sustaining the integrity of complex natural systems, such as the one articulated by George Perkins Marsh a half-century earlier, had not taken root. Indeed, anybody who raised such questions would have found little encouragement. Neither markets, nor science, nor the state rewarded anybody who pursued such questions. At a societal level, knowledge that such questions might be wise to encourage would take another century of learning.

7

Industrializing a
Biogeochemical Cycle

In the years between World War I and World War II, a major change occurred in the perception and use of fertilizers. Before World War I, most agricultural scientists and farmers saw them as a way to maintain good soil so as to sustain crop yields at typical levels. The development of the Haber-Bosch process for producing ammonia, however, encouraged agricultural scientists to think about fertilizers in a new way: as a tool for increasing yields. In the 1920s and 1930s, agricultural experts demonstrated that such increases were both possible and practical; and by the mid-1940s, when ammonia-producing plants constructed during World War II were released for nonmilitary uses, all the necessary technologies were in place. The subsequent global dissemination of nitrogen-intensive farming practices not only dramatically increased crop yields but also resulted in humans' becoming as important as nitrogen-fixing bacteria in placing new supplies of chemically active nitrogen into circulation.

By the start of World War I, the United States already had a network of agricultural experts who saw farming as an industrial activity—that is, who thought in terms of securing raw material and producing agricultural products as efficiently as possible. Three-quarters of a century earlier, Liebig's influential treatise on agricultural chemistry had given this way of thinking an important boost, but significant action did not occur in the United States until 1862. In that year, a wartime Congress passed three agriculture-related bills: first, the Homestead Act, which offered free land to potential farmers; second, the Morrill Land-Grant College Act, which gave 30,000 acres per congressional member to states for the support of colleges that would train students in the agricultural and industrial arts; and, finally, an act that established the federal Department of Agriculture. Together, these pieces of legislation articulated a vision of agriculture amenable to a rapidly growing industrial society with a high urban-to-rural population ratio.[1]

In its search for ways to increase agricultural productivity, the Department of Agriculture eventually turned to Germany. By the 1870s, the British, who previously had led the world in agricultural innovation, no longer served as much of a model. Agricultural productivity in Germany, however, was still increasing in terms of both yields per acre and acres cultivated per person. In part, the Germans had accomplished this feat by establishing a network of state-sponsored agricultural research stations and extension services to systematically acquire, disseminate, and locally adapt new agricultural practices. Impressed, Congress passed the Hatch Act in 1887, which mimicked the German model by establishing state-level agricultural research stations to complement the system of agricultural colleges already in place. In 1914, Congress took another step toward the German model by passing the Smith-Lever Act, which funded a Cooperative Extension Service to facilitate farmers' adoption of new agricultural practices. Each state received matching funds from the federal government to assemble a network of experts capable of working with farmers to disseminate new practices.[2]

Hence, by World War I and the introduction of the Haber-Bosch process for fixing nitrogen industrially, the United States had constructed an institutional network capable of directing scientific and technological knowledge toward an industrial vision of agriculture. In 1914, the nation's secretary of agriculture, D. F. Houston, could report that the acreage devoted to growing corn had risen from 34 million to more than 100 million in the half-century since the creation of the Department of Agriculture. In that same period, the acreage devoted to oats rose from about 9 million to almost 40 million, while wheat increased from 15 million to more than 50 million acres.[3] Furthermore, use of more sophisticated farming machinery (though much of it was still horse-drawn) meant that each farmer could now work more land. In addition, construction of a network of grain elevators connected by railroads had greatly simplified transactions between farmers and buyers, and staples such as corn and wheat now flowed from Midwestern fields to the mouths of urban consumers with a minimum of complication. A thriving futures market treated these grains as commodities, making it possible for farmers and food-processing companies to transfer the risks of agriculture (along with the chances of earning windfall profits) to speculators.[4]

What Secretary Houston could not report was any great increase in yields per acre. Between 1860 and 1910, the average yield of corn and oats in the United States remained steady at about twenty-five and thirty bushels per acre, respectively. Yields of wheat rose from ten to sixteen bushels per acre, but that rise had begun to flatten as well. Of course, increases in yields were not to be expected. After all, most U.S. farmers saw fertilizers as a way to maintain soil fertility rather than to increase yields. Indeed, as long as the main supply of nitrogen-based fertilizers came from nitrate deposits in Chile (which rose to nine hundred dollars per ton during the war), those views were not likely to change.[5]

Meanwhile, the nation's urban-to-rural population ratio continued to increase. In the half-century after the Civil War, the urban population rose sevenfold, expanding from about 6 million to 42 million. In that same period, the rural population had merely doubled, rising from about 25 million to 50 million. As a result, increases in U.S. food production barely kept pace with population growth.[6] For those who embraced the vision of an urban industrial society, the Haber-Bosch process looked like the perfect solution. Farmers who added more nitrogen to their soil could now be expected to increase the number of urban dwellers they were able to support.

From Weapons to the TVA's Fertilizer Program

The popular promise that less expensive nitrogen would flow into the nation's soil initially came from none other than Henry Ford. In 1921, he submitted a bid to lease one of two nitrogen-fixing plants that the U.S. government had constructed during World War I. Although Ford never acquired the facility, his rhetoric about providing American farmers with inexpensive fertilizers struck a populist chord. They did not necessarily envision any significant increases in their use of nitrogen; they just wanted to make the quantities they were already using were less costly.[7]

The government commissioned construction of the two nitrogen-fixing facilities in 1916, when imports of Chilean nitrate, needed for making explosives, were being threatened by German ships and submarines. The first facility, built in Sheffield, Alabama, at a cost of 12 million dollars, attempted to replicate the German Haber-Bosch process. However, the catalyst was still a German secret, and the material selected by American engineers did not function as hoped. The plant was a failure. The second facility, located in Muscle Shoals, Alabama, employed an older and more costly method of fixing nitrogen: the cyanamid process. This facility required huge amounts of electric power to produce calcium carbide (CaC_2), which could then be reacted with atmospheric nitrogen at high temperatures to create calcium cyanamide ($CaCN_2$). That compound then could be further processed to form other nitrogen compounds. Although expensive, the technology was proven.[8]

Most of the cost for the Muscle Shoals facility, more than 68 million dollars, went into constructing a dam and hydroelectric plant on the Tennessee River. This plant complicated the issue of what to do with the facility after the war. The original legislation had specified that the federal government would operate it in peacetime as a fertilizer plant, but production of fixed nitrogen using the cyanamid process made no economic sense. Any fertilizers produced at Muscle Shoals would be inexpensive only if they were subsidized by free power from the Tennessee River. If one factored in the cost of electricity, the nitrogen compounds produced at the plant would be quite expensive.[9]

In 1921, as debates over what to do with the two nitrogen-fixing facilities heated up, the Nitrate Division of the Army's Ordnance Bureau transferred the facilities to the Department of Agriculture. Along with the facilities came the Army's Fixed Nitrogen Research Laboratory, which had been charged with accomplishing two main tasks: getting the "direct synthetic ammonia process" (or Haber-Bosch process) up and running and figuring out the best way to transform calcium cyanamide into a fertilizer. By 1923, the research group employed seventy-five people, including thirty-five chemists, physicists, and engineers working under the leadership of Frederick Cottrell, a well-known physical chemist who had previously served as the director of the U.S. Bureau of Mines. Cottrell, who championed the development of technology for the public good, believed that knowledge created at the Fixed Nitrogen Research Laboratory should be openly shared. Under him, the lab soon began researching a variety of issues related to the production and application of fixed nitrogen. Efforts ranged from investigating the behavior of steel vessels containing nitrogen and hydrogen at high pressures and temperatures to determining the effects of various concentrations, sequences, and mixes of nitrogenous compounds on crops in the field.[10]

As discussions over what to do with the Muscle Shoals facility continued, a whirlpool of policy issues sucked participants into a series of contentious debates. Business-minded senators argued that it was not fair to expect private companies to compete with an operation heavily subsidized by the federal government. Efficiency-minded Progressives such as Gifford Pinchot were just as outraged to think that a valuable resource (hydroelectric power) might be used to subsidize Ford's operation of an inefficient industrial process. They hoped that the electricity could instead be used to improve the lives of farmers in the Tennessee Valley. Others charged that the level of regional planning encouraged by the Pinchot-led Progressives smacked of Soviet-style socialism. Meanwhile, Cottrell lobbied to make the Nitrogen Fixing Research Laboratory a permanent, well-funded experimental station focused on determining the most effective ways to produce and use fertilizers. Issues of national security revolving around the need for nitrates for explosives, questions of who really owned hydroelectric power, and Henry Ford's charge that Wall Street Jewish conspirators were working against him mired the whole debate in political quicksand.[11]

In 1933, the U.S. Congress settled the issue by passing the Tennessee Valley Authority Act. Faced with the Depression-era collapse of the nation's economy and a series of agriculture-wrecking dust storms on the high plains, federal legislators decided to take a more active role in shaping the future of various regions, including the predominantly rural area drained by the Tennessee River and its tributaries. To accomplish this, legislators created a federally owned corporation, the Tennessee Valley Authority (TVA), and charged it with bringing affordable electric power, productive agricultural practices, flood control, and navigational improvements to the region. Congress also integrated Cottrell's recommendation into the act by mandating that the TVA "improve and cheapen the production of fertilizer" and "cooperate with National, state, district, or county experimental stations or demonstration farms . . . for the use of new forms of fertilizer or fertilizer practices during the initial or experimental period of their introduction."[12]

By the time Congress created the TVA, both DuPont and Allied Chemical had already constructed large ammonia-producing facilities. Together, these two plants, one in Virginia and one in West Virginia, could fix 309,000 tons of nitrogen each year. A handful of smaller U.S. companies could fix another 44,400 tons. Worldwide, capacity exceeded 1 million tons, with Germany accounting for about half of the total.[13] Harry Curtis, the chemical engineer selected to lead the TVA's fertilizer works and an expert in the nitrogen industry, saw these facilities, when coupled with rotations of legumes and other sources of nitrogen, as being sufficient to meet farmers' needs. The American Farm Bureau Federation agreed and placed a higher priority on the production of phosphate-based fertilizers. The military, which was interested in incendiary bombs that used phosphate-based chemicals, also supported this focus. Therefore, soon after the TVA's creation, its fertilizer group shifted its attention from nitrogen-based compounds to the production of phosphorus-based fertilizers.[14]

In the mid-1930s, after constructing a new facility for manufacturing phosphate fertilizers, the TVA—in cooperation with the U.S. Department of Agriculture, state-level agricultural extension services, county soil conservation associations, and local agricultural committees—began conducting "whole-farm test demonstrations in improved farming systems using new forms of fertilizers produced by the TVA in its experimental plants."[15] The TVA initially placed the most emphasis on phosphorus-based fertilizers, with farmers who participated in the demonstration programs receiving free phosphate fertilizer for three years. After that, if they remained in the program, they could purchase phosphate fertilizer at a 50 percent discount. To keep soils well fertilized with nitrogen, agronomists with the TVA encouraged farmers to plow rotations of alfalfa, clover, or kudzu back into the soil, seeing this last plant as an especially promising, fast-growing host for nitrogen-fixing bacteria. Even though rotations of such hosts took a crop such as corn out of production for a season, the practice met the TVA's goal of building up the soil and preventing erosion. Initially, then, the farmers who participated in a TVA demonstration program typically applied more phosphorus (in the form of P_2O_5) than industrially fixed nitrogen to their soil. In 1937, for example, the sixty-six Alabama farmers participating in the TVA's demonstration programs applied, on average, thirteen pounds of phosphates per acre but only nine pounds of nitrogen. Another twenty-six pounds of nitrogen per acre came from rotations of nitrogen fixers.[16]

In the 1920s, the nation's farm-association leaders had pointed out that any increases in crop production were more likely to result in lower food prices for urban consumers than in greater profits for farmers. After all, if production rose while demand remained even, the prices farmers could get for their crops were sure to fall. The demand for grain to feed horses (which was steadily being replaced by the demand for gasoline to fuel internal combustion engines) was also on the decline. As a result, some farmers were hesitant to adopt production-increasing practices, especially those that were capital intensive. In the face of this hesitancy, demonstration farms proved to be especially important in disseminating the TVA's and the Department of Agriculture's vision of agriculture. If an entrepreneurial farmer decided to work with the local agricultural extension service and the effort proved successful, other farmers felt compelled to adopt the new practices as well. Otherwise, if prices dropped due to increases in production, farmers who did not adopt yield-increasing practices would begin to lose ground.[17]

Increasingly, farms came to be seen as a type of factory that should produce products from raw material as efficiently as possible. Those in the business of supplying products to farmers—seeds, pesticides, fertilizers, and mechanical equipment—certainly embraced this vision of agriculture. The American Agricultural Chemical Company, for example, estimated that crops harvested from U.S. farms removed 17 billion pounds of nutrients from the soil but only returned 12 billion, most of which came from cultivating nitrogen-fixing hosts. The company went on to argue that growing wheat cost farmers who did not use fertilizers $1.14 per bushel while those who used industrial fertilizers could produce the same amount for 67 cents.[18] In 1936, the chief of the Department of Agriculture's By-Product Laboratory did not hesitate to say that, "fundamentally, the farm is a chemical factory in which complex chemical products such as fats, carbohydrates, and proteins are synthesized from oxygen and carbon dioxide of the air, water, minerals, sunlight, and organic matter."[19] Increasingly, farmers were learning to manage their chemical factories more efficiently.

During World War II, officials at the TVA shifted their attention from phosphate back to nitrogen. As part of the nation's war preparedness plan, the TVA's fertilizer division constructed a new Haber-Bosch facility capable of producing 56,900 tons of ammonia each year. The federal government constructed nine other ammonia-producing facilities as well, pushing the total nitrogen-fixing capacity in the United States to more than 900,000 tons per year. Although the ammonia was intended mainly for the manufacture of explosives, production occasionally outpaced military demand and some of the nitrogen was diverted to agricultural experiments. Indeed, in 1943, county agents were asked to find enough farmers to consume thirty railroad cars' worth of the material. The results of that experiment established nitrogen as a "valuable production tool" in the effort to increase agricultural yields.[20]

After World War II ended, the federal government sold or leased eight of their newly constructed ammonia-producing facilities. Seven went to their wartime operators. For example, the largest, a facility in South Point, Ohio, capable of fixing 187,000 tons of nitrogen per year, was sold to its operator, Allied Chemical. Only the TVA facility at Muscle Shoals remained under government control. Ammonia-producing facilities constructed in Europe and Japan also remained in operation, pushing the world's capacity to fix nitrogen to more than 3 million tons per year.[21]

The Establishment of Industrial Agriculture

On an April morning in 1947, the French-flagged *Grandcamp*, a Liberty ship mass-produced during World War II, lay at anchor at an industrial dock in Texas City, Texas. At about 8:00 A.M., as longshoreman were preparing to load sacks of ammonium nitrate fertilizer onto the ship, workers spotted a plume of smoke rising from one of the holds. On the previous day, they had already loaded 2,300 tons of the fertilizer, and the source of the smoke appeared to be seven or eight layers down among the sacks. Dousing the cargo with water had no effect, so the captain ordered workers to fill the hold with steam. But the strategy failed: pressure from within blew out the hatch, and bright orange flames shot into the sky. By 9:00 A.M., firefighters had arrived on the scene and were training streams of water onto the blaze. Twelve minutes later, the *Grandcamp* disintegrated in a series of explosions strong enough to be heard 150 miles away.[22]

The ammonium nitrate (NH_4NO_3) provided the explosive power. At normal temperatures, the material is very stable, but at higher temperatures (more than several hundred degrees Fahrenheit) it decomposes rapidly into two gases: nitrous oxide (N_2O) and water vapor. On the *Grandcamp*, all 2,300 tons of the crystalline powder went from a solid to a gas in a few explosive moments, a transformation that ripped the ship apart and engulfed the docks in a massive fireball. Deadly fragments of plate steel flew in all directions, slicing through whatever structures they encountered, including another ship carrying ammonium nitrate as well as numerous oil storage tanks, thus triggering secondary fires and explosions. In all, the disaster injured approximately 2,000 people, killed about 600, and knocked one plane out of the sky.[23]

The explosion of the *Grandcamp* serves as a metaphor for how industrial society was proceeding as a whole. At the time, the world's farms were supporting about 2.5 billion people, approximately double the number they had fed a century earlier. Demographic trends suggested that the world population would soon double again, with urban numbers increasing faster than rural ones. To avoid serious food shortages, significant increases in agricultural productivity would also have to occur. Although increasing food production through the use of nitrogen-based fertilizers did not literally increase the danger of an explosive catastrophe, it did facilitate this population explosion and further entangle human activity with the nitrogen cycle. The shift to a global dependency on chemical fertilizers had begun.[24]

During the next half-century, both the application of nitrogenous fertilizers and crop yields rose steadily. By 1955, farmers in the Netherlands and Japan, two densely populated countries where high yields were especially valued, applied an average of 160 and 100 pounds of nitrogenous fertilizers per acre, respectively.[25] In the United States, the average farmer used much less, but those who increased their applications showed impressive results. A five-year TVA experiment on farms in Kentucky indicated that it was cost-effective to apply fifty to one hundred pounds of nitrogen per acre to corn. In Wise County, Virginia, yields of corn on demonstration farms had risen to seventy bushels per acre, and personnel with the TVA and the Virginia extension service were organizing a "pasture improvement contest" called the "100 bushel corn club."[26]

As agricultural scientists continued to experiment, they discovered that even larger increases in production were possible. In 1957, researchers applied increasing amounts of nitrogen, up to 520 pounds per acre, to twelve different test plots of corn. Yields rose fairly linearly up to about 200 pounds of applied nitrogen, which resulted in 130 bushels per acre. After that, the response flattened out, with 520 pounds of applied nitrogen producing only 150 bushels per acre. Basing their figures on the price of corn and fertilizer, these researchers computed the optimal amount of applied nitrogen to be 280 pounds per acre.

By 1960, the world's capacity to produce synthetically fixed nitrogen had risen to 9,500,000 metric tons per year. In United States alone, thirty-eight firms operated fifty-four facilities capable of producing 3,600,000 metric tons per year. The U.S. national average for yields of corn—for the entire nation, not just for demonstration farms—approached sixty bushels per acre, about double the national average twenty years earlier.[27]

The development of new cultivars capable of taking full advantage of the added nitrogen represented a parallel step in the industrialization of agriculture. Traditional cultivars did not necessarily respond to higher levels of nitrogen in a desirable way. For example, wheat tended to grow larger but disproportionately so, with heavier grain heads making the wheat bend, or "lodge," resulting in plants that eventually fell over. Further increases in wheat yields therefore depended on the development of varieties with shorter, stronger stalks. Varieties resistant to disease and pests were also necessary if yields were to continue their rise, and by the 1950s, agricultural colleges had assembled a small army of plant breeders and plant pathologists to continually improve the response of cultivars and keep one step ahead of pests that could destroy a vulnerable crop.[28]

To secure the latest cultivars, farmers had to purchase hybrid seeds from companies that produced them through controlled cross-pollination. Furthermore, they had to purchase new seeds each year because the second crop produced from a hybrid line did not necessarily have the desired characteristics. In 1918, when Henry A. Wallace, son of Warren G. Harding's secretary of agriculture and grandson of the founder of the influential journal *Wallace's Farmer,* started a company called Hi-Bred Corn, relatively few farmers could be convinced to buy hybrid seeds. At the time, the systematic breeding of cultivars guided by science of genetics was only a decade old, and farmers had yet to be convinced that hybrids could have characteristics significantly different from their own stock. Increased yields eventually changed minds, especially those of younger farmers. By 1960, more than 92 percent of the corn grown in the United States came from hybrid seed.[29]

Other factors also contributed to changes in agricultural practices. To reduce the quantity of crops that were being lost to pests, farmers began to apply insecticides and herbicides made from synthetic organics, a technology that had been developed during World War II. By 1960, U.S. farmers were spending about 250 million dollars on those chemicals each year. The amount of land being worked by the average farmer was also on the rise due to the use of gasoline-powered tractors and other specialized pieces of farm equipment. Between 1910 and 1964, the number of farms in the United States dropped from about 6 million to 3 million, but the average farm size increased from about 100 acres per farm to about 350 acres. The end results were higher yields and fewer people farming more land.[30]

Thus, by about 1960, a nitrogen-intensive system of industrial agriculture that could support an unprecedented urban-to-rural ratio had been constructed in the United States, Europe, and Japan. A host of other factors (such as new types of farm equipment, hybrid seeds, high-volume irrigation pumps, pesticides, efficient transportation networks, and the phosphorus fertilizers needed to keep up with inputs of nitrogen) also contributed to the change. Furthermore, this system of market-based industrial agriculture had begun to disseminate globally.

A Not-So-Green Revolution

Any nation that attempted to increase its urban-to-rural ratio without making the shift to industrial agriculture (or importing massive quantities of food) was setting itself up for disaster. Between 1958 and 1961, such a disaster happened: Mao Zedong's plan for China's economic "great leap forward" had shifted significant amounts of labor from the agricultural sector to heavy industry without first securing any gains in agricultural productivity. Droughts and floods compounded the problem, and in subsequent harvests, Chinese society simply was not able to produce the food it needed. As a result, the Chinese found themselves in the middle of a three-year famine that eventually killed between 15 and 30 million people.[31]

The famine reaffirmed the decision of one international development organization, the Rockefeller Foundation, to invest heavily in efforts to disseminate the methods of industrial agriculture. The first significant steps in this direction had been taken in the early 1940s when the foundation had initiated a project to improve crop yields in Mexico. The idea came about after Henry Wallace—by that time, a former secretary of agriculture (1933–40) and the vice president–elect of the United States—toured a Mexican farm with the Mexican secretary of agriculture. In a later conversation with Nelson Rockefeller, Wallace expressed his belief that increases in the yields of corn would contribute more to the welfare of the average Mexican than would just about any other plan that could be devised.[32]

Wallace's observation was not a casual one. In part, he had accepted the position of secretary of agriculture to improve the lives of farmers. Although he championed the use of hybrid seed and what he called the "engineering science approach" to progressive change, he also raised questions about how this change was actually playing out for farmers. "The engineers and the scientists," he told an audience in 1933, "have given us the instruments and the methods whereby we can escape much of the grind; theoretically, there ought to be far more time for living and far more with which to enjoy life. Yet the reverse, seems to be poignantly true." Wallace also believed, however, that the engineering-scientific approach could be made more beneficial to everyday people "if the planning of the engineer and the scientist in their own fields gives rise to comparable planning in our social world." Exactly what this type of planning should entail was by no means clear.[33]

Rockefeller presented the idea of a program to increase crop yields in Mexico to the president of the Rockefeller Foundation, Raymond Fosdick. At the time, Fosdick was dealing with criticisms that the foundation's health-related programs had contributed to population growth without doing anything to help feed a larger population. Initiating a program to increase agricultural productivity in nonindustrialized nations appeared to be the perfect way to address that criticism, so he sent a soil scientist, a plant breeder, a plant pathologist, and an animal husbandry specialist—experts with skills that lie at the heart of industrial agriculture—to work with Mexican officials in determining how to proceed.[34] Their effort was not without precedent: some European countries had established colonial research institutes for the purpose of increasing the production of exportable agricultural commodities. But the Rockefeller Foundation sought to change the agricultural practices of an entire nation in fundamental ways. Its goal was to set into motion what foundation members saw as the forces of modernization, and its closest model was the TVA's effort to change agricultural practices in the rural south.[35]

After discussions with Mexican officials, the foundation decided to fund a research station that would develop robust, high-yielding wheat and maize plants for Mexico's soil and climate. The research station, under the jurisdiction of the Mexican secretary of agriculture, would then help to disseminate the new cultivars along with the practices of industrial agriculture. In what turned out to be a model of technological transfer, the Rockefeller Foundation hired a small team of scientists, including Norman Borlaug, a future winner of the Nobel Peace Prize, to work closely with Mexican researchers. By 1948, after the research team started distributing new varieties of wheat, the average yield in Mexico began a spectacular rise that would continue for several decades, increasing from approximately twelve bushels per acre when Borlaug arrived to seventy bushels per acre in the early 1980s. Those gains were accompanied by increases in the use of machinery and irrigation, a shift suggesting that more fundamental changes in rural life were also under way.[36]

In the mid-1950s, the Rockefeller Foundation began sending Borlaug on trips to assess the agricultural systems of other countries, eventually charging him with bringing high-yielding wheat plants to regions of India and Pakistan. Under Borlaug's leadership and tireless devotion to the program, yields of wheat began to climb in those regions as well. One dissemination strategy involved investing resources into "top-notch demonstrations" that produced record yields by employing the "whole package of improved practices." In India and Pakistan, many of those demonstration fields produced more than 100 bushels of wheat per acre; one reached 150 bushels per acre. When other farmers began adopting even a portion of the demonstrated practices, regional yields increased dramatically. In one case, local officials failed to heed Borlaug's warning about the need to construct more storage, and the production of crops ended up overwhelming the available structures.[37]

In 1960, the Ford and Rockefeller foundations established a similar research program for rice, the International Rice Research Institute, in the

Philippines. Several years later, the Mexican research effort morphed into the International Maize and Wheat Improvement Center. As yields of wheat, corn, and rice rose in countries around the world, Borlaug began to focus on the logistics of delivering enough nutrients to the world's agricultural soils, with supplies of nitrogen being one of the critical issues. When editing a 1963 report on the program, he crossed out a statement that downplayed the importance of fertilizers and reiterated their central role in the program's success. His reason was simple: supplies of the fertilizer were not keeping up with demand. In a 1966 letter, Borlaug concluded that "our greatest obstacle now is to get sufficient fertilizer."[38] The emphasis that he and others placed on fertilizers caught people's attention. By 1972, India had fourteen facilities fixing a total of 1,326,000 tons of nitrogen each year; in addition, another twelve facilities capable of fixing 2,298,000 tons were under construction, pushing India's total capacity to a level that exceeded what had been the world's capacity three decades earlier.[39]

The TVA's fertilizer group in Muscle Shoals, by this time called the National Fertilizer Development Center, also began to turn its attention to international agricultural practices, mainly in response to the U.S. Agency for International Development's requests for information. In 1970, the TVA group prepared publications such as "A Fertilizer Program for Bolivia" and "Estimated World Fertilizer Production Capacity As Related to Future Needs," in which the authors estimated that the world's consumption of fixed nitrogen for fertilizer would rise from 25 million metric tons in 1968 to 58 million metric tons in 1980. Total ammonia production, they indicated, had to rise by approximately 6 percent per year to keep pace. The international work of the TVA's National Fertilizer Development Center, however, was not sanctioned by law. Therefore, in 1974, a private, nonprofit corporation called the International Fertilizer Development Center was established at Muscle Shoals to carry on the international work.[40]

As agricultural productivity rose in Mexico, India, and Pakistan, leaders of development agencies began to speak of a "green revolution." In this case, *green* referred not to environmental values but to increasing agricultural productivity through the use of fertilizers, pesticides, machinery, irrigation, and the breeding of robust, nitrogen-responsive crops. Not surprisingly, the producers of pesticides, fertilizers, seeds, and farm equipment embraced this revolution, providing it with a solid base of political and, in some cases, financial support.[41] Many business and political leaders also embraced agricultural programs as a critical strategy in the fight against Soviet communism. Indeed, the Rockefeller's Foundation's effort in India was partly driven by this motivation, with the goal being to help developing nations become modern industrial states capable of supporting democratic governments and market economies.[42]

Yet agricultural programs dedicated to the spread of industrial agriculture also had various critics. One line of criticism questioned the wisdom of replacing a subsistence economy, such as that based on Mexico's "three sisters" (corn, beans, and squash) with one that required landowners to invest substantial amounts of capital so that they could produce crops for a market. Carl Sauer, a leading cultural geographer and an expert on agricultural history, had articulated such concerns from the beginning. The Rockefeller Foundation had contacted Sauer in the early 1940s and asked him to tour South America in search of projects that it could fund. When asked about potential agricultural projects in Mexico, he had stressed the importance of building on traditional knowledge to improve subsistence agriculture rather than encouraging rapid modernization through the methods of industrial agriculture. Although leaders of the Rockefeller Foundation seriously wrestled with the issue, they eventually decided to focus on increases in yields.[43]

Three decades later, as international development agencies began to speak of a green revolution, another generation of critics raised issues similar to Sauer's. In part, they were responding to the rural-to-urban migration that accompanied shifts to industrial agriculture. For example, economist E. F. Schumacher questioned whether capital-intensive, labor-saving approaches to agriculture made sense for nations with large rural populations, no industrial base, and no tradition of market capitalism. Critics also noted that the shift to industrial practices was biased in favor of landowners with resources to invest in equipment and chemicals and did little for peasants who owned relatively small plots.[44]

Another set of critics believed that the green revolution was unwittingly contributing to a long-term problem because it was feeding a Malthusian pace of growth that was unsustainable. In 1948, ornithologist-turned-ecologist William Vogt published *Road to Survival* in which he argued that society's ability to manipulate nature was neither limitless nor without consequence. We should not, he emphasized, simply assume that the natural systems on which we depend can continue to support an ever-increasing population. Two decades later, Paul Ehrlich, heavily influenced by Vogt, published *The Population Bomb* and argued that radical change was necessary to avoid famine in the coming decades. He, too, suggested that increasing levels of food production without addressing the core problem only delayed the day of reckoning.[45]

Borlaug, who became the public face of the green revolution after winning the Nobel Peace Prize, did not disagree with those who placed population growth at the core of the problem. In exchanges with Ehrlich and others, he pointed out that the foundation's agricultural program was in place to make sure that people did not starve while societies addressed the problem of population growth. He saw the program as "buy[ing] time—perhaps two to three decades—in which to permit population control programs to become more effective and dynamic." Blaming the Rockefeller Foundation for causing the problem, he said, was "barking up the wrong tree."[46]

Meanwhile, the world's population—and its dependency on industrially fixed nitrogen—continued to rise. When the *Grandcamp* exploded in 1947, the world's population had stood at 2.4 billion, with about 30 percent of all people living in urban centers. By 1985, the world's population had doubled to 4.8 billion, with the urban percentage climbing to 40 percent. In that same period, the global production of nitrogen-based fertilizers had risen from about 3 million tons to approximately 70 million tons, rivaling the amount being fixed by bacteria. Industrially fixed nitrogen had become essential for feeding the world's population.[47]

PART III

Learning to Establish Human-Defined Limits

8

N in the Well

In 1957, researchers at Michigan State University conducted a straightforward experiment involving the application of nitrogenous fertilizer to fields of sugar beets. They found that "300 pounds of nitrogen an acre applied at planting time" did not supply enough of the nutrient for the entire growing season. But plants that "received the same total amount of nitrogen fertilizer at three different times—one at planting time and two later—were well supplied with nitrogen the whole season." The experiment also showed that, in the first case, only 50 percent of the nitrogen could be accounted for in plant tissue; in the second case, the amount entering the plant climbed to 70 percent. However, the researchers did not discuss, for either case, where the rest of the fertilizer ended up.[1]

It is not surprising that 1950s agricultural scientists showed little interest in the fate of nitrogenous fertilizers that flowed beyond the root zone. As Robert Rodale had suggested several years earlier in an issue of *Organic Gardening and Farming,* agricultural scientists tended to ignore questions not directly related to production.[2] Although the cost of the lost fertilizer certainly mattered, where it ended up did not. In addition, compared to applications of insecticides, herbicides, and other chemicals designed to kill organisms, one hundred pounds of lost fertilizer over an acre of land seemed to be relatively harmless. Even public health officials, who knew that high concentrations of nitrate in well water could lead to "blue baby syndrome," initially did not express much interest in the fate of fertilizers.[3] For that matter, neither did the proponents of organic agriculture. They simply recommended that farmers avoid applications of industrial fertilizer and other capital-intensive inputs, which they saw as compromising the long-term health of not only the soil but also agricultural communities in general.[4] One agronomist who did attempt to construct a nitrogen "balance sheet" concluded that the issue was too complicated to answer given the current state of knowledge.[5]

By the late 1960s, however, scientists had begun to ask sophisticated questions about the flow and fate of industrially produced chemicals in the environment, including nitrogenous compounds. Thanks to the publication of Rachel Carson's *Silent Spring*, which examined the fate of pesticides and insecticides, even the general public was becoming more aware of how small flows of material could affect ecological systems in subtle ways. At a societal level, this process of learning to ask questions about the fate of chemicals in the environment and rewarding those who pursue such questions surely represented a step toward developing a more sustainable relationship with the rest of nature.

Wells, Nitrate, and the Creation of an Environmental Standard

In the 1950s, farmers in the United States were interested in knowing more about the fertilizers they were beginning to use in larger and larger quantities, if only to make better use of their investment. In 1958, at the seventh annual meeting of the Agricultural Research Institute, an organization of "industrial, governmental, and private scientific members" formed under the auspices of the National Academy of Sciences, a session on the research and development of nitrogen fertilizers led to a discussion about the need for practical advice on how best to use the various types of fertilizers available. Everybody agreed that huge increases in yields were possible. The question was how to obtain them profitably.[6]

The director of Allied Chemical's fertilizer research program led the session. He noted that "in one corn test in 1956, a yield of 230 bushels per acre, containing about eleven percent protein, was obtained in a field across the fence from one that produced thirty-five bushels per acre and contained only seven percent protein. The difference in yield and quality, in this case, was due to the feeding." Nobody questioned the results. What they did question was the ability of untrained farmers to obtain the same results. A representative of the Greenwood Seed Company, for example, noted that his company spent 50,000 dollars each year on fertilizers but had yet to receive any assistance from the manufacturer. Similarly, a representative of the American Association of Cereal Chemists wanted to know more about the use of urea, which was beginning to be marketed as a high-nitrogen (44 percent) fertilizer that in the soil was converted into nitrate at a more even pace than were nitrogen compounds such as ammonia and ammonium nitrate.[7]

Simple answers about how to get the most benefit out of industrially produced fertilizers were not always possible. For the highest yields and most efficient use of fertilizer, nitrate must be delivered to the root zone at a pace that matches the ability of crops to draw in the nutrient. In nonagricultural ecosystems, where the gradual decomposition of organic material serves as the main source of nitrogen, the delivery of nitrogen to the root zone is less likely to overwhelm the ability of plants to draw in the nutrient. Not only are flows of nitrate regulated by a complex soil ecology, but a well-established network of roots is present during the entire growing season.

In agricultural systems, however, matching the delivery of nitrogen to the needs of crops can be complicated; and if farmers fail to manage their practices, loss of nitrogen can be significant. The rate at which the nitrogen in industrial fertilizers reaches the root zone depends on a number of factors, including the chemical form of the fertilizer, the amount applied, the timing of its application, soil conditions, the amount of sunshine and precipitation, the level of irrigation, the types of plants involved, and the extent to which a network of roots has been established.[8] High losses can occur if ammonium nitrate is applied to well-drained soils during rainy weather early in the growing season because precipitation dissolves the material more quickly than young plants can draw it in, and water seeping into the ground ends up carrying highly soluble nitrate ions out of the root zone. Losses can also occur when gases are released into the air. For example, when farmers inject anhydrous ammonia (that is, pure ammonia undiluted by water) into their soil, some of the material vaporizes and escapes. The increased activity of nitrogen-manipulating bacteria, stimulated by the application of fertilizers, can also result in higher-than-normal releases of nitrogenous gases. In harvested fields, where no plants are present to take in any nitrates, losses can also be quite high if farmers stimulate decomposition and nitrification by plowing.[9]

Manufacturers looked for ways to reduce nitrogen losses. For example, they tried coating granules of ammonium nitrate with substances to prevent the salt from dissolving too rapidly, but pinholes in the coating often defeated that strategy. In the end, what mattered most to the average farmer was not minimizing losses but optimizing profits. If the costs of purchasing and applying fertilizer were economically justified by larger yields, the fate of any lost nitrogen was an academic issue. In short, if applying fertilizers could triple yields and boost revenues in excess of what was needed to pay for the fertilizer, few people asked questions about the nitrogen that leached away.[10]

Early indications that the fate of that nitrogen might matter emerged in the late 1930s. In 1936, sixty-nine cows on a Colorado ranch died after being fed oat hay. In investigating the cause of those and subsequent livestock deaths, researchers at a Wyoming agricultural experimental station determined that a five-hundred-pound animal could be fatally poisoned by eating five and half pounds of hay containing 5 percent potassium nitrate by weight (roughly an eighty-gram dose of nitrate).[11]

Experts did not find the report particularly surprisingly. By the time the station had issued its warning, the medical community was already familiar with the effects of nitrates and nitrites. The diuretic effects of ammonium nitrate, for example, were well known, and physicians occasionally prescribed the compound to treat certain ailments. Low levels of nitrates and nitrites were also routinely used as food preservatives. Nitrites not only helped to preserve meats but also provided a fresh, reddish-pink tint to tissue that would otherwise appear brownish. However, when used as preservatives in meats, the concentrations of those compounds hovered at 100 to 200 parts per million, meaning that even the most heavily preserved meats delivered a dose that was less than a one-tenth of a gram per pound.[12]

Physicians also realized that, at higher concentrations, these compounds could interfere with the blood's ability to carry oxygen. As early as the 1860s, physiologists had noticed that blood took on a distinctive color when mixed with nitrite.[13] Thirty years later, in 1897, physiologists seeking to understand the diseases of workers engaged in the "manufacture of certain nitro-explosives" demonstrated that, in mice, the change in color occurred because nitrite converts oxygen-carrying hemoglobin into methemoglobin, a molecule incapable of carrying oxygen.[14] Over the next several decades, a variety of medical researchers examined the physiological effects of nitrates and nitrites in more detail, eventually concluding that, while nitrites caused methemoglobinemia, nitrates could also lead to the condition if bacteria were to reduce them to nitrite in the intestine. In the mid-1930s, the introduction of sulfonamide-based antibiotics increased physicians' interest in methemoglobinemia because soon after they began prescribing these drugs, they learned that sulfonamides could also trigger the conversion of hemoglobin to methemoglobin. In some cases, the drug reduced the oxygen-carrying capacity of the blood enough to produce serious symptoms. The effect was reversible, with levels of methemoglobin dropping soon after the patient stopped taking the drug.[15]

In the end, the agricultural investigators in Wyoming determined that a number of factors had influenced the concentration of nitrate in hay: the type of grass used to make the hay, the age of the plant when cut, the type of soil, the level of fertilizer use, and the weather conditions just before the cut. During rainy weather, some plants take in nitrate faster than they can process it, which results in an accumulation of nitrate in the plant. Waiting for a few good sunny days before cutting hay was one way to reduce whatever accumulation had occurred. Even raising the height of the cut could help, farmers were told, because most nitrate accumulates low in the stem. Farmers were also instructed to seek out sources of water low in nitrates because the concentration of the compound in an animal's drinking water was an important contributing factor. Farmers who paid attention to any these factors found that they could easily protect their livestock from nitrate poisoning.[16]

At the time, though, nobody had yet linked any human cases of methemoglobinemia to nitrate concentrations in water. Indeed, in February 1939, when doctors at the Saint Louis Children's Hospital diagnosed an infant with cyanosis, the general condition associated with a lack of oxygen, they assumed it was a case of methemoglobinemia caused by sulfonamides. However, the parents, who came from a farming community in Missouri, said that the child had not received any medication. After the doctors successfully treated the infant, they confirmed that no sulfonamides were present in the child's blood and publicized the case as being one of "unknown origin."[17]

A few years later, health officials did link high nitrate concentrations in well water to rural cases of infant methemoglobinemia. In 1945, Hunter Comly, a doctor in the Department of Pediatrics at the State University of Iowa, published a paper in the *Journal of the American Medical Association* in which he identified two cases similar to the earlier one in Missouri. In both of the new cases, Comly discovered that the mothers had bottle-fed their infants using well water. When water from these wells were tested, both samples contained more than 550 milligrams per liter of nitrate, an amount that suggested contamination from "water seeping from barnyards and privy pits." The presence of coliform bacteria reinforced this observation. In addition, Comly noted that similar cases of infant cyanosis had been discussed at a recent meeting of the American Academy of Physicians. He suggested that high nitrate levels in well water might be the cause of those cases as well. He examined two water surveys, one completed by the Iowa State Planning Board in 1936 and one conducted by the Iowa Department of Health in 1944, both of which contained data about nitrate concentrations in water drawn from wells. Given these data, he advised against feeding infants water that contained more than 45 to 90 milligrams per liter of nitrate, at least until further research could be performed.[18]

By the 1950s, the symptoms of nitrate-triggered blue baby syndrome were well known. If formula-fed infants took in too much nitrate, a bluish tint appeared around their lips. After moving to their toes and fingers, the tint spread to other areas and could be accompanied by vomiting and diarrhea. Research suggested that adults were less susceptible to the problem. First, the percentage of body weight that adults took in as fluid was much lower. Second, higher levels of acidity in adult intestines reduced the activity of nitrate-reducing bacteria. Finally, adults appeared to be more able to convert methemoglobin back to hemoglobin.[19]

Comly's recommended threshold for separating safe from unsafe concentrations of nitrate in drinking water proved to be as good a choice as any.

In 1951, the U.S. Public Health Service conducted a survey of the literature related to cases of infant methemoglobinemia and concluded that 97 percent of the cases involved water with concentrations of nitrate higher than 90 milligrams per liter. Only 3 percent of cases involved nitrogen concentrations below that level, and in those cases all concentrations were above 45 milligrams per liter. Although Graham Walton, the sanitary engineer who conducted the survey, hesitated to say that water containing more than 45 milligrams per liter of nitrate was unsafe, he noted that a committee formed by the American Public Health Association had suggested 45 milligrams per liter as the recommended safe permissible level for water used in preparing infant formula. Furthermore, the number meshed fairly well with studies showing that water from most drilled wells could meet this standard. In Iowa, for example, more than 95 percent of the drilled wells produced water containing less than 45 milligrams per liter of nitrate. Dug wells, which tended to be much shallower, were more problematic. Almost 40 percent of those wells contained more than 45 milligrams per liter of nitrate [20]

The bottle-feeding recommendation soon became the de facto standard for distinguishing between safe and unsafe concentrations of nitrates in well water. The World Health Organization published the guideline "50 to 100 mg/l" in its 1958 publication on drinking-water quality, and the U.S. Public Health Service adopted it in 1961.[21] In effect, the health community now had a threshold that could serve as an early warning signal for potential problems, a standard that facilitated a nested process of trial and error for determining whether water was safe for infants to drink. One no longer had to wait for an infant to fall ill before deciding that a water source was unsafe. Instead, one could now test the water for nitrate and predict what might happen if an infant were to be bottle-fed using that water.

The establishment of a nitrate standard or guideline was potentially important for other reasons as well. It served an indicator of change: a rise in the nitrate concentration of water drawn from an aquifer suggested that some activity capable of changing water quality on a relatively large scale was occurring. Whether 50 milligrams per liter was the right number to choose as a health-based threshold is certainly a legitimate issue, and some agronomists and health officials do argue that the guideline is overly cautious and based on a flawed understanding of the physiology involved.[22] After all, such guidelines and standards have important economic consequences once they become embedded in a body of law. However, in the long term, the role of such measures as markers of change may be as important as the specific threshold that is chosen.

As for the cause of the nitrate contamination, Walton identified all possible sources, including animal wastes, fertilizers, and the leaching of compounds from geological formations. He noted that, while most health officials assumed that cesspools, privies, and barnyards were the source of contamination, the data suggested that incidents of high nitrate contamination "did not seem to be associated with nearby sources of pollution." But Walton did not point to fertilizers as a likely culprit either. Instead, he noted that "40 inches of soil may contain 16,000 lbs of organic nitrogen per acre" and suggested that activities such as plowing, which oxygenated the soil, probably stimulated nitrifying bacteria and turned a portion of that 16,000 pounds into nitrates that leached away.[23] This suggestion was consistent with the observations of investigators with the Kansas State Board of Health, who concluded that the presence or absence of vegetation on agricultural soil greatly influenced how much nitrate reached groundwater. They came to this conclusion after determining that nitrate concentrations in four municipal wells varied seasonally, peaking after the harvest when the ground was bare.[24]

Few people, however, realized how fast fertilizer use was increasing and what effect that might have on flows of nitrogen that were reaching aquifers. In the 1930s, relatively few farmers in the United States applied significant quantities of industrially fixed nitrogen to their soils. Yet by the end of the 1940s, they were applying a total of about 1 million metric tons each year. Over the course of the 1950s, that amount climbed to 2.5 million metric tons. By 1970, it had tripled to 7.5 million metric tons. Worldwide, the application of nitrogenous fertilizers rose more than sevenfold between 1950 and 1970, going from about 4 million to 30 million metric tons, an increase accelerated by the spread of nitrogen-intensive industrial agricultural to countries such as Mexico and India.[25]

In the United States, inputs of nitrogen to the soil were also increasing in the nation's rapidly expanding suburban areas, where many homes were being constructed with sewage-digesting septic tanks under large lawns. Both the septic tank and the lawn had the potential to introduce relatively large quantities of nitrates into local environments.[26] Some of that nitrate came from the overuse of lawn fertilizers, which were emerging as a profitable product line. In the 1950s, executives at the O. M. Scott Company, originally a distributor of turfgrass seeds, discovered that they could make more money selling fertilizers. After all, people only seeded their lawns once, but they could be convinced to purchase fertilizers each year. The company had marketed an organic fertilizer made from soybean meal in the 1930s, but that business had been relatively low volume. In addition, during World War II, the U.S. government had redirected the company's supply of soybean meal into cattle feed. So after the war, the company began selling a new line of fertilizers using inexpensive nitrogen compounds purchased from the operators of surplus ammonia plants. Some of those products, marketed with images of bright-green, weed-free lawns, also contained wartime-developed chemicals capable of killing broadleaf plants without harming grass. These products soon became, in the words of one executive, "a sort of tail wagging the dog entity of the business."[27] The Scott Company also encouraged hardware stores to make available a line of lawn-care guides that encouraged frequent use of company products. For example, one guide advised homeowners to remove and dispose of grass clippings, which had the effect of ensuring that lawns would benefit from doses of fertilizer each growing season. The guides also provided fertilizer-friendly answers to hypothetical questions, such as how to fix a bad lawn. "The key to success," one guide explained, "is regular use of fertilizer."[28]

What most people did not know or think about was that much of the nitrogen applied to lawns ended up in local streams or in aquifers supplying nearby wells. In some communities, lawn-care companies further aggravated the problem by marketing services in which they sprayed lawns with a nitrate-rich solution that quickly boosted grass's green plushness while sending large quantities of nitrate beyond the root zone. Under many of these lawns lay a septic system that was also adding to the local nitrogen load. Usually poorly maintained, these systems often drained into soils that were ill-equipped to process the amount of nitrogen-rich liquids that the household was releasing.[29]

In the United States, a rise in meat production along with a shift to concentrated animal-feeding operations also increased the flow of nitrogen compounds into the environment. While animals are being fattened, each consumes a significant amount of feed, and about five-sixths of the nitrogen in that feed ends up being released in the animal's urine and feces. On small pasture-based farms, the waste can be directed back to agricultural soil or to land used for grazing, creating a closed loop of nitrogen flow. However, if a concentrated animal-feeding operation nourishes its livestock with feed grown elsewhere, little if any pasture is needed. As a result, the operations were generating large quantities of nitrogen-rich wastes but had little use for them. Sloppy disposal meant that nitrogen compounds were entering nearby streams and aquifers. Moreover, most of the purchased feed came from farms that were using industrial fertilizers, and one-third to one-half of the nitrogen that farmers applied to the soil never even made it into the crop's biomass. Over the entire supply chain, therefore, losses of nitrogen were high: roughly twenty molecules of nitrogen were applied to soils for every one molecule that reached the dinner table.[30]

Increases in meat consumption magnified the release of nitrogen compounds into the environment. In 1950, when the U.S. population stood at 152 million, the average person consumed about 110 pounds of meat per year for a total of about 8.4 million tons. By 1980, 227 million people were eating 165 pounds of meat per person, for a total of about 19 million tons per year.[31] In addition to increasing the amount of nitrogen that was being released into the environment during farming and fattening operations, this trend also meant that more nitrogen was being flushed into urban sewer and septic systems.

Finally, automobiles and power plants were sending more chemically active nitrogenous compounds into the environment, primarily in the form of nitrogen oxides. In the 1950s, concerns associated with the formation of photochemical smog in Los Angeles brought these emissions to the public's attention. At first, however, the smog problem seemed to have nothing to do with other nitrogen-related concerns.

Rising Interest in the Fate of Nitrogen Compounds

Until the publication of Rachel Carson's *Silent Spring* in 1962, which focused on the unintended effects of pesticides, it is safe to say that most people in the United States simply assumed that human-manufactured chemicals could not significantly affect the dynamics of natural systems. By showing a broad audience how the pesticide DDT accumulated in the tissue of organisms as it worked its way up the food chain, Carson made it clear that humans, even when using relatively small amounts of chemicals, could affect natural systems in subtle ways. In some birds, she explained, the accumulation of pesticides was great enough to weaken the shells of their eggs, preventing successful reproduction. If the large-scale use of DDT continued, she wrote, the birds we expect to hear in spring might be forever silent.[32]

Carson's way of thinking had not emerged out of a vacuum. In the 1950s, after several decades of ferment, ecological thought had disseminated widely among biologists and others in the life sciences. The 1953 publication of Eugene Odum's *Fundamentals of Ecology* focused broad attention on the value of tracing flows of energy and material through natural systems. Eugene's brother Howard Odum, who contributed to the volume, had already analyzed the global cycling of strontium for his doctoral research and visualized all such cycles as being interconnected, with each acting as a cog geared to other cogs in a complex self-regulating system powered by the sun.

Howard had earned his Ph.D. at Yale University, where he studied under George Evelyn Hutchinson, one of the first scholars to systematically study flows of nutrients through natural systems outside the boundaries of agricultural land.[33] Hutchinson, in turn, had been heavily influenced by the highly original Russian thinker, Vladimir Vernadsky, author of *The Biosphere* (1926). Vernadsky (whose son, a historian at Yale, had introduced Hutchinson to his father's work) depicted the slim film of life near the surface of the Earth as something akin to the self-regulating mix of interconnected systems that James Lovelock would later call the *Gaia*. To Vernadsky, a flock of geese was not just a flock of geese but a nitrogen-transport system as well. His influence on Hutchinson can be seen in Hutchinson's pioneering work on the dynamics of freshwater lakes, which he treated as complex systems that could be best understood in terms of energy and material flows.[34]

Hutchinson's research on eutrophication proved to be especially relevant. By 1960, many previously clean lakes and ponds had become unsightly and foul-smelling, and Hutchinson's work helped to explain what was happening. Algae growth in inland lakes, he had determined, was limited mainly by the availability of phosphorus.[35] Together, inputs of nitrogen and phosphorus could form a potent brew, something that became increasingly obvious as more of both nutrients flowed into lakes and ponds. Indeed, by the late 1950s, many inland water bodies routinely experienced unsightly algal blooms, often in the form of a thick green or reddish-brown scum covering the water surface. Because it blocked sunlight from reaching oxygen-producing phytoplankton, the scum quickly altered conditions below the surface. The decomposition of the bloom consumed whatever oxygen remained, making it difficult for other oxygen-dependent organisms—such as fish—to survive. Also, in the absence of oxygen, decomposition could be taken over by anaerobic organisms, resulting in the release of methane and foul-smelling sulfur compounds.

In response to the problem, the National Academy of Sciences formed the Planning Committee on Eutrophication to study the problem. The committee's report, published in 1965, recommended that "the general public and the whole scientific community be alerted to the deterioration of the quality of the human environment through the eutrophication of our water."[36] Two years later, the committee convened an international symposium at the University of Wisconsin attended by more than six hundred researchers. Many attendees presented nutrient budgets for individual water bodies, thus revealing that phosphorus in detergents was the most important factor in algae blooms. At the time, most detergents sold in the United States contained, by weight, about 10 percent phosphorus. Reducing or eliminating this input, the research suggested, was the obvious first step in addressing the problem.[37]

Nutrient budgets for nitrogen also proved to be useful because they gave the researchers who were studying eutrophication a more complete system of accounting and a broader perspective than either agricultural scientists or sanitary engineers had possessed. As ecologically minded biologists began to assimilate data on flows of nitrogen, a fuller picture of how humans interacted with the nitrogen cycle began to emerge. And what researchers discovered was that human fixing of nitrogen had become a significant component of this basic biogeochemical cycle.

Some ecologically minded scientists asserted that humanity should be concerned about its growing role in the cycle. In 1968, at a symposium of the American Association for the Advancement of Science, biologist Barry Commoner specifically raised the issue of human activity as a potential threat to "the integrity of the nitrogen cycle," linking larger flows of nitrogen to eutrophication, photochemical smog, nitrate accumulation, and acid rain. He later argued in *The Closing Circle* that humans had fallen out of harmony with ecological and biogeochemical systems such as the nitrogen cycle.[38]

When a global nitrogen budget appeared in a 1970 *Scientific American* article written by C. C. Delwiche, an expert on the biochemistry of nitrogen, the issue reached a wide audience. In a well-executed color diagram representing the nitrogen cycle, Delwiche included estimates for the amount of nitrogen that was stored in various biogeochemical reservoirs: the ocean, the atmosphere, organic matter, and so on. He also gave estimates, based on numbers that Hutchinson had come up with a decade earlier, for the amount of nitrogen being put into and taken out of circulation each year. Among other things, these numbers, which he admitted were rough, suggested that industrial processes now fixed almost as much nitrogen as all the bacteria in the world. (Delwiche estimated that bacteria fixed 54 million metric tons each year while humans fixed 30 million metric tons.) Although the amount of nitrogen that was being fixed and denitrified annually was small relative to the reservoir of nitrogenous compounds in the world's soils and seas, he suggested that introducing large quantities of industrially fixed nitrogen into the biogeochemical cycle could have large effects. What would happen, he wondered, if denitrifying bacteria (which, he said, processed 83 of the 84 million metric tons fixed each year) could not remove nitrogen as fast as humans were creating it?[39]

According to Delwiche, humans had injected themselves into a fundamental cycle of nature, and "the ingenuity that has been used to feed a growing world population will have to be matched quickly by an effort to keep the nitrogen cycle in reasonable balance."[40] By saying this, he reinforced an idea that recent photographs of Earth from space had communicated visually, an idea that Vernadsky had suggested a half-century earlier: materially, the world is a closed system, and humans might have to manage their industrial-scale activities if they wished to sustain its integrity.[41]

Many agricultural experts saw such concerns as being out of proportion to reality, and some referred to the growing interest in flows of nitrogen as the "nitrogen panic."[42] Norman Borlaug, who had become the face of the green revolution after winning the Nobel Peace Prize, believed that potential famine was still the primary issue and that critics of now-standard agricultural practices were being naïve: "Why don't you take on the job to sell the importance of population control to the rebellious youth of the U.S.A. and get their boundless energies behind a worthy cause?"[43]

Others, such as those who embraced the work of Sir Albert Howard and his vision of organic agriculture, did worry about the increased use of industrially fixed nitrogen but not for Delwiche's reasons. Before his death in 1947, Howard had railed against what he called the N-P-K mentality of agricultural scientists: that is, the emphasis placed on manufactured fertilizers composed of nitrogen (N), phosphorus (P), and potassium (K), often at the expense of other aspects of soil management and farming. He suggested that knowledge of how to grow food with as few inputs as possible should be integrated into both mainstream agricultural practices and the research agendas of agricultural colleges. Industrial agriculture as it was currently framed, he declared, was not right for either industrialized or industrializing nations.[44]

Howard's concern had less to do with the fate of chemicals applied to the soil and more to do with maintaining healthy soils and stable farming communities. He believed that everything should operate in ecological harmony, from microorganisms in the soil to the farmers who worked the land. While conducting research in India on how to increase the productivity of its farms, he had concluded that any practices undermining the communities of working farmers were as undesirable as practices that degraded soils; and he developed a strategy for steadily building up soil's organic matter by systematically composting plant residues. In 1931, while he was directing the agricultural research station in Indore, India, Howard and an assistant published their strategy in *The Waste Products of Agriculture: Their Utilization As Humus*.[45] A decade later, he published *An Agricultural Testament* in which he criticized the "present-day organization of agricultural research" and encouraged readers to learn from "nature's method of soil management."[46] To Howard, producing food as inexpensively as possible for a rapidly increasing urban population was not the priority; instead, the goal was to avoid the use of capital- and energy-intensive farming practices.

Howard was also familiar with Gilbert Fowler's research in India. Fowler was the consultant who had designed Milwaukee's pilot-scale activated sludge facility and advised the city to sell its waste sludge as a nitrogen-rich fertilizer.[47] In 1916, two years after designing the Milwaukee facility, he had moved to India to improve "the utilization of the waste products of human and animal life for the benefits of agriculture." That task, he said, required him "to study closely some of the numberless transformations that take place in the journey of nitrogen from the plant in the field through men and animals back to the soil again." Like Howard, he noted that farmers in India used much of their animal manure for fuel and saw the first order of business as altering this practice to prevent the associated loss of nutrients. In 1934, Fowler published *An Introduction to the Biochemistry of Nitrogen Conservation* in which he noted that "the conservation of nitrogen may indeed be said to be the most important problem confronting the human race." At the same time, he dismissed greater use of industrially fixed nitrogen as the solution, saying, "it has been found by age old practical experience that something more than mineral nitrogen is required for healthy crop development." He pointed to examples of successful nitrogen conservation from around the world, ranging from the use of night soil in Shanghai to fish ponds in Germany. To Fowler, Milwaukee's facility remained the "the most outstanding example of nitrogen conservation by completely modern methods."[48]

Fowler tended to be less harsh in his criticism of industrial agriculture than Howard was. Both men would have been dumbfounded, however, by post–World War II developments involving concentrated animal-feeding operations in the United States. To them, adding industrially fixed nitrogen to the soil for the purpose of growing corn to feed animals who were being fattened hundreds of miles away would have made no sense, especially if the resulting nitrogen-rich manure and urine were not being applied to agricultural soils. Their concern would have been less about the nitrate's effect on Earth systems and more about the wastefulness of such practices and the growing dependency of farmers and societies on industrial inputs.

Through his *Agricultural Testament* and his explicit critique of industrial agriculture, Howard had a great influence on those who rebelled against what they saw as the conversion of family farms into capital-intensive chemical factories. One such disciple was Lady Eve Balfour, an advocate of what she called *sustainable agriculture*. Balfour explicitly articulated a vision of agriculture that rejected the energy- and nitrogen-intensive practices of the green revolution. Agriculture, she argued, should rely on the biologically produced products of soil organisms to generate the nitrogen needed for productive farm nutrients. Believing that humans ought to live within the limits of the living soil, Balfour emphasized the importance of fostering symbiotic relationships and rejected any activity that undermined them. The symbiotic relationship between nitrogen-fixing bacteria and legumes, which had awakened a generation of thinkers to the implications of evolutionary processes that were being shaped by both cooperation and competition, was only one of many such examples she considered. To Balfour, the industrial scientists who successfully bypassed the symbiotic activities of nitrogen-fixing bacteria were also gradually undermining other symbiotic relationships in the soil.[49]

In the United States, the major promoter of Howard's views was Jerome Rodale, who argued that industrial interests and the profit motive were pushing agriculture in an unsustainable direction. Rodale, whom Howard had described as "the prime mover in bringing out the first American edition of *An Agricultural Testament*," began publishing the magazine *Organic*

Gardening and Farming in 1942.[50] The very first issue opened with an article titled "Who Pays for Agricultural Research?" Written by his son Robert, the article argued that industry was moving agriculture in a direction that made the best sense for companies but not necessarily for farmers and their customers. According to Rodale, topics of interest to organic farmers were receiving little attention from mainstream agricultural scientists because any scientist who raised questions unrelated to agricultural productivity was not likely to be rewarded with large grants or professional prestige.[51]

As it happened, more funds for research on the fate of nitrogen did become available, mainly because of interest in eutrophication, although they did not necessarily flow through agricultural channels. In the early 1970s, with scientists such as Commoner and Borlaug publicly debating over whether the public should be concerned about nitrate accumulation, Congress asked the National Academy of Sciences to investigate the matter. In 1972, a committee operating under the auspices of that organization released a report summarizing what scientists knew (see table 8.1).

According to the authors, inputs of ammonia and nitrate into U.S. soils now totaled an estimated 21 million metric tons, and they suggested that human activity was responsible for most of that amount. The 7.5 million metric tons of nitrogen being fixed industrially clearly involved human activity, as did much of the 3.6 million metric tons produced by nitrogen-fixing bacteria working symbiotically with plants. (After all, farmers intentionally grew those plants.) In addition, the 5.6 million metric tons supplied by precipitation included nitrogen fixed by human activity through combustion processes.

The committee estimated where those 21 million metric tons of fixed nitrogen were being used. Notable was the amount associated with the production of meat: 15.1 million metric tons. Although the meat itself contained only about 0.84 million metric tons of nitrogen, the agricultural sector needed to start with 15.1 million metric tons of nitrogen in the soil. Only about half that amount found its way into crops used as animal feed. Another 75 percent was lost as urine and feces while livestock were being fattened.[52]

How much of the 21 million metric tons of nitrogen eventually ended up back in the atmosphere? The authors' best estimate was that only about 19.5 million metric tons reached the atmosphere. Therefore, about 1.5 million metric tons were accumulating somewhere, perhaps leaching into groundwater, or being carried away by streams to the sea. The authors hesitated, though, to make any definite statements about trends associated with the nitrate concentration of groundwater. Although they had access to significant amounts of groundwater data, they had no way of determining whether nitrate concentrations were actually increasing.[53]

As for health concerns, the committee noted that infant methemoglobinemia was no longer a major concern in the United States. Most of the

TABLE 8.1

Nitrogen Inputs and Returns to U.S. Soils, 1970

	Millions of Metric Tons
Inputs to agricultural soil	
Industrially fixed N (fertilizers)	7.5
Precipitation	5.6
Symbiotic N-fixing bacteria	3.6
Mineralization of soil compounds	3.1
Nonsymbiotic N-fixing bacteria	1.2
Total	21.0
Use	
Production of animal protein	15.1
Not integrated into the food chain	4.2
Production of plant protein	0.9
Production of sugar	0.6
Production of fibers	0.2
Total	21.0
Amount returned to atmosphere	
Oxides and ammonia in moisture	5.6
Gases, denitrifying bacteria in soils	8.9
Gases, denitrifying bacteria in water	5.0
Total	19.5

Source: Committee on Nitrate Accumulation, Accumulation of Nitrate (Washington, D.C.: National Academy of Sciences, 1972), 7.

350 documented cases, the authors observed, had occurred between 1945 and 1950. Education of physicians and mothers had apparently done much to address the problem. The authors also noted concerns that nitrates and nitrites in foods could serve as precursors to nitrosamines, compounds known to be carcinogenic in laboratory animals, but they indicated that such concerns did not appear to be pressing. In sum, "the Committee finds no evidence of danger to man, animals, or the global environment from present patterns of nitrogen fertilizer use." However, committee members also found an "appalling lack of information" on key topics and recommended

"imaginative research on all ramifications of nitrogen as a fertilizer, food constituent, food additive and preservative, and waste component of the farm and city."[54] Calls for the production of such knowledge were common by the 1970s, in contrast to a half-century earlier.

How to fund the production of such knowledge was another matter. After all, markets, in general, are not particularly good at producing environmental knowledge. Why would a business bear the cost of generating such knowledge unless there were something to be gained? Government funds aimed at improving military preparedness or stimulating economic activity do not necessarily produce this knowledge either. So unless setting and reaching environmental objectives is seen as a legitimate public goal, knowledge relevant to managing a society's interactions with the environment is unlikely to be pursued. Without legally defined environmental objectives, resources tend to be made available only when problems demand immediate attention, as when infants are being diagnosed with methemoglobinemia or when once-clean lakes develop a layer of slime.

9

N in the Air

Nitrogen follows a complex path as it flows from the atmosphere through living systems and eventually back to the atmosphere, and any diagram that attempts to depict this route is bound to be confusing. The full biogeochemical cycle contains several inner loops, alternate pathways, and reservoirs that involve many chemical reactions and compounds. To represent activity in the soil, a tangle of arrows connects one set of bacteria to another. Add details of crops, animals, sewage-treatment plants, forest fires, groundwater, coal, and oceans, and the diagram becomes practically unintelligible.

Thus, to keep things simple, most diagrams do not depict the movement of chemical compounds within the atmosphere. In most cases, they represent the atmosphere as a giant reservoir of inert molecular nitrogen (N_2) capable of being converted into fixed nitrogen by one of four main processes: nitrogen-fixing bacteria, industrial fixation, lightning, and combustion. According to these depictions, nitrogen usually returns to the atmosphere through a single process: denitrification, in which denitrifying bacteria release inert molecular nitrogen, nitrous oxide (N_2O), and nitric oxide (NO) back into the atmosphere. Although diagrams sometimes note that combustion processes release nitric oxide and nitrogen dioxide (NO_2), they do not depict the fate of these chemically active gases because their atmospheric concentrations are so small.

However, as the citizens of Los Angeles discovered in the 1940s, these trace atmospheric gases cannot be ignored; and the city's response to emissions of nitrogen oxides played a pivotal role in subsequent U.S. efforts to measure, monitor, and manage all types of emissions into the atmosphere. Framed in terms of a biogeochemical imbalance, emissions of nitrogen oxides might not have seemed to be particularly serious. After all, according to a 1970 advisory committee charged with recommending an ambient-air-quality standard for nitrogen dioxide, power plants, industrial facilities, and vehicles were releasing only about 50 million tons of nitric oxide and nitrogen dioxide (together referred to as NO_x) each year, an order of magnitude less than the 500 million tons circulated by nature in the same period. According to a parallel study funded by the American Petroleum Institute, the difference in these quantities suggested that combustion sources were in no danger of overwhelming the natural biogeochemical cycle. In practice, however, anthropogenic emissions of these gases were generating concern: the advisory committee found that about 40 percent of all nitrogen oxides released from vehicles and industrial facilities was coming from sources in the United States, and most of that amount was concentrated in several highly populated areas.[1] The general process of developing a network to measure and monitor their presence in ambient air, along with the effort to manage their emissions, represented another step toward developing more sustainable interactions with Earth systems.

Learning to See the Invisible

It is no coincidence that the main constituents of the atmosphere, molecular nitrogen (78 percent) and oxygen (21 percent), are invisible to human eyes: eyeballs evolved in a way that allowed organisms to explore their environments using solar radiation that passes freely through the atmosphere. But humans are still adapting to their environments and still developing tools to explore their surroundings. In the twentieth century, for example, we learned to exploit the properties of light to "see" atmospheric gases present in extremely low concentrations, including nitric oxide and nitrogen dioxide. Such innovations are especially interesting because they were not driven solely by military needs or market forces; they were also encouraged by policy choices designed to prevent the degradation of air quality.

Although the main constituents of the atmosphere, oxygen and inert molecular nitrogen, are transparent to a large band of solar radiation, other atmospheric gases (present in much smaller concentrations) absorb a portion of that radiation. To atmospheric scientists, this ability of trace gases to absorb certain wavelengths of electromagnetic radiation is an extremely valuable characteristic. By measuring the amount absorbed at different wavelengths, they can determine the concentration of each gas in a sample of air. Each gas, in a sense, has a different fingerprint, and analytical tools for detecting those fingerprints have been key to understanding how trace gases affect atmospheric dynamics.[2]

Development of this analytic capacity began in earnest with Robert Bunsen and Gustav Kirchhoff's 1859 invention of the spectroscope. They had been studying phenomena that gave off light, such as the glow of an incandescent wire, and wanted a tool for systematically examining the emission spectra produced when that light passed through a prism. Different sources of light, they knew, produced different spectral patterns. They had also learned that passing sunlight through gases other than air could alter its normal spectral pattern, with different gases absorbing different wavelengths of light.[3]

With the methods and tools developed by Bunsen and Kirchhoff, chemists began to systematically analyze the ability of materials to emit and absorb light. One of Bunsen's students, John Tyndall, hoped to identify gases that could absorb infrared radiation. Thanks to experiments performed earlier in the century by the English astronomer Sir William Herschel, Tyndall knew that heat could be transmitted by calorific waves. Herschel had discovered this phenomenon while using a thermometer to measure the heating effect associated with different colors of the rainbow, observing that the largest effect lay just outside the red side of the visible spectrum. Tyndall, interested in recent theories about how glaciers had once covered northern Europe, wondered if any atmospheric gases could absorb these invisible calorific waves. If so, he reasoned, changes in the atmospheric concentration of those gases could help explain the melting of glaciers. He determined that molecular nitrogen and oxygen were transparent to calorific waves but that other atmospheric gases, such as water vapor, carbon dioxide, methane, and nitrous oxide, absorbed them.[4]

Characterizing materials by their light-absorbing and -emitting properties soon became a routine part of chemistry. Once those properties were documented, chemists could use that knowledge in reverse: they could determine the presence of a material in a phenomenon involving light by examining the wavelengths generated or absorbed. Initially, though, tools for generating and detecting various wavelengths of light were too crude for precisely measuring such things as the concentration of a trace gas in an air sample. These measurements continued to require the methods of "wet" chemistry. That is, chemists had to bubble the air sample through a solution designed to react with the gas to be measured and then determine how much of the gas had been captured.[5]

Practical reasons for studying the effect of light on materials certainly existed. Chemists knew, for example, that sunlight could trigger or accelerate some chemical reactions, including those associated with photography, the fading of dyes, and the degradation of materials. The ability of light to trigger fluorescence and phosphorescence in certain materials was also intriguing. Because companies involved in the manufacture of photographic film, paper, textiles, dyes, inks, and paints had a direct interest in such matters, they served as a firm base of support for chemists who were pursuing new knowledge in this area.

In 1883, Hermann Vogel, the author of *The Chemistry of Light and Photography*, explained fluorescence in terms of ethereal waves at one wavelength that were causing atoms to resonate and emit waves at another. Two decades later, in 1901, Thomas Preston, the author of *The Theory of Light*, explained the phenomenon in much the same way.[6] Yet even though this explanation was consistent with observations, it provided little insight into why specific materials emitted or absorbed particular wavelengths of light. Within a generation, however, physicists and physical chemists had produced a powerful new tool for explaining such things: the quantum model of the atom.

By the mid-1920s, all new treatises on photochemistry began with an introduction to quantum theory. Some phenomena, though, could still be described in almost purely electromechanical terms. For example, physical chemists now knew that when electrons in molecules were not symmetrically distributed, the resulting structure was more positively charged at one end than at the other. Hence, when light (an electromagnetic wave changing polarity millions of times each second) interacted with such a molecule, the molecule vibrated as it attempted to align with the rapidly changing field. If the molecule's movement happened to resonate with the frequency of the wave, some of the radiated energy could be kinetically transferred to the vibrating molecule. The ability of greenhouse gases to absorb energy from infrared waves could be explained in this fashion. But for phenomena such as fluorescence, electromechanical explanations were inadequate. Instead, scientists turned to descriptions of electrons that fell to lower quantum energy states or jumped to higher ones, accompanied by the absorption or emission of a quantum of radiation at the appropriate wavelength. In short, the quantum model of the atom could be used to explain phenomena that older models could not predict.[7]

In the 1920s and 1930s, as physical chemists continued to systematically analyze the photochemical behavior of gases, the oxides of nitrogen, like all gases known to be present in the atmosphere, received significant attention. Physical chemists learned, for example, that ultraviolet radiation could break the bonds of nitrogen dioxide (NO_2) and facilitate the creation of ozone (O_3). Treatises on photochemistry, however, noted that the formation of ozone was only temporary because it quickly recombined with another byproduct, nitric oxide (NO), to form nitrogen dioxide again:

$$\text{Sunlight} + NO_2 + O_2 \rightarrow O_3 + NO$$
$$O_3 + NO \rightarrow NO_2 + O_2$$

Hence, no build-up of ozone occurred.[8]

Chemists also knew that combustion processes associated with automobiles and power plants released nitric oxide and nitrogen dioxide into the air, but they did not have any compelling reason to study the implications.

After all, the concentrations of these gases remained low, typically much less than one part in a million. Nor did the operators of electric-power-generating stations and automobile manufacturers worry about emissions of nitrogen oxides. After all, with sooty coal smoke pouring out of almost every business and home, the idea that anybody should be concerned about relatively small releases of nitric oxide and nitrogen dioxide was almost inconceivable.

The School of Hard NOx

In the 1920s, textile manufacturers received complaints from merchants who had noticed that colored fabrics stored on shelves were fading and taking on a reddish tinge. The fading was especially noticeable with blue, green, and violet dyes on acetate rayon fabrics. By systematically fumigating fabrics with various gases and observing the results, industrial chemists soon implicated oxides of nitrogen as the probable cause. Furthermore, they guessed that most of the troublesome gases were coming from store heaters that burned coal gas.[9]

Investigative measurements showed that store heaters were releasing gases that contained a nitrogen oxide concentration of 10 to 20 parts per million (ppm). The investigators also determined that ambient concentrations in urban air hovered at 0.01 to 0.02 ppm but could rise to 0.10 to 0.15 ppm under smoky conditions. Making such measurements was not particularly easy as it required the methods of wet chemistry, which posed logistical challenges outside of the laboratory. But the investigators had to make only a few such measurements. After all, textile manufacturers had no reason to gather long-term data; they simply desired to find out why the fabrics were fading and how to make their products less sensitive to environmental conditions.[10]

It was natural for leaders in the textile industry to focus on improving their dyes and fabrics rather than lobbying for controls on emissions of nitrogen oxides. At the time, most large industrial cities were wrestling with how to control visible emissions of coal smoke: those sooty particles that were being deposited on everything in sight. Smoke inspectors' main measuring instrument was the Ringelmann chart, basically a piece of cardboard colored in varying shades of gray, from 0 percent black to 100 percent black. Inspectors assessed the smoke coming out of a stack by matching its color to one of the shades; violations occurred if the smoke was darker than a predefined threshold. Given that officials were dealing with concentrations of smoke dark enough to be measured by percentage of blackness, controlling emissions of nitrogen oxides, which were present in concentrations of less than 1 ppm, did not seem to be particularly urgent.[11]

However, when dealing with highly reactive gases, 1 ppm is not such a low concentration. In air containing 1 ppm of any gas, an average breath takes in about 10,000 trillion molecules of that gas.[12] For reactive gases, that concentration is more than sufficient to trigger a reaction. The human nose can detect the presence of nitrogen dioxide at concentrations as low as 0.12 ppm. Concentrations of 50 ppm can cause coughing and chest pain. Several times that amount can be fatal.[13] In the 1930s, though, the concentrations associated with such effects were not known, and in any case, the sooty particles that were pouring out of every stack in sight posed a more immediate concern.

While textile manufactures were busying developing fabrics and dyes capable of resisting the effects of nitrogen oxides, another problem emerged that involved trace concentrations of those reactive gases. This time the problem was in the air of Los Angeles. In the early 1940s, residents first recognized that something highly unusual was happening. The city, subject to periodic smoke-trapping temperature inversions due to its location in a basin between the ocean and a mountain range, had experienced problems with smoke in the past. Even in the mid-nineteenth century, when the population had yet to reach 10,000, residents occasionally noticed the effects of inversions: smoke would rise until it hit what appeared to be an invisible barrier and then spread out. Still, clear blue skies always returned when the weather changed, even by 1920, when the population had multiplied fifty-fold. By 1940, however, with the city's population soaring to 1.5 million people, complaints about the air grew more frequent. In the summer of 1943, one episode involved an eye-irritating haze that cut visibility to three city blocks and caused nausea and vomiting.[14]

Most large urban centers in the 1940s faced air-quality concerns, but the situation in Los Angeles differed from that in other cities. For one thing, its residents generally placed a higher value on clean air than did the residents of other cities. After all, the region's climate had been a major selling point in attracting the 1 million people who had arrived there between 1920 and 1940. So in 1945, after wartime attempts to address the haze problem had failed, the city reorganized its pollution-control effort and hired Isador A. Deutch, a Chicago expert on smoke abatement. For additional advice, the city consulted with Raymond R. Tucker, Saint Louis's top smoke fighter, and Louis C. McCabe, former head of the federal Bureau of Mines. Yet even though the city took strong action based on their recommendations, such as forcing petroleum refineries to significantly cut emissions of sulfur dioxide, air quality continued to decline.[15]

Civic leaders soon realized that their pollution problem differed significantly from that experienced in, for example, Saint Louis, Pittsburgh, and London, where the burning of sooty bituminous coal in homes and industries was the root of the most serious problems. In Los Angeles neither industry nor residents burned much coal. People did burn some fuel oil, but the most serious pollution episodes occurred in the summer and did not coincide with the main period of residential fuel use. In addition, the symptoms differed. Instead of dealing with sooty smoke that turned white shirts (and everything else) black, Los Angeles residents complained of an eye-irritating haze that left no residue but could reduce visibility and damage plants.[16]

Over time various clues about the source of the problem accumulated. On Saturdays, when football games in the northern California city of Berkeley led to traffic jams, the area experienced the same type of air pollution that Los Angeles was experiencing on weekdays. As a result, people began to associate smoggy conditions with automobiles. Chemists also noticed that, in the Los Angeles area, rubber had a greater tendency to crack, a phenomenon associated with ozone. Indeed, Arie Jan Haagen-Smit, a researcher who was studying the effect of smog on plants, recognized the smell of ozone in the hazy air of Los Angeles, which led him to look for explanations that involved the presence of this gas.[17]

By the early 1950s, Haagen-Smit and others had concluded that the emissions lying at the heart of the problem were, first, nitrogen oxides from power plants and automobiles and, second, volatile organic compounds (such as gasoline vapors and evaporated solvents) from automobiles, refineries, and industrial processes. Haagen-Smit's identification of these compounds as troublesome quickly came to the attention of executives in three powerful industries: automobile manufacturing, the oil industry, and the electric-power industry. Oil companies had acted quickly and innovatively to reduce their sulfur emissions when those emissions were thought to be the cause, but this time industrial leaders questioned Haagen-Smit's conclusions.[18] Haagen-Smit and his colleagues, however, performed a simple but convincing experiment. They first added 0.4 ppm of nitrogen dioxide to pure oxygen and exposed the mixture to sunlight. No significant buildup of ozone occurred. As the chemists expected, nitrogen dioxide in the presence of oxygen and sunlight gave rise to small concentrations of nitric oxide and ozone. But when they added volatile organics to the mix, the concentration of ozone reached levels capable of cracking rubber. The experiment suggested that, in the air over Los Angeles, compounds such as gasoline vapors were reacting with molecules of nitric oxide, preventing them from recombining with the ozone. The result: a buildup in the concentration of ozone and in the creation of compounds formed by the combination of volatile organics and nitric oxide.[19]

By the mid-1950s, officials in Los Angeles had embraced the theory that the photochemical breakdown of nitrogen dioxide in the presence of volatile organics lay at the heart of the smog problem. The exact chemistry would take years to work out, but city officials did not need to wait for the details. Air monitoring stations confirmed the results of laboratory experiments, which showed that, on a typical weekday morning, large quantities of nitric oxide and nitrogen dioxide entered the atmosphere from the tailpipes of nearly 1 million cars. Then, as the sun climbed higher in the sky, the concentrations of these two gases dropped and the concentration of ozone rose. Preventing photochemical smog clearly meant reducing the amount of nitrogen oxides and volatile hydrocarbons that were being released into the air.[20]

Constructing a Threshold

Residents genuinely expected something to be done about the Los Angeles smog problem. Blue skies and clean air were fundamental components of California's identity, and residents believed that the atmosphere over the city was a commons to be governed for the public good.[21] But civic leaders in Los Angeles soon discovered that understanding the basic cause of a pollution problem and doing something about it are two different things. Although they recognized that the problem could be addressed by reducing emissions of nitrogen oxides and volatile organic compounds, nobody knew exactly what to do next. How large a reduction was needed for both types of chemicals, and what strategy should be used to allocate and achieve those reductions?

In November 1955, the California State Chamber of Commerce, in cooperation with the Los Angeles County Board of Supervisors, the Los Angeles County Pollution Control District, and the Air Pollution Foundation (a nonprofit group representing local business interests), convened a conference to ask three questions about the nitrogen-related smog problem: what has been done, what is now being done, and what is planned for the future?[22] Among other things, organizers wanted to shape the research agenda that newly committed federal dollars had now made possible. Several months earlier, Congress had passed the Air Pollution Control Act of 1955, which authorized the U.S. Public Health Service to spend up to 5 million dollars per year over the next five years on air pollution research. At the conference, a representative from the Public Health Service, Leslie Chambers, affirmed the agency's willingness to support the city's research agenda, saying that for the foreseeable future the federal effort would be "strongly slanted toward the solution of your vexing problem."[23]

S. Smith Griswold, chief air pollution officer for Los Angeles, opened the conference by suggesting that industrial society was past the point at which cities could grow in an unplanned manner. He noted that, "under ordinary conditions, the flow of currents and eddies continually replenishes man's living zone and carries off the waste products to be diluted in the giant reservoir in the sky." According to Griswold, this was not occurring in the Los Angeles basin. The equivalent of the entire population of Salt Lake City was moving to the area each year, with the result that residents were "drowning in our own wastes."[24] Two recent air pollution episodes underscored that point: one in Donora, Pennsylvania (1948), in which a temperature inversion had trapped emissions from industrial facilities, killing twenty people and injuring thousands; the other in London (1952), in which an inversion had intensified the city's normal mix of fog and coal smoke, resulting in the deaths of thousands.[25]

Discussions of potential policies, regulatory strategies, and technological solutions dominated the conference, which at one level was a form of nested trial and error in which people had a chance to test out their ideas. Observers could listen as the group considered potential strategies and then passed judgment, dismissing some and embracing others. Certain ideas, such as grand technological fixes involving giant fans, seeding clouds to wash out the pollutants, and spraying chemicals into the air to neutralize pollutants, were dismissed without much discussion. Other ideas required more thought. For example, would industrial zoning—that is, forcing business to locate facilities in specific areas—be effective? Griswold responded by asking everybody to visualize a problematic scenario. What if zoning pushed eight refineries into a single area, and what if all eight were complying individually with emission limits but creating a problem with their combined emissions, so much so that adding a ninth refiner would be unacceptable? Should the city be able to tell the owners of the remaining land that they could not build a refinery there? When someone asked if the city should encourage mass transportation, a supporter noted that a bus pollutes only as much as two autos so that any bus carrying more than two passengers would be worthwhile, at least in terms of managing emissions. Yet choices associated with industrial zoning and mass transportation are not purely technical matters. They are also policy choices, and at this conference both received a cool reception.[26]

Most participants saw engineering solutions that reduced emissions as the most practical option. The suggestion to place catalytic mufflers on automobiles, for example, generated interest. Chemists already knew that catalysts could convert volatile organics and nitrogen oxides into a harmless mixture of carbon dioxide, water, and inert atmospheric nitrogen. Representatives from the auto industry, however, directed attention away from catalytic mufflers and to the process by which nitric oxide formed in the engine. By reducing combustion temperatures, they noted, one could reduce the amount of nitrogen oxides created in the first place. Refiners focused on their successful efforts to reduce the amount of hydrocarbon vapors escaping from storage tanks and suggested that it would help significantly if automobile manufacturers could reduce the gasoline vapors escaping from their vehicles. Refiners, too, had reason to discourage participants from placing too much hope on catalytic technology. After all, the tetraethyl lead they added to gasoline would render most catalysts ineffective.[27]

The operators of power plants also had a huge stake in the outcome. Significantly reducing the quantity of nitrogen oxides emitted from oil-burning power plants would require either a small chemical plant or a device akin to a giant catalytic converter, both of which they wished to avoid. At this conference, industry representatives focused on their efforts to reduce sulfur dioxide, which was achievable by burning low-sulfur oil. In general, though, when discussions turned to reducing emissions of nitrogen oxides, engineers in the electric-power industry pointed to the redesign of combustion chambers as the best way to achieve that goal. By reducing the number of turbulent hot spots in combustion chambers, where nitrogen and oxygen combine to form nitric oxide, engineers hoped to halve the amount of nitric oxide that was being created. Nonetheless, the amount of nitrogen oxides emitted due to the nitrogen content of the fuel would remain unchanged.[28]

Lee A. DuBridge, then president of California Institute of Technology and a former science advisor to President Harry Truman, wrapped up the conference by suggesting avenues of research. DuBridge was a physicist who had helped to develop radar during World War II, and he emphasized the importance of determining what was known and unknown. Many of the unknowns he identified involved basic technical data. Nobody, for example, knew how much of the nitrogen being emitted by power plants came from the fuel and how much was atmospheric nitrogen fixed by the heat of combustion. DuBridge also raised questions about levels of eye irritation, odor generation, low visibility, and rubber cracking. What was the best way to measure each of these symptoms? Indeed, the effort to establish tools and standards for measuring and monitoring various aspects of the problem, including human responses to atmospheric contaminants, emerged as one of the most important research tasks. In affirming DuBridge's call for the development of new measuring and monitoring techniques, Griswold observed that ordinances in some locales still made reference to Ringelmann charts. Monitoring emissions of invisible gases by comparing them to various shades of gray on a piece of paper clearly did little good. More sophisticated methods, he agreed, should be developed.[29]

DuBridge's emphasis on developing new instruments for monitoring, measuring, and characterizing the constituents of urban air was well founded. Companies had few incentives to measure and monitor air emissions or, for that matter, to monitor ambient air quality. Not surprisingly, therefore, few tools appropriate to the task had been developed. Researchers investigating the problem of coal smoke in industrial cities such as Pittsburgh had developed techniques for measuring the deposition of particulates and the average concentration of gases such as sulfur dioxide, but those devices tended to be specialized and employed only as part of special investigations. The types of emissions that officials in Los Angles hoped to reduce—hydrocarbons, nitrogen oxides, and byproducts involving reactions between the two—presented an entirely new challenge.[30]

Funding from California and the federal government did facilitate technical developments associated with measuring and monitoring air quality. Among other things, it provided an alternative to research controlled by companies with a direct interest in the problem at hand. In general, industry-funded research on pollution-related issues tended to be defensive, pursued to generate data that could be used to support arguments against potential regulations. Without federal funds, industrial interests would have been better able to control the research agenda, giving large companies a dominant role in determining the pace and direction of innovation.[31] But with state and federal funds, researchers associated with universities and private institutions could proceed more directly along the lines that DuBridge had suggested. Indeed, those who competed for funds managed by the Public Health Service were explicitly judged based on their potential for contributing to this agenda.[32]

Even before the conference, researchers had begun to develop techniques for studying the problem of photochemical smog, such as using mass spectrometers and gas chromatography to identify and measure concentrations of organics in air samples. Essentially, these tools separated molecules by mass and allowed researchers to identify compounds by comparing their observed characteristics to those of known compounds.[33] Other investigators began experimenting with infrared and ultraviolet spectrometry to measure concentrations of nitrogen oxides and ozone without the hassle of wet chemistry. For example, when scientists at the Franklin Institute in Philadelphia created a test chamber to mimic what was happening in the air of Los Angeles, they integrated infrared spectrometry into their setup. By shining infrared light through the chamber and measuring the energy that was being absorbed at various wavelengths, they could determine changes in the concentrations of nitric oxide and nitrogen dioxide in real time. They also passed air samples from the chamber through mass spectrometers and gas chromatographs to determine the identity of any chemicals being created in the smoggy mix.[34]

A network of monitoring stations capable of measuring the concentration of contaminants in urban air was also being constructed. In 1953, the U.S. Public Health Service had established its National Air Sampling Network to test particulate levels in a few large cities. Then in 1954, Los Angeles set up ten stations equipped to monitor concentrations of ozone, nitrogen dioxide, sulfur dioxide, carbon monoxide, and hydrocarbons, along with various pieces of meteorological data. In one four-month period, more than 150,000 measurements were made and "transferred to IBM cards" for processing.[35] A year later, the Public Health Service began providing support for a broader collection of air-quality data in places such as Louisville, Kentucky, where an air-pollution study initiated by the University of Louisville had been hampered by lack of data. In 1960, the Public Health Service expanded its monitoring system and established a Continuous Air Monitoring Program (CAMP) in Chicago, Cincinnati, New Orleans, Philadelphia, San Francisco, and Washington. The program provided for the continuous measurement of a variety of trace gases, with concentrations of each tracked continuously on a strip-chart recorder. In addition, a discrete reading was recorded every five minutes and stored on magnetic tape. States also established monitoring networks of their own, providing additional data to the nation's growing but loosely organized air-quality surveillance network.[36]

The participants who helped to design and administer these monitoring programs quickly saw the importance of developing instrumentation that required less human attention. For example, the initial equipment used at CAMP sites required frequent calibration, a constant supply of chemicals, and the attention of highly skilled personnel. The method used to measure nitrogen dioxide was especially problematic because it required air samples to be scrubbed with a reagent and the resulting color change to be measured with a colorimetric analyzer. Keeping this array of instrumentation in running order necessitated a Herculean effort.[37] The policy goal of developing a national air-monitoring system, however, facilitated technological advances in the direction of improved instrumentation. If nothing else, as the network grew, instrument manufacturers competing for market share increasingly became important innovators.

The data generated by these monitoring stations allowed decision makers to determine whether or not air quality was improving. Initially, making sense of the accumulating data was a challenge because many were distributed in printed tables.[38] But gradually, as digital computers became more available and researchers began to analyze and present air-quality data more systematically, it became obvious that conditions were getting worse, not better. As a result, more people began raising questions related to health standards, with the main unknown being the point at which various atmospheric contaminants became unsafe to breathe. Efforts to answer such questions motivated passage of the federal Air Quality Act of 1967, which mandated that states set air-quality standards.[39]

The 1967 act, which had no strong provisions for enforcement, is generally considered to have been ineffective. Drawing a legal line between safe and unsafe concentrations of a contaminant has significant consequences, and officials in most states moved slowly in establishing standards. Nonetheless, the act set important bureaucratic wheels in motion. For example, because it mandated that the Public Health Service provide guidance to states, the service created a network of advisory committees and charged them with reviewing existing data and making recommendations on how to proceed. For guidance on air-quality criteria related to oxides of nitrogen, it established an advisory committee consisting of fifteen people, including experts in atmospheric science, combustion and pollution-control engineering, and public health. The committee released its report in 1971 under the auspices of the recently formed U.S. Environmental Protection Agency.[40]

The advisory committee's central question was a tough one to answer: at what concentration of nitrogen dioxide does air become unhealthy to breath? Where was the line, the threshold, that should not be crossed? To address this question, the committee drew from myriad sources of data, including concentrations of nitrogen dioxide measured in major cities, epidemiological studies that correlated those concentrations with public health, and toxicity studies that determined the level at which concentrations affected various types of plants and animals. For patterns of change associated with concentrations of nitrogen dioxide in the air of major cities, the committee had plenty of raw data to draw from. By the late 1960s, continuous air-quality monitoring stations had been operating in the largest U.S. cities for more than a decade, and they had pumped out reams of numbers. Now the committee had data for the average concentrations of nitric oxide, nitrogen dioxide, and ozone in a variety of different cities for various time spans over multiple years. Committee members knew, for example, that hourly concentrations of nitrogen dioxide in Los Angeles routinely exceeded 0.2 ppm and that concentrations in cities such as Saint Louis, Philadelphia, and Bayonne typically ranged between 0.03 and 0.09 ppm. Occasionally, in Los Angeles, concentrations of nitrogen dioxide exceeded 1 ppm for short periods of time.[41]

One of the most useful measurements turned out to be the yearly average of twenty-four-hour concentrations. With this number, investigators did not have to worry about hour-to-hour, day-to-day, and season-to-season variations that occurred due to fluctuations in traffic and shifting temperatures and weather patterns. Nor did they have to be too concerned about the quantity and placement of monitoring stations in a city. All they had to deal with was a single number for the entire year; and thanks to the national air-surveillance network, they had twenty-four-hour averages for approximately 150 cities. Data from 1969 indicated that the twenty-four-hour annual average of nitrogen dioxide in most of these cities was lower than 0.1 ppm. A few large cities had annual twenty-four-hour averages that were higher than 0.1 ppm, and the highest (recorded in Chicago) was 0.16 ppm.[42]

When questions about the accuracy of the twenty-four-hour data emerged, both advocates and opponents of air-pollution regulation used them as ammunition to challenge decisions based on the data. At issue was the fact that some monitoring stations were measuring concentrations of the gas using two different types of instruments, and the averages calculated from those two sets of data did not match. The double set of data occurred whenever equipment associated with the national air-surveillance network was integrated into stations that were already holding CAMP equipment. In Saint Louis, yearly averages of nitrogen dioxide concentrations calculated from CAMP data turned out to be 4.5 times smaller than the averages calculated using the other equipment. In general, the two sets of values differed by a factor of 2.7.[43]

The two monitoring networks had been designed for different purposes, and those design differences were creating the disparity. Although both networks used the methods of wet chemistry, technical personnel for CAMP stations chose their reagents and calibrated their equipment to measure highly polluted air. Therefore, measurements of nitrogen dioxide concentrations over 0.1 ppm were accurate, but those below 0.1 ppm were less so, meaning that the resulting annual average of twenty-four-hour averages mixed reliable and unreliable data points. On the other hand, engineers associated with the national air-surveillance network had specifically designed their system to measure twenty-four-hour averages and were using a different reagent and technique. Although twenty-four-hour averages obtained by the second method were more trustworthy, several factors compromised those measurements as well, including the difficulty of calibrating equipment and potential interference from other compounds. For this reason, members of the advisory committee recommended research into other methods of measuring nitrogen dioxide, especially those based on the use of chemiluminescence and infrared spectrometry.[44]

The advisory committee also examined the results of studies involving the toxicological effects of nitrogen dioxide. In one set of studies, researchers exposed different kinds of plants to various amounts of nitrogen dioxide for a range of time periods. The most sensitive plants tended to be injured when exposed to 4 to 8 ppm of the gas for about an hour. Persistent exposure to 2 to 4 ppm of nitrogen dioxide was enough to affect growth. Other studies showed that concentrations on the order of 100 ppm were fatal to animals such as guinea pigs, rabbits, and cats. Relatively low concentrations (0.25 ppm for four hours per day over six days) were shown to have a permanent effect on the lungs of rabbits.[45]

Some studies also examined the effect of nitrogen oxide on humans. In one study involving fifty-seven healthy young men, nine subjects could detect the odor of nitrogen oxide at concentrations of 0.12 ppm. In another study, 2.5 ppm of nitrogen dioxide was shown to have an affect on the breathing patterns of subjects after thirty minutes. In the end, the committee emphasized the need for more research but suggested that nitrogen dioxide did not appear to be a concern below 0.12 ppm. In addition, nitric oxide, at the concentrations then found in the atmosphere, did not appear to be a concern at all.[46]

Finally, they turned to epidemiological data. By far, the most important source of data came from a study funded by the U.S. Public Health Service in which researchers looked for a correlation between ambient nitrogen dioxide levels and the health of schoolchildren in Chattanooga, Tennessee. In that city, an army facility that manufactured nitric acid for use in explosives was releasing significant quantities of nitrogen dioxide into the air, which kept concentrations of the gas in some neighborhoods relatively high. By correlating the exposure of schoolchildren to nitrogen oxide with occurrences of respiratory-related illness and performance on a weekly ventilation test, researchers concluded that 0.06 ppm appeared to be a potential threshold.[47]

In the end, the advisory committee focused on 0.06 ppm as a significant number. Not only did an important (though highly criticized) epidemiological study suggest this figure as a threshold, but it appeared to be a practical choice for other reasons. For one thing, it was half the concentration at which young men with the most sensitive noses could detect any odor. Second, it was well below the concentration that had a measurable effect on plants. Third, it was about the same concentration at which effects on materials were observed, with 0.07 to 0.08 ppm of nitrogen oxides leading to the corrosion of telephone-company relays due to the formation of nitric acid. Finally, it was about the concentration at which nitrogen dioxide, in the presence of sunlight and hydrocarbons, could photochemically generate enough ozone and other chemicals to be an even larger concern than the nitrogen dioxide itself.[48] The committee might have chosen a more or less cautious value, but the critical step lay in establishing a standard. The exact concentration—and whether it was expressed as an hourly, weekly, or monthly average—inevitably would be challenged and potentially would be refined, but creation of a standard established an ethical limit where none had existed before.

In the end, the interplay of producers and consumers alone could not have created a technological system capable of monitoring trace amounts of nitrogen dioxide (and other contaminants) in urban air. Neither would that interplay have funded the pieces of science that were necessary to guide the development of such a system because incentives for doing so were not embedded in the market. Instead, this effort was driven by the concerns of citizens as articulated through public debate, lawsuits, and the voting booth. The possibility of embedding that public choice in law and hence integrating the need to respect air quality into economic decisions lay on the horizon.

10

N in the Law

An ecological economy recognizes that Earth is finite and rewards activity that respects ecological limits. Although constructing such an economy involves far more than controlling the release of pollution-causing wastes, pollution-control laws passed in the 1970s were an important first step. Aimed at sustaining air and water quality, they established systematic limits on what individuals, companies, and municipalities could release into the air, discharge into the water, and bury in the soil, with the underlying assumption being that neither the atmosphere nor bodies of water could serve as an endless sink for municipal and industrial wastes.[1] The laws also laid a shaky foundation for managing more complex human interactions with the rest of nature, including the cycling of nitrogen. In the United States, three laws—the Clean Air Act of 1970, the Federal Water Pollution Control Act of 1972, and the Resource Conservation and Recovery Act of 1976—accounted for much of the change. By examining their development and implementation according to how they affected flows of nitrogen, we can identify a shift that we might otherwise easily overlook: the ambient concentrations of some naturally occurring compounds (including nitrogen compounds), long regulated by natural processes alone, had now come to be regulated by human institutions.

The idea of managing disposal practices so as prevent the deterioration of air and water quality was not new. For more than a century, sanitary engineers and health officials had been wrestling with how best to address sewage-related pollution. Efforts to reduce smoke emissions also had a long history and, by the 1960s, had expanded into concern about the release of specific gases, including nitrogen dioxide.[2] Although weak laws passed in the 1960s failed to change industrial practices, public support for improved air and water quality gave progressive legislators the political ammunition they needed to proceed. Thus, the strong pollution-control laws enacted in the 1970s were part of a decades-long process of societal-level learning that included the development of tools and bureaucracies for measuring and managing releases of material into the environment.[3]

From a strictly technical perspective, managing releases of pollution-causing wastes in order to meet air- and water-quality objectives seemed to be a straightforward goal. In a nation that had just flown two men to the moon and back, how difficult could it be to reduce the level of contaminants flowing out of industrial and municipal waste-disposal facilities? As it turned out, however, attempting to define, much less achieve, air- and water-quality goals was as challenging as the moon shot; and those who participated in the process found themselves undertaking a legal and scientific journey for which they were largely unprepared.

Almost two decades would pass before federal and state agencies succeeded in creating an administrative system capable of effectively monitoring and managing what firms and municipalities were releasing into the nation's air and water. In the meantime, a series of legal challenges tested the fledgling regulatory process, uncovering weaknesses and complications that nobody had anticipated. Addressing these issues involved a significant amount of trial-and-error learning, not only of technical and legal matters but also about what the public was willing to support. Ultimately, participants were forced to think beyond the relatively narrow framework of pollution control and focus on the complete cycle of material flow, including the cycling of nitrogen.

Managing Flows of N into Surface Water

In 1967, officials with the Union Oil Company of California announced plans to tear down an aging Chicago oil refinery. They intended to replace it with an entirely new facility capable of processing three times as much crude oil, and they promised that 37 million dollars, approximately 15 percent of the facility's total cost, would be associated with pollution control. The president of Union Oil assured everybody that the new facility would be "the most efficient and modern refinery in the world from the standpoint of air and water conservation . . . being designed to meet all foreseeable federal, state, and local regulations."[4] Company officials, however, did not anticipate the wave of strong pollution-control laws that the U.S. Congress would pass in the 1970s, laws that forced companies to manage their wastewater discharges and gaseous emissions more stringently than the designers of the new refinery had anticipated. Discharges of nitrogen in the form of ammonia were one of those regulated emissions.

Although the Union Oil refinery was not an unusually large emitter of ammonia, it is representative of an average facility affected by the passage of the 1972 Federal Water Pollution Control Act. Now nitrogenous compounds in the effluent of all such facilities, large or small, were to be measured, monitored, and managed in new ways. In other words, flows of compounds between economy and ecology had become governable transactions, even though legislators and policymakers had framed the new laws solely in terms of improving and maintaining air and water quality.

The Union Oil refinery, situated between two canals, replaced an older refinery on the same site. The original refinery, built in 1922 by the Globe Oil and Refining Company, had been designed to take advantage of the Chicago Sanitary and Ship Canal, an active navigational channel that carries barge and ship traffic between the Great Lakes and the Mississippi River. Built to flush Chicago's effluent away from the Great Lakes, the Sanitary and Ship Canal pushed a much smaller canal, the nineteenth-century Illinois and Michigan (I&M) barge canal, into obscurity.[5] Hence, when Globe Oil constructed its refinery, the company's engineers decided to use the abandoned I&M channel as a sink for the facility's wastewater. Each day, Globe Oil pumped approximately 60 million gallons of water out of the large Sanitary and Ship Canal and, after using the water for tasks such as cooling distillates, generating steam, and cleaning equipment, discharged it into the smaller I&M channel. That wastewater included oil from spills and leaks and some ammonia-containing process wastes.[6]

Unfortunately for Globe Oil, in the early 1930s, state officials decided to integrate downstream portions of the abandoned I&M canal into a public park. Complaints about oil slicks in the water soon followed, and the Illinois Department of Public Health started pressuring the refinery to reduce the amount of oil in its effluent. However, the state's newly hired public health director, Clarence Klassen, experienced only modest success in getting the refinery to change its practices. Although the company installed devices for trapping oil, poor maintenance and heavy storms resulted in significant quantities of oil periodically escaping. A new wave of complaints typically followed such events.[7]

In 1954, after a major expansion of the facility and a new wave of complaints, Klassen wrote to the refinery manager, pointing out that, although the company always seemed to be doing something to reduce its release of oily waste, conditions never seemed to improve. He asked what Globe Oil planned to do about permanently resolving the problem. In response, the manager, as usual, detailed the firm's progress and thanked Klassen for his interest. He also promised to get back to Klassen as soon as the company had completed its current construction projects. Finally, he noted that the refinery had been purchased by the Pure Oil Company, whose management fully supported efforts to improve the facility's effluent.[8]

What happened next served as a critical step in the effort to gain greater control over the industrial facility's waste-disposal practices: Klassen asked the refinery manager to begin monitoring the quality of the effluent and to submit the data in a monthly report. He requested measurements for oil content, pH, dissolved and suspended solids, odor, dissolved oxygen, chemical oxygen demand, chlorine demand, phenols, sulfides, nitrogen compounds, and mercaptans. By 1957, Pure Oil Company was sampling the refinery's effluent weekly and sending that data to Klassen at the end of each month. Although Klassen did not require the refinery to meet specific standards, simply getting an industrial firm to monitor its effluent routinely was a considerable accomplishment, one that would have been unheard of a generation earlier. If nothing else, the company's data had established a baseline of expectations.[9]

In the mid-1960s, after thirty years of pressuring the facility to better manage its waste-disposal practices, another wave of complaints motivated Klassen (who was himself under pressure from federal officials) to threaten the company with significant legal action.[10] At this point Pure Oil sold the aging refinery to Union Oil, which promptly announced plans to construct an entirely new refinery on the site, complete with a state-of-the-art wastewater-treatment system. Not only were those improvements themselves significant, but engineers had designed the new facility to use water more efficiently, reducing the refinery's daily intake from about 60 million gallons of water to fewer than 4 million gallons. For each barrel of oil processed, the new (and larger) refinery used one-fortieth of the water required by the older one. Furthermore, the new facility released all of its wastewater back into the massive Sanitary and Ship Canal rather than the much smaller I&M channel.[11]

Yet the increase in facility size and the drop in water usage created a nitrogen-related legal problem for the refinery. With more reactive nitrogen entering the refinery and less water being discharged, concentrations of ammonia in the effluent rose; and these higher concentrations came to the company's attention soon after the new Federal Water Pollution Control Act went into effect. The general approach of the 1972 legislation was simple, at least in the abstract. All facilities that discharged effluent into bodies of water were expected to (1) characterize their effluent and apply for a permit that specified the appropriate discharge standards, (2) routinely monitor the concentration of contaminants in their effluent to ensure that they were meeting those standards, and (3) report any violations. In essence, the permit served as a contract spelling out what a facility could release into a water body. Furthermore, permits were good for only five years and were expected to get more stringent over time, with the goal being discharges that were practically free of contaminants.[12]

In the first round of permits, state regulators were required to base all standards, at a minimum, on what federal regulators believed were technologically and economically practical levels. For the new Union Oil facility, federal technology standards indicated that discharges could include 775 pounds of ammonia each day, which translated to 29 ppm when discharged in the refinery's 3.3 million gallons of wastewater per day. The refinery could meet this requirement. However, when Union Oil engineers applied to the Illinois Environmental Protection Agency for their first discharge permit, they were told to keep ammonia levels below 3 ppm. The law, officials explained, allowed states to set requirements that were more stringent than the federal guidelines if stricter requirements were necessary to reach and maintain specific levels of water quality, and Illinois wanted to keep the ammonia concentration of the Sanitary and Ship Canal below 3 ppm. In response, Union Oil engineers argued that the company was being penalized for its efficient use of water. After all, if the company had not cut water consumption so drastically, concentration of ammonia in its effluent would have remained below 3 ppm.[13]

It took fifteen years of legal challenges and several cycles of permit applications before state and refinery officials could agree on the quantity of ammonia that the facility could release. Similar battles played out at industrial facilities throughout the country, not just over ammonia but over all contaminants. But by the mid-1980s, an effective permit system for managing the concentration of contaminants in industrial and municipal wastewater was in place throughout most of the United States. Now all facilities that discharged effluent into bodies of water were expected to monitor and manage those discharges, with specific expectations clearly spelt out in their permit.[14]

The implementation of the discharge permit system generated a significant amount of new knowledge, including information about what was enforceable, what courts were willing to uphold, and what actions the public was willing to support. Permits also facilitated a form of learning by nested trial and error. No longer did engineers and public officials have to wait until equipment was installed to see if community members would complain or pollution-related conflicts would emerge, either of which could lead to lengthy court battles that might or might not be successful. Engineers could now determine if their designs were acceptable by testing them against the expectations specified in the facility's discharge permit. Regulators could also make enforcement decisions based on whether facilities met the conditions of their permit instead of having to wait for complaints.

The National Pollutant Discharge Permit Elimination System (NPDES), as the permit program was officially called, also represented an important step toward the governance of entire watersheds. Theoretically, regulators could now monitor and manage the total quantity of different compounds flowing into a river system. For nitrogenous discharges, however, the program was only a step toward that level of governance. Although regulators had constructed an effective permit system for point sources (that is, effluent flowing out of a discharge pipe), most nitrogen-rich runoff did not flow through a pipe. Large quantities of chemically active nitrogen also flowed into streams from farms and well-fertilized lawns as well as from land that hosted concentrated animal-feeding operations. These so-called "non-point sources" had no controls on them. Still, the permit system, which theoretically could be expanded to include such discharges, represented a major new institutional framework for establishing ecologically justified limits and integrating them into economic activity.[15]

Managing Emissions of N into the Air

In the United States, the process of constructing a regulatory system to manage air quality was more complicated than it had been for water quality, in large part because of legislators' reduced emphasis on the development of a systematic permit system. In areas with clean air, the law allowed power plants and industrial facilities to continue operating as they always had; they did not even have to apply for a permit. Regulatory action was triggered only if local air quality did not meet the national standards. In many ways, the system was putting the cart before the horse.

The process of setting ambient air-quality standards proceeded quickly because of the Public Health Service's earlier work. Indeed, by 1970, when Congress passed the Clean Air Act amendments, the service had already formed advisory committees to decide where to draw the line between air that was safe to breathe and air that was not. Different committees had been established for each of the major contaminants released by combustion processes: sulfur dioxide, nitrogen dioxide, carbon monoxide, and particulates. Standards for ozone, which could be generated by photochemical reactions involving nitrogen oxides, were also being reviewed.

In 1971, the committee that was working on nitrogen oxides released a report recommending that nitrogen dioxide concentrations in the air be kept below 0.06 ppm. Soon thereafter, the Environmental Protection Agency officially set the standard for nitrogen dioxide at 0.053 ppm as measured by a yearly average of twenty-four-hour averages.[16] In the abstract, the law's ecological implications were profound. Humans would become an active component of the biogeochemical system that regulated concentrations of reactive nitrogen in the atmosphere. If air sampled by monitoring stations did not meet the ambient standard, state officials would have to take all necessary steps to get that number below the legal threshold.

But implementing and enforcing the law turned out to be far more difficult than anyone had imagined. In the case of nitrogen dioxide, the issues had less to do with meeting the ambient air-quality standard than with meeting the standard for photochemically produced ozone, for which nitrogen dioxide is a key precursor. In 1978, the Environmental Protection Agency reported that only eight air-quality regions were in violation of the nitrogen dioxide standard while more than six hundred were in violation of the ozone standard.[17] Complicating matters was the fact that the ozone standard included an hourly threshold while the nitrogen dioxide standard was based on an annual average. Even though heavy automobile traffic might send the concentration of nitrogen dioxide in urban air well above 0.053 ppm for several hours, that spike did not violate the nitrogen dioxide standard because only the annual average mattered. However, if the spike were to occur on a hot, sunny day in the presence of gasoline vapors, the resulting photochemical reactions might send ozone concentrations through the roof.

Therefore, keeping urban concentrations of ozone below the federal standard meant reducing spikes of nitrogen dioxide and hydrocarbons. One potential way was to cut the amount of nitrogen oxides that were flowing out of tailpipes. Indeed, the Clean Air Act required automobile manufacturers to cut emissions in new cars by 90 percent, which, in the case of nitrogen oxides, meant reducing tailpipe emissions from approximately 4 grams per mile to 0.4 grams per mile. Initially, air-quality regulators had hoped that emissions of nitrogen oxides would drop dramatically as people replaced their older vehicles with newer ones. But the Environmental Protection Agency, which was responsible for enforcing the new law, soon discovered that domestic automobile manufacturers were either incapable of developing the necessary technology or unwilling to do so.[18]

To automobile company executives, the law appeared to be unreasonable. After passage of the Clean Air Act, Charles M. Heinen of Chrysler framed his industry's engineers as "artisans" who were doing the best they could to meet the emissions levels that the ruling "Pharisees" had demanded. As these Pharisees denounced the engineers and demanded better results, Heinen said, "the artisans could only wait for the laws of thermodynamics to be repealed."[19] According to him, developing a catalytic muffler was simply impractical "from a social, scientific, medical and economic standpoint."[20]

Not everybody agreed. In fact, in the 1960s, before automobile companies had been legally expected to meet strict tailpipe emissions requirements, the federal government had threatened to bring antimonopoly charges against them for colluding to suppress the development of a practical emissions control device. However, taking action against companies for failing to invent something was problematic, and the antimonopoly charge went nowhere.[21] Indeed, expecting companies to develop pollution-control technology without any legal requirement to do so was unrealistic. Automobile companies had no incentive to add an expensive and potentially unreliable piece of equipment to their cars, especially one that provided no direct benefit to the individual consumer. Any auto manufacturer that voluntarily added this piece of equipment to its vehicles would have placed itself at a disadvantage in the market.

Another complication involved the use of tetraethyl lead, which refiners added to gasoline to prevent engine knock. Until lead could be phased out, adding a catalytic pollution-control device to automobiles made no sense because lead in the exhaust would quickly render any catalyst useless. For that reason, the 1970 Clean Air Act also included a mandate to phase out the use of leaded gasoline. However, it soon became clear that phasing out the additive, which would require oil companies to invest in new refining technology, demanded a level of coordination that the legislators had not anticipated.

Recognizing that progress toward lower tailpipe emissions had stalled, the Environmental Protection Agency decided to renegotiate compliance deadlines and take a more active role in coordinating the phase-out of leaded gasoline. Japanese advances in catalytic technology also helped to move the process along. By the mid-1990s, manufacturers of passenger cars had successfully cut emissions of nitrogen oxides to the desired level, through both engine redesign and the development of catalytic converters capable of reducing oxides to molecular nitrogen. Nonetheless, net emissions of nitrogen oxides from vehicles stayed relatively high because the number of cars on the road had increased significantly. In addition, many people continued to drive older cars. By 1995, the 12.6 million tons of nitrogen oxides emitted from passenger vehicles in 1970 had only fallen to 8.9 million tons. In the same period, emissions from off-highway vehicles had actually risen from 2.6 to 4.2 million tons.[22]

Getting electric utilities to reduce emissions of nitrogen oxides from power plants turned out to be even more difficult, partly because of Congress's decision to let existing facilities keep operating without changes unless they were located in a region that did not meet ambient standards. In essence, facilities in operation before 1970 were off the hook if they were located in an area with clean air. This grandfathering strategy might have made sense for cars, whose life spans hover at about ten years. But it did not make sense for power plants, which lie at the core of an industry's profit-making activities and, with maintenance, can be kept in service indefinitely. In fact, these exemptions gave companies a powerful incentive to maintain their old power plants and to replace equipment at a pace slow enough to avoid triggering new performance standards.[23]

Complex legal questions arose at every turn as executives, activists, regulators, legislators, judges, lawyers, engineers, and interested citizens wrestled with a tangle of interrelated issues. Even something as simple as the placement of air-quality monitoring stations mattered because the location could mean the difference between air that was classified as clean or that violated the Clean Air Act. After all, an instrument placed along a high-traffic corridor or downwind from a cluster of industrial facilities would be exposed to higher levels of contaminants than would instruments in more isolated areas, and many potentially contentious decisions involving the location of monitoring equipment were avoided only because those stations were already in place before Congress had passed the act. Still, once air-quality data became publicly available—and in some places, local weather stations were starting to report it—the general public began to raise questions about how to interpret that data.[24]

Emissions from many power plants had little effect on local monitoring stations. The hot exhaust gases that large coal-fired plants released from tall stacks generally stayed aloft for hundreds of miles, well above any nearby stations. Hence, local officials concerned with ambient air quality had no reason to take action against those plants. When local monitoring stations did detect a plant's emissions, the facility's operator could install an even taller stack to send emissions further aloft. The question of whether tall stacks legally could be used to maintain local ambient air quality was just one of many issues that policymakers had not anticipated when they were drafting the Clean Air Act.

Moreover, because firms had to secure permits only for new sources of emissions, state officials who were expected to take action to improve an area's ambient air quality had little information about which facility was releasing what contaminants. Greater complications arose when firms wanted to construct new facilities in places that were so-called "non-attainment" areas. Although officials could not let firms build new sources of emissions in areas that already had poor air quality, simply turning away investment and jobs was not politically tenable. Ultimately, the Environmental Protection Agency declared that firms could construct new facilities if they offset any new emissions with reductions at other facilities. That ruling, in effect, allowed states to create a market in emission reductions, opening the door to an entirely new way of managing emissions. But without a comprehensive permit system, that market became an accounting nightmare. Bubbles, banking, netting, and offsets (new terms that described the complex emissions-related transactions between and within facilities) pushed the regulatory system into unknown terrain. A long line of contentious issues followed, each requiring an army of lawyers, engineers, and accountants.[25]

Regardless of how the Environmental Protection Agency chose to address such issues, somebody was sure to challenge its decision. The courts facilitated resolution through a form of nested trial and error, with judges and juries standing in for the rest of the society. Advocates argued and the courts ruled, but appeals and countersuits were sure to follow until most participants accepted a line of action—or at least decided it was not worth challenging. But in the meantime, issue after issue flowed into the courts, with the result that the regulatory system was as much a creation of the courts as it was of legislative action or executive decision.

Over time, it also became clear that certain assumptions underlying the Clean Air Act were fundamentally flawed. For example, using air-quality control regions as the basis of regulatory decisions was problematic because atmospheric contaminants and the concerns they generate do not respect political boundaries. Scientists eventually confirmed, for example, that the plumes that power plants sent high into the sky carried significant quantities of sulfur dioxide and nitrogen dioxide over long distances, thus contributing to the phenomenon known as acid rain. Additional quantities of nitrogen dioxide wafted into the air from long stretches of heavily traveled highway (such as Interstate 95, which runs from Maine to Florida) and contributed to smog-related problems in cities hundreds of miles away.

The laws of chemistry were not particularly cooperative either. The ability of compounds to change form gave rise to another set of unanticipated complications. For example, some of the nitrogen dioxide that reacted with hydrocarbons on hot sunny days formed peroxyacytyl nitrate (PAN), a compound capable of irritating eyes and lungs and that can travel hundreds of miles before disassociating back into nitrogen dioxide. Indeed, state officials who were struggling to meet the ambient standards for ozone eventually discovered that their efforts were being undermined by the long-distance transport of nitrogen through compounds such as PAN.[26]

Some nitrogen-related atmospheric concerns fell outside the scope of the Clean Air Act altogether. In 1970, the same year that Congress passed the act, atmospheric chemist Paul Crutzen suggested that bacterial emissions of nitrous oxide, such as those emanating from well-fertilized farms, could interfere with Earth's protective ozone layer. Although nitrous oxide is a relatively inert gas, Crutzen hypothesized that it could rise into the upper atmosphere and release nitric oxide when bombarded with high-energy solar radiation. Given that nitric oxide converts ozone to molecular oxygen, he worried that the dynamic balance of ozone creation and destruction that continually occurs in the upper reaches of the atmosphere could be altered if too much nitrous oxide were released into the air. Not long afterward, the airline industry floated the possibility of building a fleet of high-flying supersonic jets, triggering concerns that the nitric oxide they would emit could be especially dangerous to the ozone layer.[27]

In the United States, concerns about sonic booms and the economics of operating supersonic jets eventually killed interest in the technology, but the notion that chemicals reaching the upper atmosphere might harm Earth's protective ozone layer prompted additional research into the effects of other compounds. In 1974, chemists Frank Rowland and Mario Molina alerted the world to the possibility that chlorofluorocarbons (CFCs), a class of chemicals used in industrial processes and consumer products, were threatening the integrity of the ozone layer. Like nitrous oxide, chlorofluorocarbon molecules could rise to the upper atmosphere and be broken apart by ultraviolet radiation. In the case of CFCs, one of the ions (chlorine) acts as an ozone-eating catalyst that continues to convert ozone to molecular oxygen until some other compound happens to bind up the chlorine. Nitric oxide, because of its potential to react with binding compounds, remained a concern.[28]

By the end of the 1980s, atmospheric scientists had discovered that nitrogen oxides were playing a role in the production of fine particles in the atmosphere. These particles, many times smaller than the diameter of a human hair, not only scatter light and contribute to hazy conditions but also aggravate respiratory conditions far more seriously than coarser particles do. Although nitrate droplets produced from mixtures of water and nitrogen dioxide represented only a fraction of the fine particles in the atmosphere, they contributed enough to matter. Scientists also began to reach consensus on the ability of humans to alter the heat budget of the earth by emissions of heat-absorbing greenhouse gases, mainly carbon dioxide. Again, a nitrogenous compound played a contributing role. Although the concentration of nitrous oxide in the atmosphere (about 0.32 ppm) is much less than that of other greenhouse gases, such as carbon dioxide (about 390 ppm) and methane (about 1.7 ppm), increases in emissions of nitrous oxide do have an affect. Given the lower concentrations and different absorption characteristics of nitrous oxide, each new molecule of the gas traps considerably more additional heat than each new molecule of carbon dioxide or methane does.[29]

As rules associated with the Clean Air Act were being constructed, the technology for measuring and monitoring concentrations of gases such as nitrogen dioxide improved by leaps and bounds. Both regulators and firms wanted to measure air quality as efficiently and accurately as possible, and instrument manufacturers strove to outdo their competitors. Efforts to measure low concentrations of nitrogen dioxide and nitric oxide advanced especially rapidly after manufacturers developed alternatives to wet chemistry. Portable instruments based on the principle of infrared spectroscopy eventually made it possible to measure the contents of a gas sample simply by passing a light through it and measuring how much of which frequencies are absorbed. Not only did these new instruments reduce the need for wet chemistry, but they also substantially reduced the labor involved in monitoring gases in both emissions streams and the atmosphere. In the process, the ability of regulators and firms to see what the law desired them to see improved dramatically.[30]

The Clean Air Act was also intended to be a technology-forcing piece of legislation for process and pollution control, and to some extent it succeeded. After all, companies did install appropriate control equipment when required. They had, however, few incentives to innovate beyond the state of the art. According to rules constructed by the Environmental Protection Agency, facilities that triggered various aspects of the act had to meet performance standards associated with either reasonably available control technology (RACT), the best-available control technology (BACT), the lowest-achievable control technology (LACT), or the maximum-available control technology (MACT). Specific requirements depended on the context, but the terminology implied that performance criteria would get stricter as better technology became available.[31] But companies had incentives to avoid innovation because doing so would, in the long term, simply increase regulatory expectations about what should constitute "best-available" or "reasonably available" technologies. Indeed, efforts to develop some technologies, such as those associated with reducing the quantity of nitrogen oxides that power plants were emitting, evolved very slowly, with much of the experimentation occurring in Germany and Japan, which had stricter requirements for controlling nitrogen dioxide.[32]

By the late 1980s, most people familiar with the Clean Air Act could see that the law was in need of serious reform. Basically, Congress had passed the act to address urban air-quality problems, not to manage the effect of human activity on regional or global atmospheric dynamics. In short, it was not structured to address problems associated with either the long-distance transport of atmospheric gases or the role of those gases in complex atmospheric phenomena.

What to Do with All the Sludge?

Pollution-control laws passed in the 1970s affected the flow of nitrogen that passed through urban sewers and ended up in the sludge captured by wastewater treatment plants. Unintentionally, they also revived interest in efforts to close the loop on rural-to-urban flows of nitrogen. The technology associated with capturing and recycling the nitrogen that urban dwellers flushed down their toilets had not changed much since the 1920s, when Milwaukee had constructed its fertilizer-producing sewage-treatment plant. By the time that facility came on line, industrial processes for fixing nitrogen had eliminated fears of a nitrogen shortage, and the urgency associated with recycling sewage had quickly faded. Hence, for more than fifty years, Milwaukee's wastewater treatment facility continued to be the state of the art in transforming sewage into a nitrogen-rich soil conditioner.

Between 1920 and 1970, the level to which large U.S. cities treated their sewage generally depended on the extent to which they could flush their wastes downstream or into the sea without causing a nuisance. Officials in Chicago, for example, began treating their wastes in the late 1920s after the Supreme Court ruled that water flushed down the city's Sanitary and Ship Canal had to be treated enough to prevent sewage from overwhelming the ability of downstream rivers to digest harmful materials.[33] To meet that standard, the Sanitary District of Chicago had to send a large fraction of its sewage through activated sludge plants similar to Milwaukee's. By the late 1950s, most large cities on interior rivers, such as Pittsburgh, Cincinnati, and Saint Louis, had also constructed activated sludge facilities.[34] Cities on the east coast, which had less pressure to treat sewage, generally removed only the solids that settled out due to gravity. For example, by the late 1950s, Philadelphia had three treatment facilities in operation, each relying on gravity-based settling alone. Roughly half of the solid material that flowed into those facilities remained dissolved in the wastewater that was discharged into the Delaware River.[35]

All of these plants, including those that relied solely on gravity, produced a great deal of sludge, and all of that sludge had to go somewhere. Milwaukee, which had already invested in equipment capable of drying and packaging its sludge, continued to market that material as Milorganite (for *Mil*waukee *org*anic *nitrog*en), selling it mainly as turf fertilizer. A few other cities, such as Chicago and Houston, found farmers and ranchers who were willing to use some of their sludge as a soil conditioner. In general, though, operators of municipal wastewater treatment plants disposed of sludge in any way they could. Indeed, engineering textbooks of the 1930s and 1940s advised them to get rid of their sludge as cheaply as possible, which often meant using it as fill or mixing it with coal and burning it. In Philadelphia, where ninety tons of putrid organic material settled out of the city's waste stream each day, officials turned to the ocean: operators loaded the sludge onto a barge, carried it out to open water, and dumped it.[36]

The Clean Water Act, in conjunction with the Resource Conservation and Recovery Act of 1976, indirectly made it more attractive for cities to use their nitrogen-rich sludge as a soil conditioner. Other laws, such as the Marine Protection, Research, and Sanctuaries Act of 1972, contributed to this change by prohibiting the practice of ocean dumping. By the mid-1970s, all cities had to obtain discharge permits for their sewage-treatment plants that specified limits on the amount of solids a plant could release in its effluent. Because Philadelphia's permit limited the concentration of suspended solids to 30 milligrams per liter, the city had to construct two new wastewater facilities, each of which included the type of biological treatment that Milwaukee and Chicago had installed a half-century earlier. When they were completed in 1984, the new plants captured 90 percent of the organic material that Philadelphians were flushing down their toilets.[37]

Emerging now was the important question of whether this nitrogen-rich sludge should be classified as a hazardous waste. Some people thought so; after all, it was possible for chemical wastes to end up in the sludge. Although industrial facilities that discharged wastewater into urban sewers were expected to meet strict requirements, accidents and lax practices still occurred, especially at smaller companies where systems for managing wastes were less formal.[38] Furthermore, the harmful compounds that homeowners poured down their basement sinks—waste paint, used engine oil, coolant, waste pesticides—ended up in urban sewers. Obviously, nobody wanted to see these any of these contaminants reaching agricultural soil.

If federal officials had classified sewage sludge as hazardous waste, cities would have had to meet the requirements of the Resource Conservation and Recovery Act, which, among other things, established an administrative system for tracking hazardous waste from its creation as waste to its disposal by incineration, processing, or dumping into an engineered landfill. With that act in place, industrial facilities could no longer dump their hazardous wastes (defined as wastes that were flammable, toxic, or in some other way dangerous) in poorly designed and unmanaged landfills. Neither could they pay a trucking company to haul away that material without anybody around to ask difficult questions about where it would end up. Now facilities had to track their wastes and ensure that they were being incinerated, processed, or dumped appropriately. Consequently, the expense of disposal rose tremendously.

Classifying sewage sludge as hazardous waste would have had significant consequences for the operators of municipal wastewater-treatment plants. Each day, thousands of tons of sludge would have entered a complex tracking system designed for much smaller amounts of material, and neither municipal officials nor environmental regulators wanted to deal with the monumental amount of paperwork that would have resulted. In addition, cities would not have been allowed to return any of that sludge to soils but would have had to dispose of it in engineered landfills. Not surprisingly, therefore, when the act was being drafted, managers of the nation's wastewater-treatment plants lobbied their legislators, asking them to explicitly exempt sewage sludge from its provisions. They were successful, and cities continued to dispose of sludge by selling it or giving it away as a soil conditioner.[39]

But other groups worried that metals such as lead, chromium, and cadmium were reaching agricultural soils, and they challenged the law. Why, they asked, were wastes that could potentially contain hazardous material not subject to rules governing the disposal of hazardous waste? In response, federal legislators required the Environmental Protection Agency to set guidelines for the use and disposal of sewage sludge, a provision that Congress strengthened in 1987. In addition, the agency pressured large urban sewage districts to strengthen programs aimed at eliminating problematic metals and chemicals.[40]

In 1993, when the Environmental Protection Agency announced standards that sewage sludge had to meet before being applied to agricultural soils—otherwise known as Class A standards for biosolids of "exceptional quality"—the operators of many treatment plants found that their sludge satisfied the criteria. For example, the amount of cadmium, arsenic, mercury, and selenium in Philadelphia's sludge was well below the permitted level, while the amount of lead, copper, and zinc hovered at about half.[41] In addition, wastewater-treatment professionals had started referring to sewage sludge as *biosolids,* a term calculated to stress the material's organic nature and the fact that it was no longer sewage after being processed. However, opposition to its agricultural use continued. Indeed, opponents saw the new term as misleading, and the ironic title of John C. Stauber and Sheldon Rampton's 1995 book *Toxic Sludge Is Good for You* expressed their feeling that the change was a public-relations effort to disguise risk.[42]

Where did the sludge (or biosolids) flowing out of Philadelphia actually end up? In the fifteen-year period following the construction of its new treatment plants, the city disposed of its solids in a variety of ways, including in landfills (39 percent), mine reclamation sites (28 percent), farms (18 percent), commercial compost markets (10 percent), and public works projects (5 percent). In other words, roughly 60 percent of the solids ended up being used as a soil conditioner or fertilizer; and of that amount, between one-third and one-half ended up in agricultural soil. The rest went to landfills, usually during the winter months. Like most municipal facilities, the Philadelphia Water Department did not make a profit from material used as soil conditioners, but it did save money by avoiding the cost of putting it into landfills.[43]

By the mid-1990s, therefore, a bureaucratic infrastructure governing the disposal of solid wastes, the discharge of effluent, and the release of gaseous emissions had been constructed in the United States and other nations. Although the main goal of these bureaucracies was to prevent the deterioration of air and water quality and to protect the public health, they were also connecting economies and ecologies in new ways. Industrial societies were beginning to systematically govern their relationship with natural systems; and the release of chemically active nitrogen into the environment was beginning to be measured, monitored, and managed in ways that barely could have been imagined a century earlier.

At the same time, many participants recognized significant weaknesses in the new pollution-control laws. In general, they failed to effectively address issues that arose when contaminants crossed political boundaries, were transported over long distances by natural processes, underwent a change in their chemical composition, or interacted with natural systems in complex ways. Furthermore, intentional releases of chemicals into the environment, such as the use of pesticides and fertilizers, were regulated by different laws, all of which had their own weaknesses.

Yet the 1970s federal pollution-control laws were an important step, albeit a stumbling one, toward integrating ecological limits into the structure of market capitalism. Gradually, a political economy was being created in which technological innovation (and economic activity in general) was expected to respect human-defined limits. Still, learning how to manage material that flowed through cycles, such as flows of nitrogen through a biogeochemical cycle that now included human activity, would clearly take more time.

11

N and the Seeds of an Ecological Economy

In the 1990s, more scholars began writing about the complex entanglement of human activity with natural systems, and more people began to listen.[1] Several factors fueled this interest. First, world leaders attending the 1992 U.N. Conference on Environment and Development in Rio de Janeiro identified emissions of CO_2 as a significant concern, provoking public focus on the issue. The 1987 Montreal Protocol, which facilitated the phase-out of CFCs to prevent significant change to the stratospheric ozone layer, also emphasized the link between human activity and changes to Earth systems. Second, the collapse of the Soviet Union encouraged people throughout the world to think more deeply about the relationships among capitalism, globalization, and the environment. As political and financial leaders began to construct a global market governed by a single set of rules, many others raised questions about how well those rules meshed with visions of an environmentally sustainable and socially just future. Finally, two decades of experience with environmental laws made it clear that setting and achieving environmental objectives was not as straightforward as policymakers had originally anticipated. Indeed, certain goals, such as protecting complex ecosystems to avoid the loss of critical habitats for threatened species, proved to be especially daunting.[2]

Some scholars called for a form of economic accounting that placed a value on the services of the natural world. In 1997, for example, *Nature* published "The Value of the World's Ecosystem Services and Natural Capital," which estimated the dollar value of major services provided by Earth's biogeochemical and ecological systems. Prepared by thirteen authors who had met at an interdisciplinary workshop in 1995, the article was a thought experiment in ecological economics. The authors calculated that the world's ecosystems provided about 33 trillion dollars' worth of annual benefits, which included climate regulation, nutrient cycling, pollination, purifying water through the hydrological cycle, and so on. They suggested that, until societies could account for the value of these services, the world stood in danger of squandering them.[3]

Not surprisingly, the article triggered a number of responses. Placing a dollar value on nature, critics argued, leads us down a slippery philosophical slope, one we should avoid. According to William Rees, co-author of *Our Ecological Footprint,* placing a monetary value on something suggests that substitutes are available, but the integrity of nature has no substitute. He and others suggested that articulating the value of Earth systems in terms of the services they provide to humans was ethically naïve and, in the long term, politically unwise. Another group of critics pointed out that the very notion of an ecosystem service is highly flexible, raising messy questions about which services are privileged and how their benefits are to be distributed. Should a river be managed to optimize the production of hydroelectric power, recreational opportunities, habitat and biodiversity, navigation, or something else entirely? What guiding ethic should be used in making such choices and determining who benefits and who bears the costs?[4]

Still, the thirteen authors of the *Nature* article had made a basic point. Markets, as currently structured, place little value on the commons we call nature. Even if one cannot (or should not) attach a dollar sign to that value, societies probably should work to sustain the basic integrity of the ecological and biogeochemical systems that make up these commons. How to accomplish this goal is another matter, one that the authors did not address.

N, Ecological Budgets, and Adaptive Management

When dealing with natural resources such as water and trees, one can easily visualize what it means to budget their use and why that might be necessary. Only so much water flows into a river; therefore, only so much can be taken out. Similarly, only so much biomass can be sustainably removed from a forest each year. But what about budgets for more complex flows of material, such as emissions of nitrogen oxides into the atmosphere or discharges of nitrogenous compounds into bodies of water? Unless a society places a limit on such flows, someone can always emit or discharge a little more.

Pollution-control legislation passed in the 1970s gave regulators the power to create and enforce such budgets. For instance, the Clean Water Act required regulators to establish a budget for contaminants that were entering a water body—in the form of total maximum daily loads (TMDLs)—as a way to meet a desired set of water-quality standards. In practice, though, TMDLs could not be put into place without an effective and operational permit system. As a result, most regulators initially focused on getting firms and municipalities to obtain discharge permits based on technology-based performance standards. Only after establishing an effective permit system, did regulators turn their attention to TMDLs.[5]

The case of Delaware's Broadkill River watershed exemplifies this shift to TMDLs. By the 1990s, all facilities discharging effluent into the watershed had permits to do so; but the river, which flows through a patchwork of small towns and farms, was still impaired. High levels of nitrogen and phosphorus had sparked a cycle of growth and decomposition, depleting the river's dissolved oxygen and reducing its capacity to support a healthy fish population. The heavy nutrient load also contributed to problems in the Delaware Bay. Therefore, in 1997, a federal court required Delaware to create and enforce TMDLs for nitrogen and phosphorus in the Broadkill River watershed. For state officials, this ruling set in motion the difficult public process of coming up with a budget for discharges of nitrogen and phosphorus into the river.[6]

Creating an ecologically based nutrient budget, even for a relatively small river, is not an easy task. First, someone has to figure out where the nitrogen and phosphorus are coming from and what the limit on those discharges should be. For the Broadkill River, environmental consultants determined that approximately 4,100 pounds of nitrogen was entering the river each day. Of that, about 400 pounds came from facilities with permits. The bulk of the rest entered the river as fertilizer-laden runoff from agricultural land and lawns, as organic waste from livestock, and as nitrates released by septic systems. Second, a public process is needed to allocate the load. Who gets to discharge what amount? In the case of the Broadkill River watershed, accomplishing these tasks took almost ten years of public meetings and negotiations. Officials finally determined that facilities with permits (point sources) could discharge a total of 246 pounds and that distributed sources (nonpoint sources with no permit) could release 2,224 pounds. These amounts then had to be allocated. To stay within the limit of 246 pounds, the town of Milton, for example, was expected to reduce its releases to 73 pounds per day, while a Purdue Farms facility along the river needed to reduce its releases to 117 pounds. Allocating the 2,224 pounds coming from distributed sources presented more of a challenge; at the very least, it meant getting farmers and homeowners to change their fertilization practices.[7]

But the magnitude of the Broadkill challenge paled in comparison to the complications faced in the nation's largest watershed: the Mississippi River basin. It, too, had a nitrogen problem. By 1990, officials with the U.S. Environmental Protection Agency understood that nutrients in the Mississippi River were contributing to what newspapers were calling a "dead zone" in the Gulf of Mexico. Each spring, nitrogen and phosphorus transported by the river were contributing to the growth of algae, phytoplankton, and other microorganisms in the warm gulf waters. Although this biomass is essential to aquatic food chains, too much growth can be a problem. As excessive amounts of organisms sink and decompose, concentrations of dissolved oxygen in the lower strata can drop below the levels that fish and other organisms need to survive. Researchers also associated heavy nutrient loading with the intensity and frequency of red tides—blooms of toxic microorganisms that play havoc with the ecology and economy of towns along the Gulf Coast, many of which depend on tourism and fishing.[8]

The Mississippi River's role in creating hypoxic conditions along the shores of Texas and Louisiana first received serious attention in the 1970s, when researchers explicitly identified the river's nutrient load as part of the problem. Two sets of monitoring programs—one funded by the U.S. Strategic Petroleum Reserve to document the effects of releasing brine into the gulf during the construction of oil-storage cavities in salt domes, the other associated with the Louisiana Offshore Oil Port, a mooring station for unloading oil tankers in deep water—provided researchers with valuable information. Using data from these sources as well as targeted sampling programs, scientists were able to determine that the hypoxic area (defined as water with less than 2 ppm of dissolved oxygen) was increasing in size from year to year. In the mid-1980s, the affected area hovered at about 5,000 square kilometers. A decade later, it had risen to approximately 15,000 square kilometers. Reversing this trend, scientists concluded, meant establishing and enforcing a nutrient budget for the Mississippi River.[9]

The ambitious effort to create a nitrogen budget for the entire Mississippi River watershed, with specific amounts allocated to different sub-basins, began with the federal Harmful Algal Bloom and Hypoxia Research and Control Act of 1998. Estimating that harmful algal blooms had resulted in a billion dollars' worth of economic losses over the previous decade, the act required the U.S. president, working through the National Science and Technology Council (NSTC), to create an Inter-Agency Task Force on Harmful Algal Blooms and Hypoxia consisting of representatives from a dozen different federal agencies. The goal of the task force was to assess what was known about hypoxia in coastal waters along Texas and Louisiana.[10]

A team of researchers soon determined that the amount of nitrogen that the Mississippi River was transporting and discharging into the Gulf of Mexico had increased over time. Available data showed that nitrate levels in the lower part of the river had more than doubled, increasing from about 0.6 ppm in the first half of the century to about 1.5 ppm in 1990. Levels of organic nitrogen, however, had dropped by about one-quarter, from 1.2 to 0.9 ppm. In addition, that nitrogen no longer fed the marshes and wetlands of the delta; instead, the heavily channelized and controlled river system now jetted its nutrient load further into the gulf.[11]

Researchers also estimated that, by 1995, almost 21 million metric tons of nitrogen was entering the basin each year. Of course, the entire quantity did not reach the Gulf of Mexico. Food exports carried some of it outside the basin, and even the nitrogen in food that stayed within the basin and eventually reached sewers and septic systems did not necessarily reach the gulf. Denitrifying bacteria in wetlands and wastewater-treatment plants converted a significant portion of that nitrogen into atmospheric gases. Wetlands also captured some of the nitrate-rich runoff coming from farms and feedlots. Best estimates suggested that only 1 to 2 million metric tons of nitrogen actually reached the gulf.[12]

According to the report *Integrated Assessment of Hypoxia*, which the NSTC released in 2000, the size of the gulf's dead zone could be reduced by, first, reducing the quantity of nitrogen reaching the Mississippi River and, second, increasing the number of wetlands (and hence the level of denitrification) in the basin. The 2001 action plan prepared by the NSTC-commissioned Mississippi River/Gulf of Mexico Nutrient Task Force estimated that a 30 percent drop in the amount of nitrogen that was reaching the gulf would reduce the average size of the hypoxic area from roughly 15,000 to 5,000 square kilometers. Although task force members did not know for sure if they could achieve the desired reduction in nitrogen flows or, if they did, whether it would cut the size of the dead zone by the predicted amount, they did know that this reduction would return nitrogen flows to mid-twentieth-century levels.[13]

A key strategy for securing these reductions involved developing total maximum daily loads (TMDLs) for nitrogen similar to those that were being developed for the Broadkill River watershed in Delaware. But instead of having to create a nitrogen budget for a watershed that drained a portion of tiny Delaware, task force members had to create one for more than 40 percent of the land area occupied by the contiguous forty-eight states. The sheer size of the Mississippi River basin introduced an entirely new level of uncertainty and complexity to the project. Any effective plan would have to cross multiple political, ecological, and institutional boundaries. In addition, decision making would have to occur at many different scales: some at the level of the entire basin and others at the level of major sub-watersheds, such as the areas drained by the Ohio River, the Tennessee River, and the Missouri River. Inside each of those sub-basins, officials would have to create local management plans that allocated specific releases of nitrogen. Furthermore, fertilizer manufacturers, farmers, and other stakeholders could be expected to challenge any decisions that affected them, including those made within the scientific community.

The Nutrient Task Force decided to follow a general process of adaptive management. In this process, actions are viewed as a way not only to achieve objectives but also to learn about the system one hopes to influence. In a sense, each action is a hypothesis. The process is adaptive because the results from one round of actions influence the next round of decisions, including potential adjustments to objectives. Therefore, decision makers must explicitly monitor whatever they hope to improve or expect to change. If what they expect to happen does not, both the strategy and the science must be reevaluated. Choosing the appropriate indicators to measure and monitor is a significant part of the process, as is engaging stakeholders in policy decisions that potentially affect them.[14]

The term *adaptive management* emerged in the 1970s out of the work of ecologists such as C. S. Holling, who believed that ecological systems are too chaotic for people to ever fully understand or manage with complete certainty. In this view, the best one can do is to set objectives, take actions, monitor the results, and continually adapt.[15] Ecologists tend to focus on the management of nonhuman populations, but the general approach applies to any kind of management effort, including those involving changes in human practices.

Although the term itself is relatively new, people have long been using various forms of adaptive management. Any effective business executive, for example, routinely sets objectives, takes action to achieve them, and then adjusts the course of action based on the results. The trend toward explicit efforts to adaptively manage business objectives began after World War II, when Japanese companies started merging methods of statistical quality control with participatory strategies in which teams of employees worked together to identify and solve problems. This process, known as *total quality management*, was seen as a cornerstone of the 1970s Japanese manufacturing miracle, and organizations outside of Japan began to adopt it. Rooted in the work of W. Edwards Deming (who, incidentally, began his career at the Fixed Nitrogen Research Laboratory, where he applied statistics to better understand the effect of nitrogen on farm crops), total quality management included a plan-do-check-act cycle of continual adaptation that came to be known as the Deming Cycle.[16]

In the late 1980s, a version of the cycle was enshrined in the International Organization for Standardization's quality management standard ISO 9001. To be certified as meeting that standard, a company had to explicitly set product quality objectives, develop actions to achieve them, monitor their effect, and continually improve its ability to deliver a quality product. Adaptive management had come to be seen as a powerful tool for setting and achieving long-term objectives, both private and public; and in 1996, the International Organization for Standardization released an ISO standard for certifying environmental management systems that included a similar plan-do-check-act process of continuous improvement.[17]

In its effort to adaptively manage the amount of nitrogen flowing into the Gulf of Mexico, the Nutrient Task Force was able to make use of an administrative patchwork of existing organizations. The U.S. Geological Survey and the Natural Resources Conservation Service, for example, provided significant technical assistance by collecting basic data. In addition, the Ohio River watershed had had a strong interstate group in place since 1948, and members of that group, the Ohio River Valley Water Sanitation Commission, were experienced in coordinating activity within their fourteen-state region. Furthermore, the concept of TMDLs was already embedded in the Clean Water Act, and precedents existed for developing them through watershed management plans. Finally, the task force benefited from state-level programs for reducing flows of nitrogen for other reasons (such as to prevent nitrates from leaching into groundwater) as well as existing programs for protecting and restoring wetlands to prevent urban flooding.[18]

By 2008, the task force had noted a 21 percent decrease in the amount of nitrogen that was reaching the Gulf of Mexico, in large part because of what members described as "collateral benefits resulting from actions States and Federal agencies have taken independently of the hypoxia Action Plan."[19] For example, state programs to prevent nitrate contamination of aquifers meant that many farmers were now adopting best-management practices for fertilizer use. In general, this involved taking steps to better match the application of fertilizers to the needs of plants, but in some cases farmers were installing collection systems to capture nitrate-rich seepage for reapplication to the soil. Such strategies increased the percentage of nitrogen that was reaching crops and thus reduced the amount that was entering streams and aquifers.[20]

The task force also pointed out that 1.4 million acres of wetlands had been restored and enhanced. Again, there were other motivations for restoring wetlands (with flood control being especially important), but any restoration reduced nitrogen loads. Another contribution was a regulatory shift toward requiring concentrated animal-feeding operations such as hog farms to obtain discharge permits, which encouraged feedlot operators to adopt better waste-management practices.[21]

Unfortunately, however, reductions in nitrogen flows did not have the desired effect on the gulf's dead zone. Instead, the five-year rolling average of the affected area, which peaked in 2002 at 22,000 square kilometers, appeared to be holding steady. The Nutrient Task Force's next action plan, released in 2008, identified several potential reasons for the poor response, including the possibility that phosphorus might be playing a greater-than-expected role. Through symposia, the task force continued to reevaluate the science used to model the formation of hypoxic conditions.[22]

What the task force had learned in the implementation of its 2001 action plan influenced the design of its 2008 action plan. And theoretically, if the federal government remains committed to reducing the size of the hypoxic area, the task force will apply what it has learned in the implementation of its 2008 plan to the next revision, which is expected in 2013.[23] Government commitment, however, is not a given. Many of the actions identified as important in 2001, including an expansion of the gulf monitoring program, were never funded. Indeed, the recognition that political support was not particularly strong is one of the things that the task force learned and took into account while developing its 2008 action plan.

Meanwhile, scientists have continued to work on efforts to improve the predictive power of their models. In 2009, consensus was that the size of the hypoxic area would be the largest ever, but instead it dropped to 8,000 square kilometers, leading some scientists to believe that factors other than nutrients are playing a more significant role than that accounted for in their models. Questions have also been raised about procedures for measuring the size of the dead zone. After all, trying to characterize a dynamic process that varies from point to point and fluctuates over time is not easy. For example, in 2010, the failure of a well being drilled by the Deepwater Horizon released massive amounts of oil and methane into the northern gulf. Although the disaster took place east of the area in which hypoxic conditions have been forming, a surge of oxygen-consuming bacteria that feed on methane and an oil slick capable of blocking both sunlight and oxygen may have complicated gulf dynamics enough to have some effect. Other phenomena, such as unusually large spring floods in the U.S. Midwest and extensive hurricane activity in the gulf, can also have complicating effects.[24]

Regardless of what happens next, the abstract implications of the effort to manage hypoxia in the Gulf of Mexico are profound. The process of adaptively constructing a budget for the Mississippi River's nutrient load has begun to connect the ecology and economy of the region in new ways. The Nutrient Task Force is, in effect, working to reestablish nitrogen-related limits in the river basin. Yet these new limits differ substantially from the bacteria-based limits bypassed a century ago, in part because they are socially constructed. Although they are ecologically based and scientifically influenced, they ultimately represent a public choice to establish ethical boundaries on human interactions with the natural world. In addition, they integrate human choices and actions in one location with the dynamics of an aquatic ecosystem a thousand miles away. Surely this is an important step in the development of an ecological economy that fosters sustainable interactions with Earth systems.

N in the Market

As members of the Nutrient Task Force worked to reduce the amount of nitrogen (and, after 2008, phosphorus) flowing into the Gulf of Mexico from the Mississippi River, the potential value of using what members called "innovative and market-based solutions" emerged.[25] By that phrase, they meant nitrogen-discharge trading programs. As an example, imagine that a municipality must construct a 10-million-dollar addition to its sewage-treatment plant in order to cut nitrogen discharges by a certain amount. But what if local farmers could cut their discharges by an equal amount for a few hundred thousand dollars? A nitrogen-discharge trading program would allow the municipality to pay farmers to meet the required reduction. Such programs also could be used to reallocate budgets over time. Consider a case in which regulations prevent a developer from constructing a golf course in a watershed that already exceeds its nitrogen budget. A trading program would allow the developer to offset the course's nitrogen releases by securing cuts elsewhere in the watershed.

The thoughtful construction of market-based trading programs could facilitate the long-term process of establishing TMDLs and continually reallocating them among the various dischargers of nitrogen. Such programs have the potential not only to simplify the management of a nitrogen budget but also to encourage innovation that makes it easier to stay within that budget. They are a step toward integrating ecologically justified limits (and, indirectly, the value of ecosystem services) into economic decisions. Although a TMDL-based nitrogen budget for the entire Mississippi River basin is far from a reality, some states already have begun to experiment with nitrogen-trading programs. In 2007, for example, the Miami Conservancy District for Ohio's Great Miami River watershed created one to reduce discharges of nitrogen in the watershed by 112 tons. In that program, point sources such as wastewater-treatment plants can pay upstream farmers to adopt a variety of best-management practices in return for the credit associated with the resulting drop in nitrogen loading.[26]

It is no surprise that states have begun to experiment with trading programs. By the time the Miami Conservancy District created its version, regulatory bodies throughout the world had already acquired significant experience in creating and implementing them. In the United States, the most famous example was the cap and trade program for reducing sulfur dioxide emissions from power plants. Initiated by 1990 amendments to the Clean Air Act and aimed at dealing with the problem of acid rain, the program placed a limit, or cap, on the total amount of sulfur dioxide emitted by major power plants and allowed trading within that limit. It subsequently served as a model for cap and trade programs established to manage regional emissions of nitrogen oxides.[27]

Administrators of the sulfur-trading program distributed emission credits that represented a license to emit one ton of sulfur dioxide. Each power plant received enough credits to cover 75 percent of the amount they had emitted in 1990. Therefore, plant operators had to either reduce their emissions to match the credits they had received or secure more credits from another facility. To reduce their sulfur emissions, plants could purchase fuel with less sulfur in it or install equipment to capture and remove sulfur from the gases they emitted. The trading program also gave companies an incentive to reduce their emissions by an amount greater than 25 percent. For example, assume that a power plant could achieve a 60 percent reduction in emissions for not much more than it cost to achieve a 25 percent cut. Without the trading program, a firm would have no incentive to make the extra investment. With a trading program in place, firms could sell their unneeded emissions credits and recover their investment.

In general, policy analysts see the program as successful. It achieved the same objectives as a rigidly constructed fixed-reduction program but offered more flexibility in decision making and fewer costs to companies and consumers. Each year, power plants are required to secure enough credits to match their emissions, so total emissions always remain under the cap. Yet each firm is able to choose a strategy that works best for its particular situation, including being rewarded for reducing emissions beyond a minimum requirement. The owners of new power plants can also secure the credits they need through the market. In the long term, as all companies attempt to reduce their need to secure emission credits, the program has the potential to encourage continued technological innovation in the desired direction.[28]

The 1990 amendments to the Clean Air Act also laid the foundation for trading programs involving emissions of nitrogen oxides. In this case, policymakers were most concerned about the ability of nitrogen compounds to travel long distances and contribute to the production of photochemical smog in cities hundreds of miles away. Because this long-distance transport from other states meant that officials responsible for reducing ozone levels in, say, New York City or Philadelphia had limited control over the problem, legislators mandated the creation of an Ozone Transport Commission to investigate an interstate solution for reducing the production of urban photochemical smog. Any reductions in emissions of nitrogen oxides would also help address concerns associated with acid rain.[29]

The first regional trading programs for emissions of nitrogen oxides actually emerged in California, where problematic emissions came from in-state sources that California officials did have authority over. California called the program, which was up and running by 1993, RECLAIM for *Regional Clean Air Incentive Markets*. On the east coast, the Ozone Transport Commission began work on an interstate emissions-trading program for nitrogen oxides in 1994, which the U.S. Environmental Protection Agency began administering in 2003 as the NOx Budget Trading Program. Eventually, both programs integrated some level of mandated pollution control with the use of tradable emission credits.[30]

Nobody described these trading programs as a form of adaptive management, but such trading programs can also serve as an effective tool for adaptively managing efforts to stay within an ecologically justified budget. Without a trading program, the construction of new power plants (or, in the case of water-based programs, new municipal wastewater plants, farms, golf courses, and animal-feeding operations) would be problematic. After all, without adjustments elsewhere, any new emissions or discharges would exceed the limits of the established budget. An emissions-trading program, however, allows businesses and municipalities to secure the credits they need from markets without regulators having to get involved. In addition, if meeting environmental objectives requires that total emissions be cut further, program administrators can reduce the amount of tradable credits available without getting too involved in how to allocate the associated cuts. Trading between participants can reallocate the available credits instead.[31]

Other policy instruments for integrating the value of ecosystem services into economic decisions also exist. Examples include programs that reward people for managing their land in ways that protect those services. For instance, to maintain a minimum acreage of wetlands in a watershed, states have created programs in which landowners who establish wetlands can earn credits that have value in a market. In such cases, landowners who wish to eliminate wetlands can purchase credits to mitigate their actions. It is also possible for states to reward landowners for maintaining existing wetlands, which after all are providing an ecosystem service that everybody benefits from. Regardless of how such programs are structured, the political choice to maintain a certain acreage of wetlands is the critical one. Determining how to equitably integrate the cost of maintaining wetlands (or some other ecosystem service) into a market-based system is an important but separate challenge.[32]

Even though the task of designing trading programs is separate from the task of establishing environmental objectives, the details of trading programs certainly matter. Indeed, the devil is in the details. For example, an emissions-trading program that allocates the initial round of credits in a way that most people see as unfair or that allows for vague accounting and no way to avoid local emission hotspots is going to be difficult to administer well. As in the design of a tax code or other accounting system, numerous details have to be considered and tough political choices have to be made that affect who pays for what. However, debates over these details should not be confused with debates over whether to establish limits in the first place. They are two different discussions.

The learning necessary to design policies capable of effectively integrating environmental objectives into markets is not likely to occur without broad public acceptance and political support for the goals that drive such policies. In the United States, opposition generally comes from at least two directions. On one hand, some critics reject the notion that humans can place enough stress on Earth systems to make a difference, and they oppose the creation of ecological budgets in the first place. In their mind, there is no need to adaptively manage human interactions with the rest of nature. On the other hand, some people see trading programs as an effort to place nature under the control of markets. They miss the point that the key political decision has to do with setting limits and that the market aspect of such programs is a tool for meeting those limits. In short, the construction of trading programs that are fair, effective, and efficient is unlikely to happen unless people see the need for ecological budgets and recognize the usefulness of integrating them into markets.[33]

N and the Integrated Management of Knowledge

If adaptive management and policy instruments that integrate ecological limits into economic decisions are central to the notion of sustainable development, so, too, is the integrated management of knowledge.[34] After all, acquiring and managing information is an important part any decision-making process. For example, establishing a TMDL program of any kind requires a comprehensive accounting system. Attempting to construct such a program without a technologically sophisticated network of monitoring and reporting would be extremely difficult. Allow trading, however limited, and the importance of that accounting system increases dramatically. Add efforts to set and achieve objectives through adaptive management, and even greater amounts of information must be acquired, managed, and interpreted.

We are already generating significant amounts of information. Consider efforts to cycle the nitrogen-rich biosolids generated by sewage-treatment plants into agricultural land. The benefits of doing so are obvious: every ton of material returned to the soil translates into less industrial fertilizer that needs to be manufactured and fewer landfills that need to be constructed. However, concerns remain. First, over time, if too large a quantity of biosolids is worked into a patch of soil, significant releases of nitrate can occur, potentially contaminating aquifers or adding to the nutrient load of water bodies. Second, despite the Environmental Protection Agency's assurance that Class A biosolids can be safely applied to agricultural soil, many people are still concerned that contaminants such as lead may build up over time. Hence, when some operators of large, urban wastewater-treatment facilities dispose of their biosolids, program managers keep track of where the material is applied. Doing so allows them to place limits on how often their biosolids are applied to a particular piece of land, reducing the chances that a large quantity of nitrates will escape through leaching. It also generates data relevant to potential studies involving the accumulation of contaminants.[35]

Efforts to better match the application of fertilizers to crop needs has also led to innovations in monitoring and measuring. In its report *Integrated Assessment: Hypoxia in the Northern Gulf of Mexico* (2000), the NSTC included a diagram that showed a farmer using a tractor equipped with soil-monitoring instruments as well as global positioning (GPS) and geographical information (GIS) systems. The diagram illustrated the technology that some farmers were using to adjust applications of fertilizer based on soil conditions, generating data that could be overlaid with crop yields to help them make even better decisions in future years.[36]

Developers of watershed-management plans are also generating valuable information. The U.S. Geological Service, for example, maintains a modeling system known as Sparrow, which "empirically estimates the origin and fate of contaminants in river networks."[37] In their efforts to reduce hypoxia in the Gulf of Mexico, researchers combine tools such as Sparrow with computer models capable of analyzing what happens to nutrients in the gulf. By comparing the calculated results with what actually occurs (which also involves a massive collection of data), they are steadily improving their understanding of the entire system. This is no small accomplishment.

Monitoring flows of nitrogen through soils, rivers, wetlands, and air, as well as through crops, livestock operations, supermarkets, wastewater-treatment plants, chemical plants, internal combustion engines, and power plants was never a central concern to the legislators who passed the first wave of strong pollution control laws in the 1970s. Their efforts were motivated by a desire to protect air and water quality and ultimately the public health. However, even those efforts required access to massive amounts of data, including everything from the information needed to determine health standards to knowledge about how to characterize emissions and discharges from tens of thousands of industrial facilities. As most people have come to understand, environmental concerns—including but not limited to those associated with acid rain, ozone depletion, climate change, hypoxic dead zones, photochemical smog, and nitrates in groundwater—are ecologically, geographically, and socially complex. When people attempt to address these issues or even to resolve conflicts over how to address them, acquiring, interpreting, and managing data become part of the process.

There is no way to know how the future will unfold. But as societies work to manage flows of nitrogen-related compounds, they are slowly learning to establish ecological budgets and to integrate them into economic decisions. Furthermore, this learning is occurring adaptively, through processes in which policy goals, predictive models, technological practices, and the monitoring of environmental changes interact in complex ways. The process is ongoing, rooted in efforts to resolve conflicts over changes to the environment. The question now is whether the political will exists to create and support structured processes of adaptive learning, such as the effort to address concerns associated with hypoxic conditions in the northern Gulf of Mexico, or whether sustainability-related learning will generally remain unstructured and driven primarily by crises.

Conclusion

The Challenge of Sustainability

The planet Earth did not come with a nameplate bolted to its side, complete with a serial number and carrying capacity. Nor did it come with a user's guide that includes a recommended nitrogen-flow diagram or step-by-step directions for sustaining the integrity of the complex, interconnected Earth systems we call nature. However, if many billions of people are to live on Earth peacefully and equitably in thriving economies, not just in the twenty-first century but in the twenty-second and beyond, industrialized societies have no choice but to construct a guide that places ethical and practical boundaries on human interactions with the planet.

To what extent are industrial societies creating and respecting such boundaries? As this story of society's changing interactions with the cycling of nitrogen suggests, there is some movement in that direction. Two centuries ago, nobody imagined that tiny organisms lay at the core of a biogeochemical cycle that regulated the production of biomass in ecosystems throughout the world or that humans might one day bypass that regulatory system and eventually need to establish checks and balances of their own. Today, we have sophisticated systems for measuring and monitoring concentrations of nitrogenous compounds in air, water, and soil, making it possible to manage releases of nitrogenous compounds in one place to prevent problems hundreds, even thousands, of miles away. If nothing else, this capacity suggests that societies are learning to impose ecologically justified boundaries on human interactions with Earth systems.

There is, of course, no guarantee that societies will continue to move in this direction. Efforts to reduce occurrences of large-scale hypoxia or prevent problems caused by the long-distance transport of nitrogen oxides are ambitious tasks that depend upon a strong societal commitment to achieving those goals. That level of commitment becomes even more important when

162

addressing global concerns such as climate change and loss of biodiversity. Maintaining this commitment over decades, if not centuries, will be difficult without an economy that rewards innovators who make it easier to reach these goals.

Here, I want to make three general points, based on the story of society's changing interactions with the biogeochemical cycling of nitrogen, about the challenge of constructing a sustainable ecological economy. First, societies are (albeit slowly) integrating ecologically based limits into the economic decisions of producers and consumers and, in doing so, are empowering markets to reward innovations that respect those limits. Second, efforts to integrate ecological limits into economic decisions are inherently adaptive, a process that has thus far been occurring mainly through messy cycles of conflict and resolution. Given that societies now have the capacity to swiftly alter environments and environmental systems, they would be wise to create structured processes for adaptively managing potential concerns. Third, all adaptive management processes should be public in terms of both funding and participation. Integrating ecological limits into the rules governing markets affects everybody, and reaching consensus on how to proceed is critical. In the end, the process of constructing a sustainable ecological economy is an ethical project of the first order.

Integrating Ecological Limits into Market Rules

When examining the importance of integrating ecological limits into the rules that govern markets, we can see that the nitrogen-related aspect of this story is not unique. We could tell the same story about the more familiar carbon cycle. By burning fossil fuels and bypassing solar-based limits on the availability of energy from wood, wind, water, and muscle power, industrial societies have made it possible for large numbers of people to enjoy high material-living standards. However, burning coal, oil, and gas on a large scale also has had consequences: the carbon stored in that material is released as carbon dioxide and accumulates in the atmosphere. Although carbon dioxide is a completely natural compound in the sense that animals release it whenever they exhale, it is also a heat-absorbing greenhouse gas. Over approximately 150 years, industrial societies have raised its atmospheric concentration by 35 percent, altering the heat budget of the entire planet in the process. Exactly what effect this change will have on climatic patterns is still unknown, but societies are very gradually learning to place limits on emissions of carbon dioxide.

Bypassing solar-based energy limits is linked to bypassing the activity of nitrogen-fixing bacteria. At a practical level, exploiting the energy in fossil fuels made industrial fixing of nitrogen possible in the first place, but the two

are also linked in terms of Earth system dynamics. In 2008 *Nature* published
Nicolas Gruber and James Galloway's article "An Earth-System Perspective of
the Global Nitrogen Cycle," which includes a diagram that depicts two parallel nitrogen cycles, terrestrial and marine.[1] Each is positioned between two
other cycles, one smaller (phosphorus) and one larger (carbon). Visually, the
diagram is similar to an illustration of different-sized gears in which movement in one gear turns all the others. Gruber and Galloway, both prominent
Earth scientists known for their research on the nitrogen cycle, wanted the
diagram to emphasize the importance and difficulty of integrating interactions between biogeochemical cycles into computer projections of climate
change. Among other things, they were concerned that inaccurate models
and discrepancies between the predicted and observed pace of climate
change could undermine policymakers' faith in computer projections. The
authors noted that greater levels of carbon dioxide absorbed by the world's
oceans could be altering the marine nitrogen cycle in ways that increase
the production of marine biomass. If so, greater-than-expected amounts of
carbon dioxide are being absorbed from the atmosphere, slowing climate
change to a pace below what computer models have predicted.

Gruber and Galloway also noted that other nutrients, such as phosphorus or iron, might be limiting the capacity of the ocean to take in more
carbon dioxide through the production of more biomass. However, they did
not recommend, as others have, that societies should attempt to apply this
knowledge and start fertilizing the ocean with iron to slow climate change.
On the contrary, they suggested that efforts to geo-engineer the ocean on a
large scale would be very risky. After all, large-scale ocean fertilization could
set in motion a string of unintended consequences. Furthermore, it does not
even address the basic problem: humans failing to think sustainably. What
would prevent societies from simply increasing their carbon emissions even
more? At some point and in some form, societies must agree on a limit and
integrate it into the global economic system to avoid significant human-
induced changes to Earth systems.

The first step toward environmentally sustainable practices may be to
recognize the obvious: only when an economic system reward practices that
respect ecological limits can people be expected to innovate in ways that
make it easier to respect those limits. If the rules governing economic activity reward unsustainable practices, some people will inevitably innovate in
ways that exploit those practices to their advantage. In short, harnessing
market capitalism to work within an ethical system that recognizes ecological limits is central to the notion of sustainability. Only then will technological systems consistently evolve in a direction that reflects the intimate
connection between economies and ecologies.

Integrating ecological limits into market-based economic decisions is not necessarily easy. Without a crisis, political will to proceed is often weak and, in the United States, is compounded by the belief that producers and consumers should regulate themselves. Among those who embrace that ideology, Adam Smith's phrase "the invisible hand of the market" has taken on a significance far beyond its due.[2] Smith used the phrase mainly to argue for free trade between nations and against placing tariffs on goods that cross political borders. Markets unencumbered by tariffs, he said, result in the most efficient use of resources and hence the most efficient creation of wealth. That logic, however, is an argument against tariffs, not against markets in which everybody is expected to play by the same rules. Anybody who borrows Smith's words to argue against market-wide child labor laws or pollution-control regulations is making a leap that neither Smith nor his logic would support.

Sustainable economic growth—not just in the next few decades but for centuries to come—requires societies to make tough choices about how to proceed, which inevitably involves making choices about limits and how not to proceed. Furthermore, these are public decisions that need to be made through a political process. Relying solely on the unfettered interactions of producers and consumers may be acceptable when only private property is involved but does not work well for decisions involving the common good. For example, before limits on emissions of nitrogen oxides existed, the most efficient choice for producers and consumers was to ignore those emissions. Indeed, in the 1950s, the cost of reducing tailpipe emissions placed both auto manufacturers and consumers who cared about low emissions at a disadvantage in the market. Thus, by themselves, the forces of supply and demand were unlikely to reduce tailpipe emissions and prevent incidents of photochemical smog in major cities. Only when limits were put into place were the incentives reversed. Today, auto manufacturers embrace innovations that allow them to meet those standards as efficiently as possible, and the consumer who wants a car with low emissions is no longer at an economic disadvantage.

What would a mature ecological economy look like? Although adaptively learning how to integrate ecologically based limits into economic decisions is an integral part of the process, a thought experiment can help us visualize possibilities. Imagine that world leaders, with broad support, decide to place a cap of 150 million metric tons on the amount of nitrogen that societies are allowed to fix through industrial means. Assume that licenses to fix portions of that nitrogen are allocated to different nations throughout the world, based on a formula and set of rules that, miraculously, everybody has agreed is fair. In addition, each nation can sell any extra food or nitrogen-based chemicals it produces or, alternatively, trade some of its nitrogen credits for goods produced in other countries.

Although a global cap is probably too blunt an instrument for a biogeochemical cycle with large regional components, one could make an argument for the general approach. From an Earth systems perspective, pumping industrially fixed nitrogen into the terrestrial nitrogen cycle is akin to jacking the planet up on steroids. The short-term results are visible and impressive: massive amounts of corn, wheat, and rice flow from agricultural soils that would otherwise be able to support only a fraction of their current production. Indeed, the world's population now depends on the muscular harvest that industrially fixed nitrogen makes possible. But as I have shown throughout this book, there have been direct consequences associated with putting more nitrogen into circulation. Just as important are the indirect consequences, which includes draining aquifers to support large harvests and increasing inputs of phosphorous into watersheds. One might even claim that all stresses associated with population increases are nitrogen-related.

So rather than seeking out strategies to buffer the effects of those stresses (which may or may not work as expected), societies could address the problem by placing a cap on industrially fixed nitrogen. The cap would have to be set high enough and allocated so that societies could feed their populations. Over time, however, as markets began to reflect the cost of industrially fixed nitrogen, technologies, diets, and practices would evolve in ways that would make industrially fixed nitrogen less important. Meat would grow more expensive, perhaps leading to dietary shifts. More resources would certainly be invested in the technology to extract nitrogen from urban sewage and feedlots. Perhaps agricultural practices would facilitate greater uses of leguminous crops. Power companies might innovate in ways that allow them to convert emissions of nitrogen oxides into salable nitrogenous compounds such as nitric acid. All of these changes would place less stress on Earth systems; and over time, as producers and consumers made decisions with these limits in place, their practices would evolve in ways consistent with them.

Other changes would also occur, some pushing the world into new ethical territory. A cap on industrially fixed nitrogen could lead to a greater division between the haves and have-nots, with one segment of the population bearing much of the burden and the other proceeding as if no limits existed. It would no longer be possible to throw food at famine-related problems and avoid having to address the distribution of land and wealth, access to education and jobs, and the role of family planning. Facing up to such concerns and addressing them would be an integral part of the larger effort to create a sustainable ecological economy.

My point here is not to argue for a cap but to emphasize that innovations are highly influenced by market rules, that technologies and policy choices co-evolve and become entangled. If the goal is to construct an ecological economy, one that rewards firms and individuals for embracing innovations that respect the integrity of Earth systems, then markets that respect the integrity of Earth systems must be in place. The world cannot expect to achieve a more sustainable global economy through technological innovation without first adjusting the rules that govern markets.

Establishing Limits Adaptively

Moving toward more sustainable practices involves real learning, which can only be acquired adaptively through trial and error. In general, decisions about how to manage human activity so as to sustain the integrity of natural systems require the integration of several different types of knowledge: (1) what people hope to sustain and are willing to support through political and economic choices, (2) the extent to which human actions are affecting the dynamics of ecological and biogeochemical systems, and (3) how to translate what people hope to sustain into policies that channel innovation in the desired direction. Acquiring this mix of value-laden and technical knowledge is an iterative process that is continually affected by new technologies, scientific theories, policies, and political realities.

Some level of adaptive management, even if it not formally articulated, has been involved in all efforts to address environmental concerns. Take the response of Los Angelinos to the problem of photochemical smog. In the 1940s, when residents began complaining about an irritating haze, people generally agreed on what they hoped to sustain—air quality in Los Angeles—and officials mobilized the resources to address the concern. However, solving the problem was more difficult than anybody had expected. At first, no one had a clue about what was happening in the atmosphere. Officials tried first one solution, then another. Scientists and engineers came up with theory after theory. Even after scientists and civic leaders reached consensus on the cause of the problem, they still had to construct effective policies. Gradually, over many decades, each piece of science, advance in technology, and new policy contributed to the process of learning. Today, levels of photochemical smog are continually monitored, and regional cap-and-trade programs for nitrogen oxides, along with limits on emissions, have gone a long way toward helping Los Angeles and other large cities manage air quality.

There were similar informal, chaotic processes of adaptive management in efforts to deal with nitrates that leach into groundwater and sulfur and nitrogen oxides that contribute to acid rain. As with photochemical smog, a concern or conflict initiated the problem-solving process, with the main goal being to address the issue at hand. As various policy actions were taken and new practices and technologies adopted, scientists, policymakers, and the public learned more about the problem. That knowledge, in turn, led to refinements in goals, policies, and practices. Today, we have systems for monitoring the acidity of precipitation and the concentration of nitrates in groundwater, making it possible for regulators to detect significant change and produce data for future assessments.

More formal systems of adaptive management are also emerging—for instance, the effort to reduce the nitrogen-triggered dead zone in the northern Gulf of Mexico. Here, a national task force set measurable objectives, articulated and implemented a plan for achieving them, and has since adjusted both its objectives and strategies based on the information it has gained during the process. Today, multi-state organizations, individual states, and watershed groups are constructing programs for managing nitrogen throughout the basin, many of which also follow adaptive management procedures. Furthermore, specific entities such as sewage districts, fertilizer manufacturers, individual farmers, and feedlot operators are gradually changing their practices to meet new expectations. Some are even using an adaptive, continuous improvement process of environmental management (such as that certified by ISO 14001) to systematically meet those expectations.

The structure provided by a formal or semiformal process of adaptive management is surely warranted in efforts to address major environmental concerns. The alternative—relying on a focusing event that mobilizes political will for a year or two before attention turns to another problem, only to be twisted back by another focusing event—is increasingly risky. In a global economy in which large machines can be used to remove the top of a mountain to uncover the riches inside or when the daily practices of 7 billion people can alter climatic patterns, societies must become more purposeful in their efforts to determine what to sustain and how.

Structured processes of adaptive management are messy and still involve learning by trial and error, but the trials and errors are discussed, debated, and analyzed. Thus, they are a form of science-based decision making in which the science and decision-making are tightly coupled. Indeed, a major challenge of creating a sustainable ecological economy lies in better integrating the process (and funding mechanisms) of science into systems for adaptively managing significant concerns.

The three societal-level cycles of nested variation and selection that have served as powerful engines of knowledge production for a half-millennium remain critical: the adaptive rule of law, market capitalism, and the process of science. The difference lies in using the adaptive rule of law and the process of science to integrate ecological limits into the engine of market capitalism. The rule of law, of course, has always been essential to market capitalism. Without laws that define and enforce societal rules, complex markets would not be possible. Anarchists tend to see market capitalism as having hijacked the rule of law to do its bidding, but the adaptive rule of law has also made market capitalism possible by facilitating the resolution of conflicts brought about by market-driven innovations. Surely any society that embraces constant innovation without a mechanism for resolving conflicts places itself at great risk.

The challenge now is for societies to harness these engines of knowledge production to help people develop sustainable interactions with Earth systems—and ultimately each other. To do so, societies must create institutions that encourage people to continually ask and answer questions such as "What do we hope to sustain?" "Are we actually sustaining it?" and "If not, what are we going to do about it?" Until such questions (and mechanisms for addressing them) are woven into the fabric of social institutions, we have no guarantee that efforts to develop sustainable practices will be either encouraged or rewarded.

The Value of Broad Participation

The question of what a society should work to sustain is a political one. After all, who gets to decide what constitutes or qualifies as the common good? Who gets to decide which ecological limits should be integrated into markets or how much stress economic activity in one region should be allowed to place on ecological systems in another? Even if everybody agrees on the general objectives, who gets to decide on the specifics? Different groups of people are likely to make different choices.

Answering "What should a society seek to sustain?" is particularly difficult in a democracy, where broad participation means that many different perspectives and interests are represented. Groups with vested interests always attempt to sway individual choices, and often, powerful people who do not want their actions to be governed argue that the question is not legitimate and that the interplay of producers and consumers is sufficient for governing human interactions with the rest of nature. Others simply choose to ignore what is known about phenomena (for instance, the bioaccumulation of synthetic organics and the effects of CFCs on the ozone layer) and argue that human activity is incapable of affecting Earth systems.

Given the messiness of deciding anything in a democracy, one might imagine that a nation headed by a benign dictator or a ruling party with the best interest of the masses in mind would stand a better chance of moving a society toward sustainable practices. In the short term, dictatorial powers certainly go a long way in facilitating change toward clear objectives. The notion of sustainability, however, is a long-term process with objectives that are not particularly clear. Unless mechanisms for making sustainability-related decisions are woven into the fabric of society, there is no guarantee that commitment to those issues will survive from one generation of leaders to the next.

Furthermore, it is not enough to have a handful of trusted leaders who make key decisions. In practice, different people at different levels are constantly making value-laden decisions. Many tasks, of course, can and should be delegated to experts; for example, determining the acreage of wetlands needed to denitrify a certain quantity of nitrate certainly requires the skill of a wetland ecologist, and designing a market-based program to reward the maintenance of wetlands should involve an expert who is knowledgeable about integrating ecosystem services into markets. However, the decision as to whether a certain wetland should receive special consideration or whether one program design is better than another is value-laden, and such choices always have to be made. No handful of trusted leaders can be involved in all decisions at all levels.

Even many choices that seem to be purely technical can be value-laden. Consider the question of what procedure to use in calculating the size of a dead zone or how to measure whether a city has violated the ambient air-quality standard for nitrogen dioxide. At first glance, answers to both questions seem to depend on the skills of experts. However, both involve choices about everything from the placement of sensors to how and when various measurements are taken and weighted. Different sets of experts could easily arrive at different choices, which could mean the difference between a city's routinely meeting a national ambient air-quality standard and routinely violating it, between a water body's being labeled as degraded or not. Hence, broad participation is sometimes valuable even in what looks like technical decision making.

Another complicating factor is unpredictability. Oil spills, hurricanes, wars, economic disasters, technological failures, and even political shifts constantly intervene, and sometimes people have to make decisions quickly. Their choices, made in haste and with limited knowledge, sometimes matter as much as grand decisions made at a slower, more deliberate pace. If mechanisms for making sustainability-related decisions are woven into the fabric of society, people are more likely to be prepared for such events and processes, perhaps even anticipating them rather than being taken by surprise.

Constructing a sustainable global economy also involves achieving consensus on how to address key international issues such as climate change, the health of the world's fisheries, threats to the stratospheric ozone layer, and any concern affecting multiple states. Even some issues that seem to be purely local also have an international component, for in a global economy the economic decisions of producers and consumers in one nation can affect environments throughout the world. In the end, reaching consensus on how to sustain the integrity of Earth systems is an adaptive process requiring continual evaluation and adjustment. Choices abound, and billions of individuals and millions of collectives—families, firms, local and regional governments, nongovernmental and religious organizations, and sovereign states—are making nested and entangled decisions in a world structured by complex technological, bureaucratic, and legal systems. These choices are taking place in a decision-making landscape that is burdened with tremendously unequal distributions of wealth and power and that is constantly being altered by technological innovation, new scientific knowledge, and shifts in policy and values.

Sustaining the basic integrity of complex natural systems in a global, urban, industrial society with 10 billion or so inhabitants may be the great challenge of the twenty-first century. Without explicit policy choices, we have no guarantee about what, if anything, will be sustained. Traditional systems of land use and resource management based on local knowledge and well-enforced social norms might have been sufficient for pre-industrial societies. Today, however, with global markets and an unimaginably complex set of technologies linking ecologies and economies throughout the world, we need additional forms of governance. Societies must be clear about what private parties are free to change and what should be subject to ecologically justified limits.

NOTES

INTRODUCTION

1. Joan Houston Hall and Frederic G. Cassidy, eds., *Dictionary of American Regional English*, vol. I–O (Cambridge, Mass.: Belknap, 1996), 168.

2. For a descriptive account of a jubilee, see Anne George, *This One and Magic Life: A Novel of a Southern Family* (New York: Avon, 1999), 3–5.

3. M. Timothy O'Keefe, *Seasonal Guide to the Natural Year—Florida, with Georgia and Alabama Coasts: A Month by Month Guide to Natural Events* (Golden, Colo.: Fulcrum, 1996), 148–51.

4. Robert J. Diaz and Rutger Rosenberg, "Spreading Dead Zones and Consequences for Marine Ecosystems," *Science* 321 (2008): 926, 929.

5. National Oceanic and Atmospheric Administration, "Smaller Than Expected, but Severe, Dead Zone in Gulf of Mexico," NOAA website (www.noaanews.noaa.gov), July 27, 2009.

6. James N. Galloway et al., "The Nitrogen Cascade," *Bioscience* 53 (2002): 341–56.

7. Sonke Zaehle, Pierre Friedlingstein, and Andrew D. Friend, "Terrestrial Nitrogen Feedbacks May Accelerate Future Climate Change" (L01401), *Geophysical Research Letters* 37 (2010): 1–5; Nicolas Gruber and James N. Galloway, "An Earth-System Perspective of the Global Nitrogen Cycle," *Nature* 451 (2008): 293–96.

8. See G. J. Leigh, *The World's Greatest Fix: A History of Nitrogen and Agriculture* (New York: Oxford University Press, 2004).

9. Ibid., 94–121; Richard P Aulie, "Boussingault and the Nitrogen Cycle," *Proceedings of the American Philosophical Society* 114 (1970): 435–79.

10. J. C. Nesbit, *On Agricultural Chemistry and the Nature and Properties of Peruvian Guano* (London: Longman, 1856); Daniel J. Browne, *The American Muck Book* (New York: Saxton, 1851).

11. William Phillips Dunbar, *Principles of Sewage Treatment,* trans. H. T. Calvert (London: Griffin, 1908), 265–66.

12. Hoyt S. Gale, *Nitrate Deposits,* U.S. Geological Survey Bulletin 523 (Washington, D.C: Government Printing Office, 1912).

13. Vaclav Smil, *Enriching the Earth: Fritz Haber, Carl Bosch, and the Transformation of World Food Production* (Cambridge, Mass.: MIT Press, 2001).

14. Leigh, *World's Greatest Fix,* 6.

15. J. R. Partington, *A History of Greek Fire and Gunpowder* (1960; reprint, Baltimore: Johns Hopkins University Press, 1999); William H. McNeill, *The Age of Gunpowder*

Empires, 1450–1800 (Washington, D.C.: American Historical Association, 1989); Brenda J. Buchanan, ed., *Gunpowder, Explosives, and the State: A Technological History* (Burlington, Vt.: Ashgate, 2006).

16. Robert P. Multhauf, "The French Crash Program for Saltpeter Production, 1776–94," *Technology and Culture* 12 (1971): 163–81.

17. Edward D. Melillo, "Strangers on Familiar Soil: Chile and the Making of California, 1848–1940" (Ph.D. diss., Yale University, 2006).

18. James N. Galloway et al., "Nitrogen Cycles: Past, Present, and Future," *Biogeochemistry* 70 (2004): 153–226.

19. Smil, *Enriching the Earth.*

20. "In part" because other factors, such as the ability of Europe to draw on New World resources, also mattered: Kenneth Pomeranz, *The Great Divergence: China, Europe, and the Making of Modern World Economy* (Princeton, N.J.: Princeton University Press, 2000).

21. David Stradling, *Smokestacks and Progressives: Environmentalists, Engineers, and Air Quality in America, 1881–1951* (Baltimore: Johns Hopkins University Press, 1999); E. Melanie DuPuis, ed., *Smoke and Mirrors: The Politics and Culture of Air Pollution* (New York: New York University Press, 2004).

CHAPTER 1   THE EMERGENCE OF A BIOGEOCHEMICAL CYCLE

1. Paul F. Lurquin, *The Origins of Life and the Universe* (New York: Columbia University Press, 2003); D. E. Brownlee, "The Origin and Early Evolution of the Earth," in *Global Biogeochemical Cycles,* ed. Samuel S. Butcher, Robert J. Charlson, Gordon H. Orians, and Gordon V. Wolfe (New York: Academic Press, 1992), 9–10; John Gribben, *In Search of the Big Bang: The Life and Death of the Universe* (New York: Penguin, 1998); Stephen Hawking, *A Brief History of Time: From the Big Bang to Black Holes* (New York: Bantam, 1990); Thanu Padmanabhan, *After the First Three Minutes: The Story of Our Universe* (New York: Cambridge University Press, 1998); Steven Weinberg, *The First Three Minutes: A Modern View of the Origin of the Universe* (New York: Basic Books, 1993).

2. Cesare Emiliani, *Planet Earth: Cosmology, Geology, and the Evolution of Life and the Environment* (New York: Cambridge University Press, 1992), 371; R. S. Martin, T. A. Mather, and D. M. Pyle, "Volcanic Emissions and the Early Earth Atmosphere," *Geochimica et Cosmochimica Acta* 71 (2007): 3673–85.

3. The famous experiments by Stanley Miller in which amino acids were created under simulated primitive conditions is described in S. L. Miller, "A Production of Amino Acids under Possible Primitive Earth Conditions," *Science* 117 (1953): 528. Subsequent experiments similar to Miller's have produced the nitrogenous bases: Lurquin, *Origins of Life,* 96. Critiques have been made of such experiments based on arguments that the Archean atmosphere differs from the one Miller assumed, encouraging discussion of a wide range of possibilities, including whether the atmosphere around early volcanoes might have matched Miller's assumptions: Adam P. Johnson et al., "The Miller Volcanic Spark Discharge Experiment," *Science* 17 (2008): 404.

4. Karl J. Niklas, *The Evolutionary Biology of Plants* (Chicago: University of Chicago Press, 1997), 120; Manfred Eigen, *The Hypercycle: A Principle of Natural Self-Organization*

(New York: Springer Verlag, 1979); Masatoshi Nei and Richard K. Koehn, eds., *Evolution of Genes and Proteins* (Sunderland, Mass.: Sinauer Associates, 1983).

5. Freeman Dyson, *Origins of Life* (New York: Cambridge University Press, 1985); Stuart A. Kauffman, *The Origins of Order: Self-Organization and Selection in Evolution* (New York: Oxford University Press, 1993); M. Eigen et al., "The Origin of Genetic Information," *Scientific American* 244 (1993): 88–92.

6. Lurquin, *Origins of Life,* 134–39; H. D. Holland, "Geochemistry—Evidence for Life on Earth More than 3850 Years Ago," *Science* 275 (1997): 38–39; Sidney W. Fox and Klaus Dose, *Molecular Evolution and the Origin of Life* (San Francisco: Freeman, 1972); Emiliani, *Planet Earth,* 272–83.

7. Niklas, *Evolutionary Biology of Plants,* 128.

8. Donald E. Canfield, Alexander N. Glazer, and Paul G. Falkowski, "The Evolution and Future of Earth's Nitrogen Cycle," *Science* 8 (2010): 192–94; Martin G. Klotz, "Nitrifier Genomics and the Evolution of the Nitrogen Cycle," *FEMS Microbiology Letters* 278 (2008): 146–56; R. L. Mancinelli and C. P. McKay, "The Evolution of Nitrogen Cycling," *Origins of Life and Evolution of the Biosphere* 18 (1988): 311–25; Y. L. Yung and M. C. McElroy, "Fixation of Nitrogen in the Prebiotic Atmosphere," *Science* 203 (1979): 1002–4; Paul G. Falkowski, "Evolution of the Nitrogen Cycle and Its Influence on the Biological Sequestration of CO_2 in the Ocean," *Nature* 387 (1997): 272–75; John L. Ingraham, "Microbiology and Genetics of Denitrifiers," in *Denitrification, Nitrification, and Atmospheric Nitrous Oxide,* ed. C. C. Delwiche (New York: Wiley, 1981); and Mark Z. Jacobson, *Atmospheric Pollution: History, Science, and Regulation* (New York: Cambridge University Press, 2002): 29–48.

9. P. Lopez-Garcia et al., "Ancient Fossil Record and Early Evolution (ca. 3.8 to 0.5 Ga)," *Earth, Moon, and Planets* 98 (2006): 247–90; Lucas J. Stal, "Cyanobacterial Mats and Stomatolites," in *The Ecology of Cyanobacteria,* ed. Brian Whitton and Malcolm Potts (Boston: Kluwer, 2000), 62–121; Rafael Navarro-González, Christopher P. McKay, and Delphine N. Mvondo, "A Possible Nitrogen Crisis for Archaean Life Due to Reduced Nitrogen Fixation by Lightning," *Nature* 412 (2001): 61–64.

10. Jason Raymond et al., "The Natural History of Nitrogen Fixation," *Molecular Biology and Evolution* 21 (2004): 541–54. On the availability of another key nutrient: Kurt O. Konhauser et al., "Was There Really an Archean Phosphate Crisis?" *Science* 2 (2007): 1234. On the emergence of the tight link between photosynthesis and nitrogen fixation, John W. Grula, "Evolution of Photosynthesis and Biospheric Oxygenation Contingent upon Nitrogen Fixation?" *International Journal of Astrobiology* 4 (2005): 251–57.

11. Euan Nisbet and C. Mary R. Fowler, "The Evolution of the Atmosphere in the Archaean and Early Proterozoic," *Chinese Society Bulletin* 56 (2011): 4–13; James Farquhar, Aubrey L. Zerkle, and Andrey Bekker, "Geological Constraints on the Origin of Oxygenic Photosynthesis," *Photosynthesis Research* 107 (2011): 11–36.

12. Jessica Garvin et al., "Isotopic Evidence for an Aerobic Nitrogen Cycle in the Latest Archean," *Science* 323 (2009): 1045–48.

13. Paul G. Falkowski and Linda V. Godfrey, "Electrons, Life, and the Evolution of the World's Oxygen Cycle," *Philosophical Transaction of the Royal Society, Series B, Biological Sciences* 363 (2008): 2705–16; Lucas J. Stal and Jonathan P. Zehr, "Cyanobacterial Nitrogen Fixation in the Ocean: Diversity, Regulation, and Ecology," in *The Cyanobacteria: Microbiology, Genetics, and Evolution,* ed. Antonia Herrero and Enrique

Flores (San Diego: Caister, 2007), 423–46; James T. Staley and Gordon H. Orians, "Evolution and the Biosphere," in *Global Biogeochemical Cycles,* ed. Samuel S. Butcher, Robert J. Charlson, Gordon H. Orians, and Gordon V. Wolfe (New York: Academic Press, 1992), 21–54.

14. Niklas, *Evolutionary Biology of Plants,* 136–63.

15. Christopher P. McKay and Rafael Navarro-González, "The Absence of Nitrogen-Fixing Organelles Due to Timing of the Nitrogen Crisis," in *Symbiosis: Mechanisms and Model Systems,* ed. Joseph Seckbach (Dordrecht, the Netherlands: Kluwer, 2002), 223–28.

16. Anthony M. Poole and David Penny, "Evaluating Hypotheses for the Origin of Eukaryotes," *BioEssays* 29 (2007): 74–84.

17. J. Maynard Smith, *The Theory of Evolution* (Harmondsworth, U.K.: Penguin, 1966), 185–90; Niklas, *Evolutionary Biology of Plants,* 144–53.

18. Niklas, *Evolutionary Biology of Plants,* 153–63.

19. The notion of nested variation and selection is from Donald T. Campbell, "Evolutionary Epistemology," in *The Philosophy of Karl Popper,* ed. Paul A. Schilpp (La Salle, Ill.: Open Court, 1974), 412–63. Campbell uses the term *vicarious selection* to describe cycles of variation and selection that guide other cycles of variation and selection.

20. Robert H. Dott and Roger L. Batten, *Evolution of the Earth* (New York: McGraw-Hill, 1976), 304–13; J. E. Andrews et al., *An Introduction to Environmental Chemistry* (Oxford: Blackwell, 1996), 30–31.

21. Dott and Batten, *Evolution of the Earth,* 337–457.

22. Janet I. Sprent, *The Ecology of the Nitrogen Cycle* (New York: Cambridge University Press, 1987). Archaea capable of nitrifying ammonia have also been discovered: Christopher A. Francis, J. Michael Beman, and Marcel M. M. Kuypers, "New Processes and Players in the Nitrogen Cycle: The Microbial Ecology of Anaerobic and Archaeal Ammonia Oxidation," *ISME Journal* 1 (2007): 19–27.

23. T. Rosswall, "The Biogeochemical Nitrogen Cycle," in *Some Perspectives of the Major Biogeochemical Cycles,* ed. Gene. E. Likens (New York: SCOPE, 1981), 25–49.

24. W.D.P. Stewart, "Biological and Ecological Aspects of Nitrogen Fixation by Free-Living Micro-Organisms," *Proceedings of the Royal Society of London, Series B, Biological Sciences* 172 (1969): 367–88; John Postgate, *Nitrogen Fixation* (New York: Cambridge University Press, 1998), 8–10, 46–75; J. I. Baldani and V.L.D. Baldani, "History of the Biological Nitrogen Fixation Research in Gramineous Plants: Special Emphasis on the Brazilian Experience," *Annals of the Brazilian Academy of Sciences* 77 (2005): 549–79.

25. A. A. Mulder et al., "Anaerobic Ammonium Oxidation Discovered in a Denitrifying Fluidized Bed Reactor," *FEMS Microbiology Ecology* 16 (1995): 177–84; W. Koeve and P. Kahler, "Heterotrophic Denitrification vs. Autotrophic Anammox—Quantifying Collateral Effects on the Oceanic Carbon Cycle," *Biogeosciences Discussions* 7 (2010): 1813–37.

26. Mark Denny, *How the Ocean Works: An Introduction to Oceanography* (Princeton, N.J.: Princeton University Press, 2008), 69–106; Stal, "Cyanobacterial Mats and Stromatolites," 62–120; Robert W. Howarth and Roxanne Marino, "Nitrogen As the Limiting Nutrient for Eutrophication in Coastal Marine Systems: Evolving Views over Three Decades," *Limnology and Oceanography* 51 (2006): 364–76.

27. L. A. Codispoti et al., "The Oceanic Fixed Nitrogen and Nitrous Oxide Budgets: Moving Targets As We Enter the Anthropocene?" *Scientia Marina* 65 (2001): 85–105.

28. James N. Galloway and Ellis B. Cowling, "Reactive Nitrogen and the World: 200 Years of Change," *Ambio* 31 (2002): 64–71; Peter M. Vitousek et al., "Human Alteration of the Global Nitrogen Cycle: Sources and Consequences," *Ecological Applications* 7 (1997): 737–50.

29. Rosswall, "The Biogeochemical Nitrogen Cycle," 25–49; James N. Galloway et al., "Nitrogen Cycles: Past, Present, and Future," *Biogeochemistry* 70 (2004): 153–226; Gregory McIsaac and Mark B. David, "On the Need for Consistent and Comprehensive Treatment of the N Cycle," *Science of the Total Environment* 305 (2003): 249–55.

30. Jan Zalasiewicz et al., "Are We Now Living in the Anthropocene?" *GSA Today* 18 (February 2008): 4–8; James J. Elser, "A World Awash with Nitrogen," *Science* 334 (2011): 1504–5.

CHAPTER 2   FROM ADAPTATION TO INNOVATION

1. Pamela R. Willoughby, *The Evolution of Modern Humans in Africa: A Comprehensive Guide* (New York: AltaMira, 2007); Matthew H. Nitecki and Doris V. Nitecki, eds., *Origins of Anatomically Modern Humans* (New York: Plenum, 1994); David W. Cameron and Colin P. Groves, *Bones, Stones and Molecules: "Out of Africa" and Human Origins* (Burlington, Mass.: Elsevier, 2004).

2. David Christian, *Maps of Time: An Introduction to Big History* (Berkeley: University of California Press, 2004), 171–206; Ian Tattersall, *The World from Beginnings to 4000 B.C.E.* (New York: Oxford University Press, 2008).

3. Elman R. Service, *Profiles in Ethnology: A Revision of a Profile of Primitive Culture* (New York: Harper and Row, 1963); C. Loring Brace, *The Stages of Human Evolution* (Englewood Cliffs, N.J.: Prentice Hall, 1995); Robert L. Bettinger, *Hunter-Gatherers: Archaeological and Evolutionary Theory* (New York: Plenum, 1991); Alan Barnard, ed., *Hunter-Gatherers in History, Archaeology, and Anthropology* (New York: Berg, 2004).

4. Robert Boyd and Peter J. Richerson, *The Origins and Evolution of Culture* (New York: Oxford University Press, 2005); Richard B. Lee and Richard Daly, eds., *The Cambridge Encyclopedia of Hunters and Gatherers* (New York: Cambridge University Press, 1999).

5. Cecilia Heyes and David L. Hull, eds., *Selection Theory and Social Construction: The Evolutionary Naturalistic Epistemology of Donald T. Campbell* (Albany: State University of New York Press, 2001); Gary Cziko, *Without Miracles: Universal Selection Theory and the Second Darwinian Revolution* (Cambridge, Mass.: MIT Press, 1995); Marion Blute, "The Evolutionary Socioecology of Gestural Communication," *Gesture* 6 (2006): 177–88; Richard Dawkins, *The Selfish Gene* (New York: Oxford University Press, 1976).

6. Donald T. Campbell, "Evolutionary Epistemology," in *The Philosophy of Karl Popper*, ed. Paul A. Schilpp (La Salle, Ill.: Open Court, 1974), 412–63.

7. For a description of the brain that describes various levels of filtering, see Jeff Hawkins and Sandra Blakeslee, *On Intelligence* (New York: Times Books, 2004).

8. Erik Nordenskiold, *The History of Biology* (New York: Tutor, 1928), 316–30.

9. David Perkins, "The Evolution of Adaptive Form," in *Technological Innovation As an Evolutionary Process*, ed. John Ziman (New York: Cambridge University Press, 2000), 159–73.

10. Fekri A. Hassan, *Demographic Archaeology* (New York: Academic Press, 1981); W.M.S. Russell, "Population, Swidden Farming and the Tropical Environment," *Population and Environment* 10 (1988): 77–94.

11. Peter Bellwood, *The First Farmers: The Origins of Agricultural Societies* (Malden, Mass.: Blackwell, 2005); David Rindos, *The Origins of Agriculture: An Evolutionary Perspective* (Orlando, Fla.: Academic Press, 1984); Gregory K. Dow, Nancy Olewiler, and Clyde G. Reed, "The Transition to Agriculture: Climate Reversals, Population Density, and Technical Change" (2005), Research Papers in Economics, http://repec.org; Mark Nathan Cohen, *The Food Crisis in Prehistory: Overpopulation and the Origins of Agriculture* (New Haven: Yale University Press, 1977); David Russell Harris, ed. *The Origins and Spread of Agriculture and Pastoralism in Eurasia* (Washington, D.C.: Smithsonian Institution Press, 1996).

12. T. A. Surovell, "Early Paleoindian Women, Children, Mobility, and Fertility," *American Antiquity* 65 (2000): 493–508; Fekri A. Hassan, "On Mechanisms of Population Growth during the Neolithic," *Current Anthropology* 14 (1973): 535–42.

13. Leslie A. White, *The Evolution of Culture: The Development of Civilization to the Fall of Rome* (New York: McGraw-Hill, 1959).

14. Y. Liu and J. Chen, "Phosphorus Cycle," in *Global Ecology,* ed. Sven Erik Jorgensen (Amsterdam: Elsevier, 2010), 204–14; Daniel D. Richter, Jr., and Daniel Markewitz, *Understanding Soil Change: Soil Sustainability over Millennia, Centuries, and Decades* (New York: Cambridge University Press, 2001).

15. G. J. Leigh, *The World's Greatest Fix: A History of Nitrogen and Agriculture* (New York: Oxford University Press, 2004); Bruce Smith, *The Emergence of Agriculture* (New York: Scientific American Library, 1995).

16. Richard L. Burger, *Chavin and the Origins of Andean Civilization* (New York: Thames and Hudson, 1992), 29.

17. D. B. Grigg, *The Agricultural Systems of the World: An Evolutionary Approach* (New York: Cambridge University Press, 1974); Tim Denham and Peter White, *The Emergence of Agriculture: A Global View* (New York: Routledge, 2007).

18. Leigh, *The World's Greatest Fix,* 23–53; Mark A. Blumler, "Modelling the Origins of Legume Domestication and Cultivation," *Economic Botany* 45 (1991) 243–50.

19. Jared M. Diamond, *Guns, Germs, and Steel: The Fates of Human Societies* (New York: Norton, 1997).

20. Stanley A. Cook, *The Laws of Moses and the Code of Hammurabi* (London: Black, 1903); Hermann L. Strack and Gunter Stemberger, *Introduction to the Talmud and Midrash* (New York: Meridian, 1959); Michael Gagarin and David Cohen, *The Cambridge Companion to Ancient Greek Law* (New York: Cambridge University Press, 2005).

CHAPTER 3   INNOVATION WITHIN AN ECOLOGICAL LIMIT

1. Lynn Meskell, *Private Life in New Kingdom Egypt* (Princeton, N.J.: Princeton University Press, 2004), 26; Stephen K. Sanderson, "World System and Social Change in Agrarian Societies, 3000 B.C. to 1500 A.D.," in *World System History: The Social Science of Long Term Change,* ed. Robert Allen Denemark et al. (New York: Routledge, 2000), 185–98.

2. Jason W. Clay, *World Agriculture and the Environment* (Washington, D.C.: Island, 2004), 174; Bruce G. Trigger, *Understanding Early Civilizations* (New York: Cambridge

University Press, 2003), 289; Milton W. Meyer, *A Concise History of China* (Lanham, Md.: Rowman and Littlefield, 1994), 135.

3. If 50 grams of protein (16 percent nitrogen) were consumed per person per day and 4 grams of N were fixed for every gram consumed, the total amount of fixed nitrogen would be 5.8 kilograms per hectare per year.

4. William M. Lewis, Jr., "Yield of Nitrogen from Minimally Disturbed Watersheds of the United States," in *The Nitrogen Cycle at Regional to Global Scales,* ed. Elizabeth W. Boyer and Robert W. Howarth (Boston: Kluwer, 2002), 375–85.

5. Peter N. Stearns, *The Industrial Revolution in World History* (Boulder, Colo.: Westview, 1993), 11; Lynn White, Jr., *Medieval Technology and Social Change* (Oxford: Clarendon, 1962), 39. Stearns points to 20 percent as the upper limit in the fraction of people freed to do nonagricultural work in preindustrial societies. White puts the upper limit for societies before 1900 at 10 percent.

6. N. K. Fageria, *Maximizing Crop Yields* (New York: Dekker, 1992); D. B. Grigg, *The Agricultural Systems of the World: An Evolutionary Approach* (New York: Cambridge University Press, 1974); Vaclav Smil, *Energy in Nature and Society: General Energetics of Complex Systems,* (Cambridge, Mass.: MIT Press, 2008), 65–84.

7. Yosaburō Takekoshi, *The Economic Aspects of the History of the Civilization of Japan* (New York: Routledge, 2004), 3:386–407; Harumi Befu, *Japan: An Anthropological Introduction* (New York: Harper and Row, 1971).

8. Peter B. Golden, "Nomads and Sedentary Societies in Eurasia," in *Agricultural and Pastoral Societies in Ancient and Classical History,* ed. Michael Adas (Philadelphia: Temple University Press, 2001), 71–115; Smil, *Energy in Nature and Society,* 149–52.

9. Peter J. Heather, *The Fall of The Roman Empire: A New History of Rome and the Barbarians* (New York: Oxford University Press, 2005); John Man, *Genghis Khan: Life, Death, and Resurrection* (New York: St. Martin's, 2005).

10. Mary Anne Murray, "Cereal Production and Processing," in *Ancient Egyptian Material and Technologies,* ed. Paul Nicholson and Ian Shaw (New York: Cambridge University Press, 2000), 505–36; Elinor M. Husselman, "The Granaries of Karanis," *Transactions and Proceedings of the American Philological Association* 83 (1952): 56–73.

11. Robert L. Heilbroner and William Milberg, *The Making of Economic Society* (Upper Saddle River, N.J.: Prentice Hall, 2002), 15–22.

12. Leslie A. White, *The Evolution of Culture: The Development of Civilization to the Fall of Rome* (New York: McGraw-Hill, 1959), 3–280.

13. Randolf Barker and Robert Herdt, *The Rice Economy of Asia* (Washington, D.C.: Resources for the Future, 1985), 14–16; Robert E. Murowchick, *China: Ancient Culture, Modern Land* (Norman: University of Oklahoma Press, 1994), 25–27; Daniel R. Headrick, *Technology: A World History* (New York: Oxford University Press, 2009), 51–53; Ian C. Glover and Charles F. W. Higham, "New Evidence for Early Rice Cultivation in South, Southeast, and Southeast Asia," in *The Origins and Spread of Agriculture and Pastoralism in Eurasia,* ed. David R. Harris (New York: Routledge, 1996), 413–41; Kenneth R. Hall, "Economic History of Early Southeast Asia," in *The Cambridge History of Southeast Asia,* vol. 1, *From Early Times to c. 1500,* ed. Nicholas Tarling (New York: Cambridge University Press, 1993), 183–272; Deepak Lal, *Unintended Consequences: The Impact of Factor Endowments, Culture, and Politics on Long-Run Economic Performance* (Cambridge, Mass.: MIT Press, 2001), 39–41.

14. Mary Allerton Kilbourne Matossian, *Shaping World History: Breakthroughs in Ecology, Technology, Science, and Politics* (New York: Sharp, 1997), 69–70; Joseph Needham and Francesca Bray, *Science and Civilisation in China*, vol. 6, *Biology and Biological Technology*, part 2, *Agriculture* (New York: Cambridge University Press, 1984), 477–95.

15. D. O. Hall, S. Kannaiyan, and M. van der Leij, "Ammonia Production in Rice Paddies Using Immobilized Cyanobacteria," in *Biotechnology of Biofertilizers*, ed. Sadasivam Kannaiyan (Boston: Kluwer, 2002), 370–79.

16. Yi-Fu Tuan, *A Historical Geography of China* (Piscataway, N.J.: Aldine Transaction, 2008), 126–34; Zitong Gong et al., "Classical Farming Systems of China," in *Nature Farming and Microbial Applications*, ed. Hui-lian Xu, James F. Parr, and Hiroshi Umemura (Binghamton, N.Y: Food Products Press, 2000), 11–22; Mustafizur Rahman et al., eds., *Biological Nitrogen Fixation Associated with Rice Production* (Boston: Kluwer, 1996); Donald H. Grist, *Rice* (London: Longmans, 1953).

17. Joseph Needham, *Science and Civilisation in China*, vol. 4, *Physics and Physical Technology*, part 2, *Mechanical Engineering* (New York: Cambridge University Press, 1985); Tuan, *Historical Geography of China*, 75–146; Terry Reynolds, *Stronger Than a Hundred Men: A History of the Vertical Water Wheel* (Baltimore: Johns Hopkins University Press, 1983), 116.

18. Needham and Bray, *Agriculture*, 477–95; Patricia Buckley Ebrey, *The Cambridge Illustrated History of China* (New York: Cambridge University Press, 1999), 108–61.

19. Fairfax Harrison, *Roman Farm Management: The Treatises of Cato and Varro* (New York: Macmillan, 1918), 40–41; White, *Medieval Technology and Social Change*, 70.

20. R. S. Loomis and D. J. Conner, *Crop Ecology: Productivity and Management in Agricultural Systems* (New York: Cambridge University Press, 2011), 215–16.

21. White, *Medieval Technology and Social Change*, 39–78; M. M. Postan, ed., *The Cambridge Economic History of Europe from the Decline of the Roman Empire*, vol. 1, *Agrarian Life of the Middle Ages* (New York: Cambridge University Press, 1966); Paul Erdkamp, *The Grain Market in the Roman Empire: A Social, Political, and Economic Study* (New York: Cambridge University Press, 2005).

22. Georges Comet, "Technology and Agricultural Expansion in the Middle Ages: The Example of France North of the Loire," in *Medieval Farming and Technology: The Impact of Agricultural Change in Northwest Europe*, ed. Grenville Astill and John Langdon (New York: Brill, 1997), 11–40; Rosemary Lynn Hopcroft, *Regions, Institutions, and Agrarian Change in European History* (Ann Arbor: University of Michigan Press, 1999), 15–28; Jeffrey R. Wigelsworth, *Science and Technology in Medieval European Life* (Westport, Conn.: Greenwood, 2006), 1–20; H. E. Hallam, ed., *The Agrarian History of England and Wales*, vol. 2, *1042–1350* (New York: Cambridge University Press, 1988); White, *Medieval Technology and Social Change*, 70.

23. Wigelsworth, *Science and Technology in Medieval European Life*, 7.

24. Comet, "Technology and Agricultural Expansion in the Middle Ages," 11–40.

25. White, *Medieval Technology and Social Change*, 39–79.

26. Jared M. Diamond, *Guns, Germs, and Steel: The Fates of Human Societies* (New York: Norton, 1997), 176–92.

27. Clive Ponting, *A Green History of the World: The Environment and the Collapse of Great Civilizations* (New York: St. Martin's, 1991); Denys Lionel Page, *The Santorini Volcano and the Desolation of Minoan Crete* (London: Society for the Promotion of Greek

Studies, 1970); J. Donald Hughes, *Ecology in Ancient Civilizations* (Albuquerque: University of New Mexico Press, 1975).

28. Diamond, *Guns, Germs, and Steel,* 176–92.

29. J. R. Partington, *A History of Greek Fire and Gunpowder* (1960; reprint, Baltimore: Johns Hopkins University Press, 1999), xv–xxx, 237–339; Asitesh Bhattacharya, "Gunpowder and Its Applications in Ancient India," in *Gunpowder, Explosives, and the State: A Technological History,* ed. Brenda J. Buchanan (Burlington, Vt.: Ashgate, 2007), 42–50; Joseph Needham et al., *Science and Civilisation in China,* vol. 5, *Military Technology,* part 7, *The Gunpowder Epic* (New York: Cambridge University Press, 1986).

CHAPTER 4   N AND THE EMERGENCE OF MARKET CAPITALISM

1. Fulcher of Chartres, "The Speech of Urban II at the Council of Clermont, 1095," in *A Source Book for Medieval History,* ed. Oliver J. Thatcher and Edgar Holmes McNeal (New York: Scribner, 1905), 513–17.

2. Jonathan Riley-Smith, *The Crusades: A History* (New Haven: Yale University Press, 2005), 1–12; David Luscombe and Jonathan Riley-Smith, eds., *The New Cambridge Medieval History,* vol. 4, part 2, *c. 1024–c. 1198* (New York: Cambridge University Press, 2004).

3. Francois Crouzet, *A History of the European Economy, 1000–2000* (Charlottesville: University of Virginia Press, 2001), 27–33.

4. Gillian R. Evans, *Philosophy and Theology in the Middle Ages* (New York: Routledge, 1993); Jeremiah Hackett, "Roger Bacon," in *Medieval Philosophers,* ed. Jeremiah Hackett (Detroit: Gale, 1992), 90–102.

5. J. R. Partington, *A History of Greek Fire and Gunpowder* (1960; reprint, Baltimore: Johns Hopkins University Press, 1999). Partington credits Bacon with publishing a recipe for gunpowder, but other scholars are skeptical of Bacon's central role; see the introduction by Bert S. Hall, xv–xxx.

6. Joseph Needham and Peter Golas, *Science and Civilisation in China,* vol. 5, *Chemistry and Chemical Technology,* part 13, *Mining* (Cambridge University Press, 1999), 184–85; Partington, *History of Greek Fire,* 312–22; Dennis W. Barnum, "Some History of Nitrates," *Journal of Chemical Education* 80 (2003): 1393–96; Brenda J. Buchanan, "Saltpetre: A Commodity of Empire," in *Gunpowder, Explosives and the State: A Technological History,* ed. Brenda J. Buchanan (Burlington, Vt.: Ashgate, 2006), 67–90.

7. Partington, *History of Greek Fire,* 312–22; Buchanan, "Saltpetre," 67–90. Hall's introduction in *History of Greek Fire* also addresses the problem of impure saltpeter.

8. Carlo Cipolla, *Guns, Sails, and Empires: Technological Innovation and the Early Phases of European Expansion, 1400–1700* (New York: Pantheon, 1966); Buchanan, *Gunpowder, Explosives, and the State.*

9. Gábor Ágoston, *Guns for the Sultan: Military Power and the Weapons Industry in the Ottoman Empire* (New York: Cambridge University Press, 2005); John A. Wagner, *Encyclopedia of the Hundred Years War* (Westport, Conn.: Greenwood, 2006), 34–35; Weston F. Cook, Jr., "The Cannon Conquest of Nasrid Spain and the End of the Reconquista," in *Crusaders, Condottieri, and Cannon: Medieval Warfare in Societies around the Mediterranean,* ed. Donald J. Kagay and L. J. Andrew Villalon (Boston: Brill, 2002), 253–84; Peter Kirsch, *The Galleon: The Great Ships of the Armada Era*

(London: Conway Maritime, 1990); Geoffrey Parker, *The Military Revolution: Military Innovation and the Rise of the West* (New York: Cambridge University Press, 1988); William H. McNeill, *The Age of Gunpowder Empires, 1450–1800* (Washington, D.C.: American Historical Association, 1989).

10. Buchanan, "Saltpetre," 67–90.

11. Robert P. Multhauf, "The French Crash Program for Saltpeter Production, 1776–94," *Technology and Culture* 12 (1971): 163–81; Buchanan, "Saltpetre," 67–90; Joseph LeConte, *Instruction for the Manufacture of Saltpetre* (Columbia: South Carolina Executive Council, 1862).

12. Thomas Kaiserfeld, "Saltpetre at the Intersection of Military and Agricultural Interests in Eighteenth-Century Sweden," in Buchanan, *Gunpowder, Explosives and the State,* 142–57.

13. Stephen R. Bown, *A Most Damnable Invention: Dynamite, Nitrates, and the Making of the Modern World* (New York: St. Martin's, 2005), 33–38.

14. William Milburn, *Oriental Commerce: Containing a Geographic Description of the Principle Places in the East Indies, China, and Japan with the Produce, Manufacture and Trade* (London: Black, Parry, 1813), i.xxxviii.

15. Multhauf, "French Crash Program," 163–81.

16. Colin McEvedy and Richard Jones, *Atlas of World Population History* (New York: Penguin, 1978).

17. Sheilagh C. Ogilvie and Markus Cerman, eds., *European Proto-Industrialization: An Introductory Handbook* (New York: Cambridge University Press, 1996).

18. Karl Marx, *Capital: A Critique of Political Economy,* trans. Samuel Moore and Edward Aveling (New York: Cerf, 1906); Wally Seccombe, *A Millennium of Family Change: Feudalism to Capitalism in Northwestern Europe* (New York: Verso, 1992).

19. Edward Miller, ed., *The Agrarian History of England and Wales,* vol. 3, *1348–1500* (New York: Cambridge University Press, 1991); Joan Thirsk, ed., *The Agrarian History of England and Wales,* vol. 5, *1500–1750* (New York: Cambridge University Press, 1991).

20. Fernand Braudel, *Civilization and Capitalism, 15th–18th Centuries,* 3 vols. (New York: Harper and Row, 1982–84); C.G.A. Clay, *Economic Expansion and Social Change: England, 1500–1700,* 3 vols. (New York: Cambridge University Press, 1985).

21. Robert C. Allen, "The Nitrogen Hypothesis and the English Agricultural Revolution: A Biological Analysis," *Journal of Economic History* 68 (2008): 182–210; Harry Kitsikopoulos, "Convertible Husbandry vs. Regular Common Fields: A Model on the Relative Efficiency of Medieval Field Systems," *Journal of Economic History* 64 (2004): 462–99; Mark Overton, *Agricultural Revolution in England: The Transformation of the Agrarian Economy, 1500–1850* (New York: Cambridge University Press, 1996); R. S. Loomis and D. J. Conner, *Crop Ecology: Productivity and Management in Agricultural Systems* (New York: Cambridge University Press, 2011), 212–16.

22. Edward A. Wrigley and Roger Schofield, *The Population History of England, 1541–1871: A Reconstruction* (New York: Cambridge University Press, 2002).

23. Estimate of the tons of N flowing into cities is based on the average individual's consumption of fifty-five grams of protein per day. The need to feed urban horses is not included in this estimate.

24. Tertius Chandler, *Four Thousand Years of Urban Growth: An Historical Census* (Lewiston, Me.: Mellen, 1987).

25. Edward A. Wrigley, *Population and History* (New York: McGraw-Hill, 1969); G. William Skinner, *The City in Late Imperial China* (Stanford, Calif.: Stanford University Press, 1977).

26. Thomas R. Malthus, *An Essay on the Principle of Population* (1798; reprint, New York: Penguin, 1986); M. E. Turner, J. V. Beckett, and B. Afton, *Agricultural Rent in England, 1690–1914* (New York: Cambridge University Press, 2004), 233.

27. Immanuel Wallerstein, *The Modern World-System,* vol. 1, *Capitalist Agriculture and the Origins of the European World-Economy in the Sixteenth Century* (New York: Academic Press, 1974); Immanuel Wallerstein, *The Modern World-System,* vol. 2, *Mercantilism and the Consolidation of the European World-Economy, 1600–1750* (New York: Academic Press, 1980.)

28. Verena Winiwarter, "Saltpeter: An Explosive Environmental History in Early Modern Europe" (paper delivered at the American Society of Environmental History's annual conference, Saint Paul, Minn., 2006); Richard Glover, *Peninsular Preparation: The Reform of the British Army, 1795–1809* (New York: Cambridge University Press, 1963), 64.

CHAPTER 5   N AND THE RISE OF SCIENCE

1. Lynwood Bryant, "The Role of Thermodynamics in the Evolution of Heat Engines," *Technology and Culture* 14 (1973): 152–65; Robert P. Multhauf, "The French Crash Program for Saltpeter Production, 1776–94," *Technology and Culture* 12 (1971): 163–81; Edwin Layton, "Mirror-Image Twins: The Communities of Science and Technology in 19th-Century America," *Technology and Culture* 12 (1971): 562–80.

2. Stanton J. Linden, ed., *The Alchemy Reader: From Hermes Trismegistus to Isaac Newton* (New York: Cambridge University Press, 2003); William R. Newman and Lawrence M. Principe, *Alchemy Tried in the Fire: Starkey, Boyle, and the Fate of Helmontian Chymistry* (Chicago: University of Chicago Press, 2002); Trevor H. Levere, *Transforming Matter: A History of Chemistry from Alchemy to the Buckyball* (Baltimore: Johns Hopkins University Press, 2001).

3. Linden, *Alchemy Reader,* 103.

4. William R. Newman and Anthony Grafton, "Introduction: The Problematic Status of Astrology and Alchemy in Early Modern Europe," in *Secrets of Nature: Astrology and Alchemy in Early Modern Europe,* ed. William R. Newman and Anthony Grafton (Cambridge, Mass.: MIT Press, 2006), 1–37.

5. "Jabir Ibn Hayyan, from 'Of the Investigation or Search for Perfection,' 'Of the Sum of Perfection,' and 'His Book of Furnaces,'" in Linden, *Alchemy Reader,* 80–94.

6. Henry M. Leicester, *The Historical Background of Chemistry* (New York: Wiley, 1956); John Read, *From Alchemy to Chemistry* (1955; reprint, Mineola, N.Y.: Dover, 1995); Maurice Crosland, "The Chemical Revolution of the Eighteenth Century and the Eclipse of Alchemy in the 'Age of Enlightenment,'" in *Alchemy Revisited: Proceedings of the International Conference on the History of Alchemy,* ed. Z.R.W.M. von Martels (Leiden, the Netherlands: Brill, 1990), 67–80.

7. Thomas S. Kuhn, *The Copernican Revolution: Planetary Astronomy in the Development of Western Thought* (Cambridge, Mass.: Harvard University Press, 1957).

8. Ibid., 42, 100–133.

9. Elizabeth L. Eisenstein, *The Printing Press As an Agent of Change: Communications and Cultural Transformations in Early-Modern Europe*, 2 vols. (New York: Cambridge University Press, 1979); Owen Gingerich, "Copernicus and the Impact of Printing," *Vistas in Astronomy* 17 (1975): 201–20.

10. Galileo Galilei, *Dialogues Concerning Two New Sciences* [1638], trans. Henry Crew and Alfonso de Salvio (New York: Macmillan, 1914); Laura Fermi and Gilberto Bernardini, *Galileo and the Scientific Revolution* (New York: Basic Books, 1961); Mario Biagioli, *Galileo, Courtier: The Practice of Science in the Culture of Absolutism* (Chicago: University of Chicago Press, 1994).

11. Francis Bacon, *The New Atlantis* (1627; reprint, Minneapolis: Filiquarian, 2007), 46; Paolo Rossi, *Francis Bacon: From Magic to Science,* trans. Sacha Rabinovitch (Chicago: University of Chicago Press, 1978); Stephen Gaukroger, *Francis Bacon and the Transformation of Early-Modern Philosophy* (New York: Cambridge University Press, 2001); Barry Gower, *Scientific Method: A Historical and Philosophical Introduction* (New York: Routledge, 1997); Carolyn Merchant, *The Death of Nature: Women, Ecology, and the Scientific Revolution* (New York: Harper and Row, 1980), 164–92.

12. Ken Alder, "French Engineers Become Professionals; or How Meritocracy Made Knowledge Objective," in *The Sciences in Enlightened Europe,* ed. William Clark, Jan Golinski, and Simon Schaffer (Chicago: University of Chicago Press, 1999), 94–125.

13. Pamela O. Long, *Openness, Secrecy, Authorship: Technical Arts and the Culture of Knowledge from Antiquity to the Renaissance* (Baltimore: Johns Hopkins University Press, 2001); Robert P. Multhauf, "Sal Ammoniac: A Case History in Industrialization," *Technology and Culture* 6 (1965): 569–86.

14. Betty Jo Teeter Dobbs, *The Janus Faces of Genius: The Role of Alchemy in Newton's Thought* (New York: Cambridge University Press, 1991); Rossi, *Francis Bacon.*

15. Rose-Mary Sargent, *The Diffident Naturalist: Robert Boyle and the Philosophy of Experiment* (Chicago: University of Chicago Press, 1995); Robert Boyle, *The Sceptical Chymist; or: Chymico-Physical Doubts & Paradoxes, Touching the Spagyrist's Principles Commonly call'd Hypostatical* (1661; reprint, Boston: Elibron, 2006).

16. Boyle, *Sceptical Chymist,* 194.

17. John F. Fulton, "Sir Kenelm Digby, F.R.S. (1603–1665)," *Notes and Records of the Royal Society of London* 15 (1960): 199–210.

18. Edward John Russell, *Soil Conditions and Plant Growth* (London: Longmans, Green, 1917); Kathleen Ahonen, "Glauber, Johann Rudolph," in *Dictionary of Scientific Biography,* ed. Charles C. Gillispie (New York: Scribner, 1970–80), 5:419–23.

19. John Evelyn, *A Philosophical Discourse of Earth, Relating to the Culture and Improvement of It for Vegetation, and the Propagation of Plants As It Was Presented to the Royal Society, April 29, 1675* (London: Royal Society, 1676), 98, 110; Gillian Darley, *John Evelyn, Living for Ingenuity* (New Haven: Yale University Press, 2006).

20. Julius Sachs, *History of Botany, 1530–1860* (Oxford: Clarendon, 1890), 461–76; Richard M. Klein et al., "Precipitation As a Source of Assimilable Nitrogen: A Historical Survey," *American Journal of Botany* 75 (1988): 928–37.

21. Aaron John Ihde, *The Development of Modern Chemistry* (New York: Dover, 1984), 25–31; Ferenc Szabadváry, *History of Analytical Chemistry,* trans. Gyula Svehla (Langhorn, Pa.: Gordon and Breach, 1992), 42–49.

22. Ebbe Almqvist, *History of Industrial Gases* (New York: Kluwer/Plenum, 2003).

23. Seymour H. Mauskopf, "Gunpowder and the Chemical Revolution," *Osiris* 4 (1988): 93–118; Arthur Donovan, *Antoine Lavoisier: Science, Administration and Revolution* (New York: Cambridge University Press, 1993).

24. John Dalton, *A New System of Chemical Philosophy* (London: Strand, 1808); Henry E. Roscoe, *John Dalton and the Rise of Modern Chemistry* (New York: Macmillan, 1895).

25. June Z. Fullmer, *Young Humphry Davy: The Making of an Experimental Chemist* (Philadelphia: America Philosophical Society, 2000); Humphry Davy, *Researches, Chemical and Philosophical: Chiefly Concerning Nitrous Oxide, or Dephlogisticated Nitrous Air, and its Respiration* (London: Johnson, 1800); David Knight, *Humphry Davy: Science and Power* (New York: Cambridge University Press, 1998).

26. "Editor's Alphabetical List of Authorities Cited by Malthus," in Thomas R. Malthus, *An Essay on the Principle of Population,* ed. Patricia James (New York: Cambridge University Press, 1990), 2:332.

27. John Davy, ed., *The Collected Works of Sir Humphry Davy* (London: Smith, Elder, 1840), 187–88, 213, 244, 356.

28. Gerard Helferich, *Humboldt's Cosmos: Alexander Von Humboldt and the Latin American Journey That Changed the Way We See the World* (New York: Gotham, 2004), 258–59; Gregory Todd Cushman, "The Lords of Guano: Science and Management of of Peru's Marine Environment, 1800–1973" (Ph.D. diss.: University of Texas at Austin, 2003), 53–66.

29. G. J. Leigh, *The World's Greatest Fix: A History of Nitrogen and Agriculture* (New York: Oxford University Press, 2004), 78–79; Joseph Cummins, *History's Great Untold Stories: Obscure and Fascinating Accounts with Important Lessons for the World* (London: Pier 9, 2006), 220–29; Gilbert T. Rowe et al., "Benthic Nutrient Regeneration and Its Coupling to Primary Productivity in Coastal Waters," *Nature* 255 (1975): 215–17.

30. Daniel J. Browne, *The American Muck Book* (New York: Saxton, 1851), 280–82.

31. Ibid., 429; Charles M. Aikman, *Manures and Principles of Manuring* (London: Blackwood, 1894), 318–20.

32. Justus [von] Liebig, *Chemistry in Its Application to Agriculture and Physiology,* ed. Lyon Playfair, (Cambridge: Owen, 1842), 85–105; William H. Brock, *Justus von Liebig: The Chemical Gatekeeper* (New York: Cambridge University Press, 1997).

33. Frederick W. J. McCosh, *Boussingault: Chemist and Agriculturist* (Boston: Kluwer, 1984), 17–26; Richard P. Aulie, "Boussingault and the Nitrogen Cycle," *Proceedings of the American Philosophical Society* 114 (1970): 435–79.

34. Aulie, "Boussingault and the Nitrogen Cycle"; J. B. Boussingault, *Rural Economy, in Its Relations with Chemistry, Physics, and Meterology,* trans. George Law (London: Bailliere, 1845), 341–74.

35. Aulie, "Boussingault and the Nitrogen Cycle"; McCosh, *Boussingault,* 123–38.

36. John Bennet Lawes, *The Rothamsted Memoirs on Agricultural Chemistry and Physiology,* vol. 1, *Containing Reports of Field Experiments on Vegetation, Published 1847–1863 Inclusive* (London: Clowes, 1893); Leigh, *World's Greatest Fix,* 110–12; T. M. Addiscott, *Nitrate, Agriculture, and the Environment* (Cambridge, Mass.: CABI, 2006), 1–13.

37. Leigh, *World's Greatest Fix,* 110–16; Vaclav Smil, *Enriching the Earth: Fritz Haber, Carl Bosch, and the Transformation of World Food Production* (Cambridge, Mass.: MIT Press, 2001), 13–15; Aikman, *Manures,* 161–95.

38. Smil, *Enriching the Earth,* 16; Marika Blondel, "Agrochemistry and Bacterial Autotrophy," in *The European Origins of Scientific Ecology, 1800–1901,* ed. Pascal Acot (Amsterdam: Gordon and Breach, 1998), 309–24; Thomas D. Brock, *Milestones in Microbiology: 1546 to 1940* (Englewood Cliffs, N.J.: Prentice Hall, 1961), 231–33.

CHAPTER 6   BYPASSING AN ECOLOGICAL LIMIT

1. Joe Hicks and Grahame Allen, "A Century of Change: Trends in UK Statistics Since 1900," research paper 99/111 (London: House of Commons Library, December 21, 1999); Kenneth D. Brown, *Britain and Japan: A Comparative Economic and Social History Since 1900* (New York: Manchester University Press, 1998), 9.

2. Thomas R. Malthus, *An Essay on the Principle of Population* (1798; reprint, New York: Penguin, 1986); Ronald L. Meek, *Marx and Engels on Malthus* (London: Lawrence and Wishart, 1953); George Perkins Marsh, *Man and Nature; or, Physical Geography As Modified by Human Action* (New York: Scribner, 1865).

3. D. B. Grigg, *The Agricultural Systems of the World: An Evolutionary Approach* (New York: Cambridge University Press, 1974), 48.

4. A. B. Allen and R. L. Allen, *The American Agriculturalist* (New York: Saxton, 1850), 9:55–56, 117, 181, 202–4; *British Farmer's Magazine* (London: Rogerson and Tuxford, 1869), 57:102–3, 145, 159, 225, 374, 494; J. C. Nesbit, *On Agricultural Chemistry and the Nature and Properties of Peruvian Guano* (London: Longman, 1856); Percy Wells Bidwell and John I. Falconer, *History of Agriculture in the Northern United States, 1620–1860* (New York: Smith, 1941), 321.

5. F.M.L. Thomson, "The Second Agricultural Revolution, 1815–1880," *Economic History Review* 21 (1968): 62–77; J. L. Van Zanden, "The First Green Revolution: The Growth of Production and Productivity in European Agriculture, 1870–1914," *Economic History Review* 44 (1991): 215–39.

6. Daniel Stuart Margolies, "Guano and the State in British and American Foreign Policy, 1840–1860" (Ph.D. diss., University of Wisconsin–Madison, 1993); Joseph Cummins, *History's Great Untold Stories: Obscure and Fascinating Accounts with Important Lessons for the World* (London: Pier 9, 2006), 220–29.

7. W. M. Mathew, "Peru and the British Guano Market, 1840–1870," *Economic History Review* 23 (1970): 112–28.

8. Bruno Waeser, *The Atmospheric Nitrogen Industry,* trans. Ernest Fyleman (Philadelphia: Blakiston's Sons, 1936), xix–xx.

9. Harvey W. Wiley, *Principles and Practice of Agricultural Analysis,* vol. 2, *Fertilizers* (Easton, Pa.: Chemical Publishing Company, 1895), 168; Hoyt S. Gale, *Nitrate Deposits,* U.S. Geological Survey Bulletin 523 (Washington, D.C.: Government Printing Office, 1912); Jamie Arias, "On the Origin of Saltpeter, Northern Chile Coast" (paper delivered at the twenty-sixth INQUA Congress, Reno, Nevada, July 24–30, 2003); J. K. Böhlke, G. E. Ericksen, and K. Revesz, "Stable Isotope Evidence for an Atmospheric Origin of Desert Nitrate Deposits in Northern Chile and Southern California, U.S.A," *Chemical Geology* 136 (1997): 135–52.

10. Thomas T. Veblen, Kenneth R. Young, and A. R. Orme, *The Physical Geography of South America* (New York: Oxford University Press, 2007), 26.

11. Allin Cottrell, *The Manufacture of Nitric Acid and Nitrates* (London: Gurney and Jackson, 1923), 1–7.

12. Edward D. Melillo, "Strangers on Familiar Soil: Chile and the Making of California, 1848–1940" (Ph.D. diss., Yale University, 2006); Bruce W. Farcau, *The Ten Cents War: Chile, Peru, and Bolivia in the War of the Pacific, 1879–1884* (Westport, Conn.: Praeger, 2000); Stephen R. Bown, *A Most Damnable Invention: Dynamite, Nitrates, and the Making of the Modern World* (New York: Dunne, 2005), 160–63; Wiley, *Principles and Practice of Agricultural Analysis,* 166.

13. Cottrell, *Manufacture of Nitric Acid,* 1–7, 200; Frank A. Ernst, *The Fixation of Atmospheric Nitrogen* (New York: Van Nostrand, 1928), 5; William Mott Steuart, *Manufacturers, 1905,* part 4, *Special Report on Selected Industries* (Washington, D.C.: U.S. Bureau of the Census, 1908), 470.

14. Jules Pelouze and Edmond Fremy, *General Notions of Chemistry,* trans. Edmund C. Evans (Philadelphia: Lippincott, 1854), 323–27; John Read, *Explosives* (Harmondsworth, U.K.: Penguin, 1943), 84–88; Bown, *A Most Damnable Invention,* 51–69; Jack Kelly, *Gunpowder: Alchemy, Bombards, and Pyrotechnic: The History of the Explosive That Changed the World* (New York: Basic Books, 2004), 225–27.

15. Phokion Naoum, *Nitroglycerine and Nitroglycerine Explosives,* trans. E. M. Symmes (Las Vegas: Angriff, 1928), 1–22; Bown, *A Most Damnable Invention,* 134–41.

16. G. Carlton Smith, *TNT: Trinitrotoluenes and Mono- and Dinitrotoluenes, Their Manufacture and Properties* (New York: Van Nostrand, 1918); Norman Youngblood, *The Development of Mine Warfare: A Most Murderous and Barbarous Conduct* (Westport, Conn.: Greenwood , 2006), 76–84.

17. Sir William Crookes and Sir Robert Henry Rew, *The Wheat Problem: Based on Remarks Made in the Presidential Address to the British Association at Bristol in 1898* (New York: Longmans, Green, 1917); 6, 39; William H. Brock, *William Crookes (1832–1919) and the Commercialization of Science* (Burlington, Vt.: Ashgate, 2008).

18. W. R. Dodson, "Forage Crops for the Cotton States," in *Crop Report of the Louisiana State Board* (Baton Rouge, December 1901), 126.

19. James N. Galloway et al., "Nitrogen Cycles: Past, Present, and Future," *Biogeochemistry* 70 (2004): 153–226.

20. David Stradling, *Smokestacks and Progressives: Environmentalists, Engineers, and Air Quality in America, 1881–1951* (Baltimore: Johns Hopkins University Press, 1999); Joel Tarr, *The Search for the Ultimate Sink: Urban Pollution in Historical Perspective* (Akron, Ohio: University of Akron Press, 1996).

21. Olof Hammarsten, *A Text-Book of Physiological Chemistry* (New York: Scientific Press, 1914), 435–43; James N. Galloway et al., "The Nitrogen Cascade," *Bioscience* 53 (2003): 341–56.

22. B. Watt and A. Merill, *Composition of Foods,* Agricultural Handbook 8 (Washington, D.C.: U.S. Department of Agriculture, 1975); Aaron M. Altschul, *Proteins: Their Chemistry and Politics* (New York: Basic Books, 1965).

23. Philip J. Waller, *Town, City, and Nation: England, 1850–1914* (New York: Oxford University Press, 1983); Ann Durkin Keating, Eugene P. Moehring, and Joel Tarr, *Infrastructure and Urban Growth in the Nineteenth Century* (Chicago: Public Works Historical Society, 1985); Peter Elmer, "The Early Modern City," in *Pre-industrial Cities and Technology,* ed. Colin Chant and David Goodman (New York: Routledge, 1999), 227–95.

24. Steven Johnson, *The Ghost Map: The Story of London's Most Terrifying Epidemic—and How It Changed Science, Cities, and the Modern World* (New York: Riverhead, 2006),

1–24; R. J. Morris, *Cholera, 1832: The Social Response to an Epidemic* (New York: Holmes and Meier, 1976); Lawrence Wright, *Clean and Decent: The Fascinating History of the Bathroom and the Water Closet* (New York: Viking, 1960).

25. Peter Vinten-Johansen, *Cholera, Chloroform, and the Science of Medicine: A Life of John Snow* (New York: Oxford University Press, 2003); Johnson, *Ghost Map.*

26. John Snow, "On the Mode of Communication of Cholera" (1854), excerpted and adapted as *Snow on Cholera* (New York: Hafner, 1965); Vinten-Johansen, *Life of John Snow;* Johnson, *Ghost Map.*

27. Johnson, *Ghost Map,* 205–6.

28. Thomas D. Brock, *Robert Koch: A Life in Medicine and Bacteriology* (Washington, D.C.: ASM, 1988); Patrice Debré, *Louis Pasteur,* trans. Elborg Foster (Baltimore: Johns Hopkins University Press, 2003).

29. John M. Woodworth, *Cholera Epidemic of 1873 in the United States: The Introduction of Epidemic Cholera through the Agency of the Mercantile Marine: Suggestions of Measures of Prevention* (Washington, D.C.: Government Printing Office, 1875).

30. Martin V. Melosi, *The Sanitary City: Urban Infrastructure in America from Colonial Times to the Present* (Baltimore: Johns Hopkins University Press, 2000).

31. Johnson, *Ghost Map,* 115–16.

32. J. W. Slater, *Sewage Treatment, Purification, and Utilization* (London: Whittaker, 1888), 180.

33. Sharon Beder, "From Sewage Farms to Septic Tanks: Trials and Tribulations in Sydney," *Journal of the Royal Australian Historical Society* 79 (1993): 72–95; "The Sewers and Sewage Farms of Berlin," *Engineering News and American Railway Journal* 36 (1896): 139–41; N. T. Veatch, Jr., "The Use of Sewage Effluents in Agriculture," in *Modern Sewage Disposal,* ed. Langdon Pearse (New York: Federation of Sewer Works Associations, 1938), 180–89; Slater, *Sewage Treatment,* 43–67.

34. Leonard Metcalf and Harrison P. Eddy, *Sewerage and Sewage Disposal* (New York: McGraw-Hill, 1922), 541–50; Harold E. Babbitt, *Sewerage and Sewage Treatment* (New York: Wiley, 1922), 343; Leonard P. Kinnicutt, C.E.A. Winslow, and R. Winthrop Pratt, *Sewage Disposal* (Boston: Gilson, 1919), 204–32.

35. "Largest Cities in the World," in *The World Almanac and Encyclopedia* (New York: Press Publishing Company, 1904), 382; A. M. Carr-Saunders, *World Population: Past Growth and Present Trends* (London: Cass, 1964).

36. Slater, *Sewage Treatment,* 134–71.

37. C. M. Tidy, "The Process for Determining the Organic Purity of Potable Waters," *Journal of the Chemical Society* 35 (1879): 46–106; Gilbert J. Fowler, *Sewage Works Analyses* (New York: Wiley, 1902), 31–34; American Public Health Association, *Standard Methods for the Examination of Water and Sewage* (New York: American Public Health Association, 1920), 25–28.

38. Slater, *Sewage Treatment,* 14.

39. Ibid., 13, 159–63.

40. Mansfield Merriman, *Elements of Sanitary Engineering* (New York: Mansfield Merriman, 1918), 200–205; Kinnicutt et al., *Sewage Disposal,* 86–192; Slater, *Sewage Treatment,* 83–133.

41. Slater, *Sewage Treatment,* 126.

42. Donald Cameron, "A Year's Experience with the Septic Tank System of Sewage Disposal at Exeter," *Journal of the Sanitary Institute* 43 (1897): 563–70; Babbitt, *Sewerage and Sewage Treatment,* 417–25.

43. Kinnicutt et al., *Sewage Disposal,* 316–77; C.E.A. Winslow, "The Scientific Disposal of City Sewage: Historical Development and the Present Status of the Problem," *Technological Quarterly* 28 (1905): 317–32.

44. William Phillips Dunbar, *Principles of Sewage Treatment,* trans. H. T. Calvert (London: Griffin, 1908), 266.

45. Babbitt, *Sewerage and Sewage Treatment,* 470–71; Massachusetts Department of Public Health, *Fifth Annual Report* (Boston: Wright and Potter, 1920), 104–6; Harrison P. Eddy, "A Comparison of the Activated Sludge and Imhoff Tank-Trickling Filter Processes of Sewage Treatment," *Journal of the Western Society of Engineers* 21 (1916): 816–52.

46. E. Ardern and W. T. Lockett, "Experiments on the Oxidation of Sewage without the Aid of Filters," *Journal of the Society of Chemical Industry* 33 (1914): 523–39; Babbitt, *Sewerage and Sewage Treatment,* 465–70.

47. Gilbert Fowler, letter to T. Chalkley Hatton, November 2, 1914, record of the Sewerage Commission of the City of Milwaukee.

48. Frank P. Zeidler, "Sewer Socialism and Labor: The Pragmatics of Running a Good City," in *Labor in Cross-Cultural Perspective,* ed. E. Paul Durrenberger and Judith E. Martí (Lanham, Md.: AltaMira, 2005), 27–42; "Socialists Again Elect Milwaukee's Mayor," *Survey* 36 (1916): 69–70.

49. Melosi, *Sanitary City.*

50. Tarr, *Search for the Ultimate Sink,* 103–218.

51. Libby Hill, *The Chicago River: A Natural and Unnatural History* (Chicago: Lake Claremont, 2000).

52. "Playing Politics with Public Health?" *Public Service* 22 (1917), 156–57; Kate Foss-Mollan, *Hard Water: Politics and Water Supply in Milwaukee, 1870–1995* (West Lafayette, Ind.: Purdue University Press, 2001), 80–116.

53. G. H. Benzenberg, "The Sewerage System of the Milwaukee and the Milwaukee River Flushing Systems," *Transactions of the American Society of Civil Engineers* 30 (1893): 367–85; Zeidler, "Sewer Socialism and Labor," 27–42; Foss-Mollan, *Hard Water,* 80–116.

54. Record of the Sewerage Commission of the City of Milwaukee, May 26–September 17, 1914.

55. Louise E. Howard, *Sir Albert Howard in India* (London: Faber and Faber, 1953); Gilbert J. Fowler, *An Introduction to the Biochemistry of Nitrogen Conservation* (London: Arnold, 1934).

56. Babbitt, *Sewerage and Sewage Treatment,* 471.

57. T. Chalkley Hatton, "A Year's Progress in Activated Sludge Sewage Treatment," in *Official Proceedings of the [American Society of Municipal Improvements] Annual Convention, 1916* (Indianapolis, 1917), 404–15; *Annual Report of the Sewerage Commissioner of the City of Milwaukee, Wisconsin* (1916–26), Milwaukee Sewerage District records; George W. Fuller and James R. McClintlock, *Solving Sewage Problems* (New York: McGraw-Hill, 1926), 426–97.

58. *Annual Report of the Sewerage Commissioner of the City of Milwaukee, Wisconsin* (1930–31, Milwaukee Sewerage District records. In 1974, the Jones Island Wastewater Treatment Plant was named a National Historic Engineering Site by the American Society of Civil Engineers because of its revolutionary design.

59. Waeser, *Atmospheric Nitrogen Industry,* 10–11; Harry Curtis, ed., *Fixed Nitrogen* (New York: Chemical Catalog Company, 1932), 469; Williams Haynes, *American Chemical Industry: A History,* vol. 2, *1912–1922* (New York: Van Nostrand, 1945), 55–123.

60. Vaclav Smil, *Enriching the Earth: Fritz Haber, Carl Bosch, and the Transformation of World Food Production* (Cambridge, Mass.: MIT Press, 2001).

61. Smil, *Enriching the Earth,* 61–108; Werner Abelshauser, Wolfgang von Hippel, Jeffrey Allan Johnson, and Raymond G. Stokes, *German Industry and Global Enterprise: BASF: The History of a Company* (New York: Cambridge University Press, 2004), 151–57; Dietrich Stoltzenberg, *Fritz Haber: Chemist, Nobel Laureate, German, Jew* (Philadelphia: Chemical Heritage Press, 2005).

62. Waeser, *Atmospheric Nitrogen Industry,* 63–66.

63. Ernst, *Fixation of Atmospheric Nitrogen,* 21–52; Waeser, *Atmospheric Nitrogen Industry,* xv, 25–39.

64. Robert Barr, "Within an Ace of the End of the World, being some account of the fearful disaster which overtook the inhabitants of this earth through scientific miscalculation in the year 1904," *Windsor Magazine* 13 (1901): 17–26.

65. Samuel P. Hays, *Conservation and the Gospel of Efficiency: The Progressive Conservation Movement, 1890–1920* (Cambridge, Mass.: Harvard University Press, 1959); Leo Marx, "Does Improved Technology Mean Progress?" in *Technology and the Future,* ed. Albert H. Teich (New York: St. Martin's, 2008), 3–12; John McDermott, "Technology: The Opiate of the Intellectuals," in *Technology and Values,* ed. Kristin Schrader-Frechette and Laura Westra (Lanham, Md.: Rowman and Littlefield, 1977), 87–106.

66. Curtis, *Fixed Nitrogen,* 18.

67. Samuel P. Hays, *The Response to Industrialism, 1885–1914* (Chicago: University of Chicago Press, 1957); William Cronon, *Nature's Metropolis: Chicago and the Great West* (New York: Norton, 1991).

68. Abelshauser et al., *German Industry and Global Enterprise,* 151–59.

CHAPTER 7   INDUSTRIALIZING A BIOGEOCHEMICAL CYCLE

1. Percy Wells Bidwell and John I. Falconer, *History of Agriculture in the Northern United States, 1620–1860* (New York: Smith, 1941); John M. Gaus, Leon O. Wolcott, and Verne B. Lewis, *Public Administration and the United States Department of Agriculture* (Chicago: Social Science Research Council, Committee on Public Administration, 1940); Willard W. Cochrane, *The Development of American Agriculture: A Historical Analysis* (Minneapolis: University of Minnesota Press, 1993).

2. Mark R. Finlay, "The German Agricultural Experiment Stations and the Beginnings of American Agricultural Research," *Agricultural History* 62 (1988): 41–50; J. L. Van Zanden, "The First Green Revolution: The Growth of Production and Productivity in European Agriculture, 1870–1914," *Economic History Review* 44 (1991): 215–39; Thomas F. Hunt, "Report of the Director of the Agricultural Experiment Station," in *Report of the College of Agriculture and the Agricultural Experimental Station of the University of California* (Berkeley: University of California Press, 1914), 11–51.

3. D. F. Houston, "Report of the Secretary," in U.S. Department of Agriculture, *Yearbook of the U.S. Department of Agriculture* (Washington, D.C.: Government Printing Office, 1915), 9–64; F.M.L. Thompson, "The Second Agricultural Revolution, 1815–1880," *Economic History Review* 21 (1968): 62–77.

4. William Cronon, *Nature's Metropolis: Chicago and the Great West* (New York: Norton, 1991).

5. J. Enrique Zanetti, *The Significance of Nitrogen* (New York: Chemical Foundation, 1932), 19.

6. Statistics for corn, wheat, and oats (1866–1914), in U.S. Department of Agriculture, *Yearbook of the U.S. Department of Agriculture* (Washington, D.C.: Government Printing Office, 1914), 513, 522, 534.

7. Preston J. Hubbard, *Origins of the TVA: The Muscle Shoals Controversy, 1920–1932* (New York: Norton, 1961); Chester H. Gray, "Nitrogen at Muscle Shoals," *Annals of the American Academy of Political and Social Science* 135 (1928): 166–71.

8. Nitrate Division, Ordnance Office, War Department, assisted by the Fixed Nitrogen Research Laboratory, U.S. Department of Agriculture, *Report on the Fixation and Utilization of Nitrogen* (Washington, D.C.: Government Printing Office, 1922); Hugh J. Casey, "Muscle Shoals," *Kansas Engineer* 10 (January 1925): 5–10, 20.

9. Arthur Lamb and R. C. Tolman, "Utilization of Nitrate Plant #2," report 1, April 21, 1919, box 1, technical reports, series 205 (records of the Fixed Nitrogen Research Laboratory, 1919–1925), record group 54 (records of the Bureau of Plant Industry, Soils, and Agricultural Engineering), National Archives and Records Administration, College Park, Md., hereafter referred to as "records of the Bureau of Plant Industry, Soils, and Agricultural Engineering."

10. Report 26, December 21, 1919, box 1, technical reports, series 205 (records of the Fixed Nitrogen Research Laboratory, 1919–1925), records of the Bureau of Plant Industry, Soils, and Agricultural Engineering; F. G. Cottrell, "Fixed Nitrogen Research Laboratory," *Transactions of the American Institute of Chemical Engineers* 15 (1923): 209–20; Frank T. Cameron, *Cottrell, Samaritan of Science* (New York: Doubleday, 1952), 242–58.

11. Hubbard, *Origins of the TVA;* U.S. House of Representatives, Committee on Military Affairs, *Muscle Shoals Propositions,* 67th Cong., 2nd sess., 1922; U.S. Congress, Joint Committee on Muscle Shoals, *Leasing of Muscle Shoals,* 69th Cong., 1st sess., 1926.

12. Tennessee Valley Authority Act of 1933, 48 stat. 58–59, 16 U.S.C., sec. 831; Cameron, *Cottrell,* 242–58.

13. William H. Martin, "Public Policy and Increased Competition in the Synthetic Ammonia Industry," *Quarterly Journal of Economics* 73 (1959): 373–92.

14. Philip Selznick, *TVA and the Grass Roots: A Study in the Sociology of Formal Organizations* (Berkeley: University of California Press, 1949), 98–99; W. Dean of the Fertilizer Industry Contact Committee, letter to H. A. Morgan, director of the Tennessee Valley Authority, October 23, 1934, folder "Correspondence with H. A. Morgan," box 3, files of Dr. Harry Curtis, record group 142 (records of the Tennessee Valley Authority), National Archives and Records Administration, Atlanta, hereafter referred to as "records of the TVA"; Harry A. Curtis, "Draft," October 5, 1934, folder "Correspondence with H. A. Morgan," box 3, files of Dr. Harry Curtis, record group 142 (records of the TVA); "Fertilizer at Muscle Shoals," folder "Arthur Miller 10-1-35 to 7-31-34," box 2, files of Dr. Harry Curtis, record group 142 (records of the TVA).

15. J. L. McCormick, Jr., "Annual Narrative and Statistical Report of Extension-TVA Demonstration Program in Wise County, Virginia," box 18, files of A. C. Davis, record group 142 (records of the TVA).

16. Report, "New Wealth from Soils," folder "Key Variable Rate Eval.," box 19, files of A. C. Davis, record group 142 (records of the TVA).

17. National Agricultural Statistics Service and the Animal and Plant Health Inspection Service, "Equine 2005, Part II: Changes in the U.S. Equine Industry, 1998–2005" (Washington, D.C.: U.S. Department of Agriculture, 2007), 2–3; David B. Danbom, *The Resisted Revolution: Urban America and the Industrialization of Agriculture, 1900–1930* (Ames: Iowa State University Press, 1979).

18. Horace Bowker, "A Survey of the Farm Problem," brochure of the American Agricultural Chemical Company, July 1930, folder "1930," box 5, series 136 (Division of Soil Fertility Investigations), record group 54 (records of the Bureau of Plant Industry, Soils, and Agricultural Engineering).

19. P. Burke Jacobs, "Technological Trends and Their Social Implications," 1936, folder "38620," box 13, series 32 (general correspondence, 1935–39), record group 97 (Bureau of Agriculture and Industrial Chemistry), National Archives and Record Administration, College Park, Md.

20. George A. Schweppe, "Nitrate Plant No. 2 in the National Defense Activities for the Chemical Warfare Service—World War II," Tennessee Valley Authority, Department of Chemical Engineering, 1945, report 151, box 4, Office of Agricultural and Chemical Development, record group 124 (records of the TVA).

21. Martin, "Synthetic Ammonia Industry," 379; Vaclav Smil, *Enriching the Earth: Fritz Haber, Carl Bosch, and the Transformation of World Food Production* (Cambridge, Mass.: MIT Press, 2002), 245.

22. Hugh W. Stephens, *The Texas City Disaster* (Austin: University of Texas Press, 1997).

23. Ibid., 3–50.

24. William Vogt, *Road to Survival: A Discussion of Food in Relation to the Problem of Growing Population* (New York: Sloane Associates, 1948).

25. Kokusai Shokuryō Nōgyō Kyōka, *Agriculture in Japan* (Tokyo: Japan FAO Association, 1958), 25; Mirko Lamer, *The World Fertilizer Economy* (Stanford, Calif.: Stanford University Press, 1957), 91–98.

26. "Five Years' Experience in Variable Fertilizer Rate Test Demonstration Farms in Kentucky," folder "Key Variable Rate Eval.," box 19, files of A. C. Davis, record group 142 (records of the TVA); "Annual Narrative and Statistical Report of Extension–TVA Demonstration Report in Wise County, Virginia, December 1950–December 1951," folder "Wise County, Virginia," box 18, files of A. C. Davis, record group 142 (records of the TVA).

27. L. B. Nelson and B. B. Ibach, "The Economics of Fertilizers," in U.S. Department of Agriculture, *Soil: The 1957 Yearbook of Agriculture* (Washington, D.C.: Government Printing Office, 1957), 267–76; Smil, *Enriching the Earth,* 245; Martin, "Synthetic Ammonia Industry," 384; James O. Bray and Patricia Watkins, "Technical Change in Corn Production in the United States, 1870–1960," *Journal of Farm Economics* 46 (1964): 751–65.

28. John H. Perkins, *Geopolitics and the Green Revolution: Wheat, Genes, and the Cold War* (New York: Oxford University Press, 1997).

29. J. L Anderson, *Industrializing the Corn Belt: Agriculture, Technology, and Environment, 1945–1972* (Dekalb: Northern Illinois University Press, 2009), 51–67; Orvin J. Scoville, Lewis B. Nelson, and Elco L. Greenshields, "Land and Advances in Technology" in U.S. Department of Agriculture, *Land: The 1958 Yearbook of Agriculture* (Washington, D.C.: Government Printing Office, 1958), 474–502.

30. Rachel Carson, *Silent Spring* (Boston: Houghton Mifflin, 1962), 17; Sam B. Hilliard, "The Dynamics of Power: Recent Trends in Mechanization on the American Farm," *Technology and Culture* 13 (1972): 1–24.

31. Basil Ashton et al., "Famine in China, 1958–61," *Population and Development Review* 10 (1984): 613–45.

32. Raymond B. Fosdick, *The Story of the Rockefeller Foundation* (New York: Harper, 1952), 184–86.

33. Henry A. Wallace, "The Engineering-Scientific Approach" (paper delivered before the American Association for the Advancement of Science, Boston, December 29, 1933).

34. Fosdick, *Story of the Rockefeller Foundation,* 184–86; "Chronology of the Development of CIMMYT," October 20, 1978, folder "Mexican Program, 1941–66," box 34, Norman Borlaug papers, University Archive, University of Minnesota, hereafter referred to as "Borlaug papers"; John H. Perkins, "The Rockefeller Foundation and the Green Revolution, 1941–1956," *Agriculture and Human Values* 7 (1990): 6–18.

35. Vernon W. Ruttan and Yujiro Hayami, "Technology Transfer and Agricultural Development," *Technology and Culture* 14 (1973): 119–51; Perkins, *Geopolitics and the Green Revolution,* 101.

36. Food and Agriculture Organization, http://faostat.fao.org; Perkins, *Geopolitics and the Green Revolution,* 223–25; Ruttan and Hayami, "Technology Transfer and Agricultural Development," 119–52; Vernon W. Ruttan, "Research Institutions: Organizations," in *Institutions in Agricultural Development,* ed. Melvin G. Blase (Ames: Iowa State University Press, 1971), 131–38. Complicating the narrative of the Rockefeller Foundation in Mexico, especially in regards to corn production, is Karin Matchett, "At Odds over Inbreeding: An Abandoned Attempt at Mexico/United States Collaboration to 'Improve' Mexican Corn, 1940–1950," *Journal of the History of Biology* 39 (2006): 345–72, which argues that, in the area of corn production, the foundation had advocated for the use of open-pollinated corn, which would have allowed small farmers to save seeds.

37. J. G. Harrar, letter to Norman E. Borlaug, November 19, 1954, folder "Correspondence 1954, 1969–01"; Norman E. Borlaug, letter to William I. Myers, July 12, 1966, folder "Correspondence 1964–66"; Robert D. Havener, letter to Norman E. Borlaug, September 23, 1967, folder "Correspondence 1967"; Norman E. Borlaug, letter to Robert Havener, October 20, 1967, folder "Correspondence 1967"; Norman Borlaug, letter to Paul Clark, September 2, 1970, folder "Correspondence 1970." All can be found in box 3, Borlaug papers.

38. Norman E. Borlaug, letter to Dr. A. H. Moseman, July 15, 1963, folder "Correspondence Jan Jun 1963"; Norman E. Borlaug, letter to Frank W. Parker, February 12, 1963, folder "Correspondence Jan Jun 1963"; Norman E. Borlaug, letter to William I. Myers, July 12, 1966, folder "Correspondence 1964–66. All can be found in box 3, Borlaug papers. Also see Raymond Ewell, "Estimates of Fertilizer Production/Consumption in 1980 and 1985" (paper presented at the Ninth National Fertilizer Seminar, New Delhi, India, December 14–15, 1973), folder "Ewell, Estimates," box 37, Borlaug papers.

39. Raymond Ewell, letter to Norman Borlaug, March 13, 1973, folder "Correspondence, Jan–Apr 1973," box 4, Borlaug papers; Ewell, "Estimates of Fertilizer Production/ Consumption"; Raymond Ewell, "Fertilizer—The Limiting Factor in the Success or Failure of the Green Revolution" (paper presented to the Pontifical Academy of Sciences, Vatican City, April 1972), folder "Ewell, Estimates," box 37, Borlaug papers.

40. "Estimated World Fertilizer Production Capacity As Related to Future Needs," 1970, box 1, Agricultural and Chemical Division Publications, Y Series, record group 142 (records of the TVA); Tennessee Valley Authority, "A Fertilizer Program for Bolivia," 1970, box 1, Agricultural and Chemical Division Publications, Y Series, record group 142 (records of the TVA); E. A. Harre and J. R. Douglas, "World Crop Needs for Nitrogen Fertilizers—Will the Supply Be Adequate?" in *Proceedings of the First International Symposium on Nitrogen Fixation,* ed. W. Newton and C. J. Nyman (Pullman: Washington University Press, 1975), 2:674–92; "Brief History," http:// www.ifdc.org/About/History.

41. The term *green revolution* has been attributed to William Gaud, director of the U.S. Agency of International Development, in his speech "The Green Revolution: Accomplishments and Apprehensions" (presented to the Society for International Development, March 8, 1968). For examples of fertilizer and equipment manufacturers' interest in Borlaug's work, see Frank W. Parker, letter to Norman Borlaug, January 16, 1963, folder "Correspondence Jan–Jun 1963," box 3, Borlaug papers; Norman Borlaug, letter to Robert Havener, October 20, 1967, folder "Correspondence 1967," box 3, Borlaug papers.

42. John H. Perkins, "The Rockefeller Foundation and the Green Revolution, 1941–1956," *Agriculture and Human Values* 7 (June 1990): 6–18; U.S. House of Representatives, Subcommittee on National Security Policy and Scientific Developments, *The Green Revolution: Symposium on Science and Foreign Policy,* 91st Cong., 2nd sess., 1969.

43. Correspondence of Joseph H. Willits, folder "35, Sauer Carl O., 1943–54," record group 2A39 (Joseph H. Willits papers), Rockefeller Related Special Collection, Rockefeller Foundation Archives, Sleepy Hollow, N.Y.; J. Nicholas Entrikin, "Carl O. Sauer, Philosopher in Spite of Himself," *Geographical Review* 74 (1984): 387–408.

44. Keith Griffin, *The Political Economy of Agrarian Change: An Essay on the Green Revolution* (New York: Macmillan, 1974); E. F. Schumacher, *Small Is Beautiful: Economics As If People Mattered* (New York: Perennial, 1973); Billie R. DeWalt, "Appropriate Technology in Rural Mexico: Antecedents and Consequences of an Indigenous Peasant Innovation," *Technology and Culture* 19 (1978): 32–52; Perkins, *Geopolitics and the Green Revolution,* 114.

45. Vogt, *Road to Survival;* Paul Ehrlich, *The Population Bomb* (New York: Ballantine, 1968).

46. Norman Borlaug, letter to William Paddock, September 7, 1970, folder "Correspondence, April–Dec. 1970," box 3, Borlaug papers.

47. Smil, *Enriching the Earth,* 155–56; James N. Galloway et al., "Nitrogen Cycles: Past, Present, and Future," *Biogeochemistry* 70 (2004): 153–226.

CHAPTER 8   N IN THE WELL

1. R. L. Cook and Walter C. Hulbert, "Applying Fertilizers," in U.S. Department of Agriculture, *Soil: 1957 Yearbook of Agriculture* (Washington, D.C.: Government Printing Office, 1957), 216–28.

2. Robert Rodale, "Who Pays for Agricultural Research?" *Organic Gardening and Farming* 1 (1954): 16–20.

3. Graham Walton, "Survey of Literature Relating to Infant Methemoglobinemia Due to Nitrate-Contaminated Water," *American Journal of Public Health* 41 (1951): 986–95.

4. Sir Albert Howard, *An Agricultural Testament* (New York: Oxford University Press, 1940).

5. F. E. Allison, "The Enigma of Soil Nitrogen Balance Sheets," *Advances in Agronomy* 7 (1955): 213–50.

6. Eugene D. Crittenden, "Research and Development Problems," in National Academy of Sciences, *Proceedings of the Seventh Annual Meeting of the Agricultural Research Institute, Oct. 13–14, 1958,* pub. 644 (Washington, D.C.: National Academy of Sciences/National Research Council, 1958), 46–51.

7. Ibid.

8. Vethaiya Balasubramanian et al., "Crop, Environmental, and Management Factors Affecting Nitrogen Use Efficiency," in *Agriculture and the Nitrogen Cycle: Assessing the Impacts of Fertilizer Use on Food Production and the Environment,* ed. Arvin R. Mosier, J. Keith Syers, and John R. Freney (Washington, D.C.: Island, 2004), 19–34.

9. T. M. Addiscott, *Nitrate, Agriculture, and the Environment* (Cambridge, Mass.: CABI, 2005), 62–92; L. B. Nelson and R. E. Uhland, "Factors That Influence Loss of Fall Applied Fertilizers and Their Probable Importance in Different Parts of the United States," *Soil Science Society of America Proceeding* 19 (1955): 492–96; R. D. Meyer, R. A. Olson, and H. F. Rhoades, "Ammonia Losses from Fertilized Nebraska Soils," *Agronomy Journal* 53 (1961): 241–44; "Conclusions," in Food and Agricultural Organization of the United Nations, *Effects of Intensive Fertilizer Use on the Human Environment* (Rome: Swedish International Development Authority, 1972), 11.

10. D. W. Rindt, G. M. Blouin, and J. G. Getsinger, "Sulfur Coating on Nitrogen Fertilizer to Reduce Dissolution Rate," *Journal of Agricultural Food Chemistry* 16 (1968): 773–78; Committee on the Economics of Fertilizer Use, *Status and Methods of Research in Economic and Agronomic Aspects of Fertilizer Response and Use,* pub. 918 (Washington, D.C.: National Academy of Sciences/National Research Council, 1961); R. F. Hutton, *An Appraisal of Research on the Economics of Fertilizer Use,* report T 55–1 (Knoxville: Tennessee Valley Authority, 1955).

11. W. B. Davidson, J. L. Doughty, and J. L. Boughton, "Nitrate Poisoning of Livestock," *Canadian Journal of Comparative Medicine and Veterinary Science* 5 (1941): 303–13; W. B. Bradley, H. F. Eppson, and O. A. Beath, *Livestock Poisoning by Oat, Hay, and Other Plants Containing Nitrate,* bulletin 241 (Laramie: Wyoming Agricultural Experimental Station, 1940).

12. Ralph Hoagland, "Coloring Matter of Raw and Cooked Salted Meats," *Journal of Agricultural Research* 43 (1914): 211–26.

13. William Rutherford, Arthur Gamgee, and Thomas Fraser, "Report on the Progress of Physiology," *Journal of Anatomy and Physiology* 2 (1868): 177–93.

14. John Haldane, R. H. Makgill, and A. E. Mavrogordato, "The Action As Poisons of Nitrites and Other Physiologically Related Substances," *Journal of Physiology* 21 (1897): 160–89.

15. Donald D. Van Slyke and Erik Vollmund, "Studies of Methemoglobin Formation," *Journal of Biological Chemistry* 66 (1925): 415–24; C. E. Zobell, "Factors Influencing

the Reduction of Nitrates and Nitrites by Bacteria in Semisolid Media," *Journal of Bacteriology* 24 (1932): 273-81; Alexis F. Hartmann, Anne M. Perley, and Henry L. Barnett, "A Study of Some of the Physiological Effects of Sulfanilamide: II. Methemoglobin Formation and Its Control," *Journal of Clinical Investigation* 17 (1938): 699-710; William B. Wendel, "The Control of Methemoglobinemia with Methylene Blue," *Journal of Clinical Investigation* 18 (1939): 179-85.

16. Bradley et al., *Livestock Poisoning.*

17. A. S. Schwartz, "Methemoglobinemia of Unknown Origin in a Two-Week-Old Infant," *American Journal of Diseases of Children* 60 (1940): 652-59.

18. Hunter H. Comly, "Cyanosis in Infants Caused by Nitrates in Well Water," *Journal of the American Medical Association* 129 (1945): 112-16. Comly gives concentrations in units of nitrate nitrogen: 10 to 20 milligrams per liter of nitrate nitrogen equal a nitrate concentration of 45 to 90 milligrams per liter.

19. Dwight F. Metzler and Howard A. Stoltenberg., "The Public Health Significance of High Nitrate Waters As a Cause of Infant Cyanosis and Methods of Control," *Transactions of the Kansas Academy of Science* 53 (1950): 194-211; H. E. Robertson and W. A. Riddell, "Cyanosis of Infants Produced by High Nitrate Concentration in Rural Waters of Saskatchewan," *Canadian Journal of Public Health* 40 (1949): 72-77.

20. Walton, "Survey of Literature," 986-95.

21. World Health Organization, *International Standards for Drinking Water* (Geneva: World Health Organization, 1958), 28; U.S. Public Health Service, *Drinking Water Standards* (Washington, D.C.: U.S. Department of Health, Education, and Welfare, 1962).

22. For arguments that the nitrate standard is overly cautious, see David S. Powlson et al., "When Does Nitrate Become a Risk for Humans?" *Journal of Environmental Quality* 37 (2008): 291-95; J. L'hirondel and J. L. L'hirondel, *Nitrate and Man: Toxic, Harmless, or Beneficial* (New York: CABI, 2002); Addiscott, *Nitrate, Agriculture and the Environment;* Michael J. Hill, "Nitrate Toxicity: Myth or Reality," *British Journal of Nutrition* 81 (1999): 343-44.

23. Walton, "Survey of Literature."

24. Metzler and Stoltenberg, "Public Health Significance," 194-211.

25. Frederick R. Troeh and Louis M. Thompson, *Soils and Soil Fertility* (New York: Blackwell, 2005), 189; U.S. Department of Agriculture, Economic Research Service, "Table 1: U.S. Consumption of Nitrogen, Phosphate, and Potash, 1960-2009," http://www.ers.usda.gov/Data/FertilizerUse/; Vaclav Smil, *Enriching the Earth: Fritz Haber, Carl Bosch, and the Transformation of World Food Production* (Cambridge, Mass.: MIT Press, 2001), 245.

26. Adam W. Rome, *The Bulldozer in the Countryside: Suburban Sprawl and the Rise of American Environmentalism* (New York: Cambridge University Press, 2001).

27. "Dedication of Purpose" [speech], April 8, 1960, box 13, manuscript no. 254, Scott Company, Special Collections, Michigan State University.

28. "The 1966 Lawn Book," box 5, manuscript no. 254, Scott Company, Special Collections, Michigan State University.

29. Kristoffer Whitney, "Living Lawns, Dying Waters: The Suburban Boom, Nitrogenous Fertilizers, and the Nonpoint Source Pollution Dilemma," *Technology and Culture* 51 (2010): 652-74; Larry W. Canter and Robert C. Knox, *Septic Tank System Effects on Ground Water Quality* (Chelsea, Mich.: Lewis, 1985), 77-81.

30. Smil, *Enriching the Earth,* 157, 186; J. J. Meisinger, F. J. Calderón, and D. S. Jenkinson, "Soil Nitrogen Budgets," in *Nitrogen in Agricultural Systems,* ed. J. S. Schepers and W. R. Raun (Madison, Wisc.: American Society of Agronomy, 2008), 505–62; Committee on Nitrate Accumulation, *Accumulation of Nitrate* (Washington, D.C.: National Academy of Sciences, 1972), 6–10, 30–37; James M. McDonald et al., *Consolidation in U.S. Meatpacking,* Agricultural Economic Report 785 (Washington, D.C.: U.S. Dept. of Agriculture, 2000); Michael Pollan, *The Omnivore's Dilemma: A Natural History of Four Meals* (New York: Penguin, 2006).

31. Vaclav Smil, "Eating Meat: Evolution, Patterns, and Consequences," *Population and Development Review* 28 (2002): 599–639.

32. Rachel Carson, *Silent Spring* (Boston: Houghton-Mifflin, 1962).

33. Eugene P. Odum, *Fundamentals of Ecology* (Philadelphia: Saunders, 1953); Peter J. Taylor, "Technocratic Optimism, H. T. Odum, and the Partial Transformation of Ecological Metaphor after World War II," *Journal of the History of Biology* 21 (1988): 213–44; Karin E. Limburg, "The Biogeochemistry of Strontium: A Review of H. T. Odum's Contributions," *Ecological Modelling* 178 (2004): 31–33.

34. Vladimir I. Vernadsky, *The Biosphere,* trans. David B. Langmuir, revised and annotated by Mark A. S. McMenamin (New York: Copernicus, 1998); Joel B. Hagen, *An Entangled Bank: The Origins of Ecosystem Ecology* (New Brunswick, N.J.: Rutgers University Press, 1992), 50–77.

35. G. Evelyn Hutchinson, *A Treatise on Limnology,* vol. 1, *Geography, Physics and Chemistry* (New York: Wiley, 1957); G. Evelyn Hutchinson, *A Treatise on Limnology,* vol. 2, *Introduction to Lake Biology and the Limnoplankton* (New York: Wiley, 1967).

36. Planning Committee on Eutrophication, *Report of the Planning Committee on Eutrophication* (Washington, D.C.: National Academy of Sciences/National Research Council, 1965), 1.

37. National Academy of Sciences, *Eutrophication: Causes, Consequences, Correctives* (Washington, D.C.: National Academy of Sciences, 1969); Chris Knud-Hansen, "Historical Perspective of the Phosphate Detergent Conflict," working paper 94–54 (Boulder, Colo. Conflict Research Consortium, February 1994).

38. Barry Commoner, "Threats to the Integrity of the Nitrogen Cycle: Nitrogen Compounds in Soil, Water, Atmosphere, and Precipitation" (paper presented at the annual conference of the American Association for the Advancement of Science, Dallas, December 1968); Barry Commoner, *The Closing Circle* (New York: Knopf, 1971).

39. C. C. Delwiche, "The Nitrogen Cycle," *Scientific American* 223 (1970): 137–46; G. E. Hutchinson, "The Biochemistry of the Terrestrial Atmosphere," in *The Solar System,* vol. 3. *The Earth As a Planet,* ed. G. P. Kuiper (Chicago: University of Chicago Press, 1954), 371–433.

40. Delwiche, "Nitrogen Cycle," 146.

41. K. E. Boulding, "The Economics of the Coming Spaceship Earth," in *Environmental Quality in a Growing Economy,* ed. H. Jarrett (Baltimore: Johns Hopkins University Press, 1966), 3–14.

42. George E. Smith, "The Nitrogen Panic Button—What Are the Facts?" (paper presented to the Michigan Fertilizer Conference, December 4, 1970), folder "Fertilizer, Nitrates, 1969–1970s," box 37, Borlaug papers.

43. Norman Borlaug, letter to William Paddock, September 7, 1970, folder "1970, Correspondence, April–Dec. 1970," box 3, Borlaug papers.

44. Sir Albert Howard, *An Agricultural Testament* (New York: Oxford University Press, 1940); Philip Conford, *The Origins of the Organic Movement* (Edinburgh: Foris, 2001).

45. Sir Albert Howard and Yeshwant D. Wad, *The Waste Products of Agriculture: Their Utilization As Humus* (New York: Oxford University Press, 1931).

46. Howard, *Agricultural Testament*, 22, 41.

47. Louise E. Howard, *Sir Albert Howard in India* (London: Faber and Faber, 1953); Howard, *Waste Products of Agriculture*, 54, 123, 145.

48. Gilbert J. Fowler, *An Introduction to the Biochemistry of Nitrogen Conservation* (London: Arnold, 1934), 3, 1–9, 244.

49. Lady Eve Balfour, *The Living Soil* (London: Faber and Faber, 1943); Lady Eve Balfour, "Towards a Sustainable Agriculture—The Living Soil" (speech to the conference of the International Federation of Organic Agriculture Movements, Sissach, Switzerland, October 1977). On the perception of symbiotic relations as a counterpoint to competition, see Mark R. Finlay, "The Nitrogen Crisis and Its Miraculous Solution: The Legume Inoculation Industry in the United States" (paper presented to the American Society for Environmental History, Tallahassee, Florida, February 25–March 1, 2009).

50. Sir Albert Howard, *The Soil and Health: A Study of Organic Agriculture* (Lexington: University Press of Kentucky, 2006), xxvii.

51. Rodale, "Who Pays for Agricultural Research?" 16–20.

52. Committee on Nitrate Accumulation, *Accumulation of Nitrate*, 6–10, 30–37.

53. Ibid., 53.

54. Ibid., 91.

CHAPTER 9   N IN THE AIR

1. U.S. Environmental Protection Agency, *Air Quality Criteria for Nitrogen Oxides*, Air Pollution Control Office Pub. AP-84 (Washington, D.C.: Government Printing Office, 1971), 2.1–3.4; Elmer Robinson and Robert C. Robbins, "Gaseous Nitrogen Compounds from Urban and Natural Sources," *Journal of the Air Pollution Control Association* 20 (1970): 303–6.

2. Alexander E. Farrell, "Learning to See the Invisible: Discovery and Measurement of Ozone," *Environmental Monitoring and Assessment* 106 (2005): 59–80.

3. D. B. Brace, ed., *The Laws of Radiation and Absorption: Memoirs by Prévost, Steward, Kirchhoff, and Kirchhoff and Bunsen* (New York: American Book Company, 1901); Florian Cajori, *A History of Physics in Its Elementary Branches: Including the Evolution of Physical Laboratories* (London: Macmillan, 1899), 140–88; John C. D. Brand, *Lines of Light: The Sources of Dispersive Spectroscopy, 1800–1930* (Amsterdam: Gordon and Breach, 1995).

4. John Tyndall, *New Fragments* (London: Longmans, Green, 1892), 169–93; Cajori, *History of Physics*, 189–214; Spencer R. Weart, *The Discovery of Global Warming* (Cambridge, Mass.: Harvard University Press, 2003), 1–19.

5. E.C.C. Baly, *Spectroscopy* (London: Longmans, Green, 1905); Heinrich Schellen, *Spectrum Analysis in Its Application to Terrestrial Substances* (New York: Appleton, 1872); Ferenc Szabadváry, *History of Analytical Chemistry*, trans. Gyula Svehla (Langhorn, Pa.: Gordon and Breach, 1992), 318–74.

6. Hermann Vogel, *The Chemistry of Light and Photography* (New York: Appleton, 1889), 66; Thomas Preston, *The Theory of Light* (London: Macmillan, 1901), 481.

7. Carleton Ellis and Alfred Wells, *The Chemical Action of Ultraviolet Rays* (New York: Chemical Catalog Company, 1925); George B. Kistiakowsky, *Photochemical Processes* (New York: American Chemical Society, 1928); R. O. Griffith and A. McKeown, *Photo-Processes in Gaseous and Liquid Systems* (New York: Longmans, Green, 1929); William A. Noyes, Jr., and Philip A. Leighton, *The Photochemistry of Gases* (New York: Reinhold, 1941); Armin Hermann, *The Genesis of the Quantum Theory, 1899–1913* (Cambridge, Mass.: MIT Press, 1971); D.W.G. Style, *Photochemistry* (New York: Dutton, 1930), 23; Philip A. Leighton, *Photochemistry of Air Pollution* (New York: Academic Press, 1961), 3.

8. Noyes and Leighton, *Photochemistry of Gases,* 327–414.

9. Carleton Ellis, Alfred Wells, and Francis F. Heyroth, *The Chemical Action of Ultraviolet Rays,* rev. ed. (New York: Reinhold, 1941), 633–35; Frank P. Greenspan and Paul E. Spoerri "A Study of Gas Fading of Acetate Dyes," *American Dyestuff Reporter* 30 (1941): 645–50; F. M. Rowe and K.A.J. Chamberlain, "The Fading of Dyeings on Cellulose Acetate Rayon," *Journal of the Society of Dyers and Colourists* 53 (1937): 268–378.

10. V. J. Altieri, *Gas Analysis and Testing of Gaseous Materials* (New York: American Gas Association, 1945), 227–39; V. S. Salvin, W. D. Paist, and W. J. Myles, "Advances in Theoretical and Practical Studies of Gas Fading," *American Dyestuff Reporter 41* (1952): 297–302.

11. David Stradling, *Smokestacks and Progressives: Environmentalists, Engineers, and Air Quality in America, 1881–1951* (Baltimore: Johns Hopkins University Press, 1999); Frank Uekoetter, "The Strange Career of the Ringelmann Smoke Chart," *Environmental Monitoring and Assessment* 106 (2005): 11–26.

12. C. Donald Ahrens, *Meteorology Today: An Introduction to Weather, Climate, and the Environment* (Belmont, Calif: Thompson Brooks/Cole, 2006), 4.

13. National Research Council, Committee on the Medical and Biological Effects of Environmental Pollution, *Nitrogen Oxides* (Washington, D.C.: National Academy of Sciences, 1977), 242–50.

14. Marvin Brienes, "The Fight against Smog in Los Angeles, 1943–1957" (Ph.D. diss., University of California, Davis, 1975); Scott Hamilton Dewey, *Don't Breathe the Air: Air Pollution and U.S. Environmental Politics, 1945–1970* (College Station: Texas A&M University Press, 2000); California Air Resources Board, *Clearing California Skies* [video], http://www.arb.ca.gov/videos/clskies.htm.

15. Joshua Dunsby, "Localizing Smog: Transgressions in the Therapeutic Landscape," in *Smoke and Mirrors: The Politics and Culture of Air Pollution,* ed. E. Melanie DuPuis (New York: New York University Press, 2004), 170–200; Dewey, *Don't Breathe the Air,* 34–56; James E. Krier and Edmund Ursin, *Pollution and Policy: A Case Essay on California and Federal Experience with Motor Vehicle Air Pollution, 1940–1975* (Berkeley: University of California Press, 1977), 52–61.

16. A. J. Haagen-Smit, "Air Conservation," *Science* 128 (1958): 869–78.

17. Krier and Ursin, *Pollution and Policy,* 75; Farrell, "Learning to See the Invisible," 59–80.

18. A. J. Haagen-Smit, "Chemistry and Physiology of Los Angeles Smog," *Industrial and Engineering Chemistry* 44 (1952): 1342–46; F. E. Blacet, "Photochemistry in the

Lower Atmosphere," *Industrial Engineering Chemistry* 44 (1952): 1339–42; Stanford Research Institute, *The Smog Problem in Los Angeles County: Report on the First Twelve Months of Research* (Los Angeles: Western Oil and Gas Association, 1948); Stanford Research Institute, *The Smog Problem in Los Angeles County: Second Interim Report on Studies to Determine the Nature and Sources of the Smog* (Los Angeles: Western Oil and Gas Association, 1949); Stanford Research Institute, *The Smog Problem in Los Angeles County: A Report on Studies to Determine the Nature and Causes of Smog* (Los Angeles: Western Oil and Gas Association, 1954).

19. A. J. Haagen-Smit, C. E. Bradley, and M. M. Fox, "Ozone Formation in Photochemical Oxidation of Organic Substances," *Industrial and Engineering Chemistry* 45 (1953): 2086–89; Harold S. Johnson, "Photochemical Oxidation of Hydrocarbons," *Industrial and Engineering Chemistry* 48 (1956): 1489–91.

20. F. E. Littman, H. W. Ford, and N. Endow, "Formation of Ozone in the Los Angeles Atmosphere," *Industrial and Engineering Chemistry* 48 (1956): 1492–97.

21. Dunsby, "Localizing Smog," 170–200.

22. California State Chamber of Commerce, *Proceedings of the Southern California Conference on Elimination of Air Pollution: What Has Been Done, What Is Now Being Done, What Will Be Done to Eliminate Air Pollution, November 10, 1955* (Los Angeles: California State Chamber of Commerce, 1955).

23. Leslie A. Chambers, "What Has Been Done, Is Now Being Done, Will Be Done about Smog in Southern California: The Role of the Federal Government," in *Proceedings of the Southern California Conference*, 39–44.

24. S. Smith Griswold, "The Smog Problem in Los Angeles County," in *Proceedings of the Southern California Conference*, 2–25.

25. Lester Breslow, "The California State Government . . . Health Effects of Air Pollution," in *Proceedings of the Southern California Conference*, 26–32; Lynn Page Snyder, "Revisiting Donora, Pennsylvania's 1948 Air Pollution Disaster," in *Devastation and Renewal: An Environmental History of Pittsburgh and Its Region,* ed. Joel A. Tarr (Pittsburgh: University of Pittsburgh, 2005), 126–144; William Wise, *Killer Smog: The World's Worst Air Pollution Disaster* (Chicago: Rand McNally, 1968).

26. *Proceedings of the Southern California Conference,* 45–63, 103, 122–30.

27. Ibid., 61–63, 83–95, 112–14.

28. Ibid, 102–4; John L. Mills et al., "A Preliminary Report on Available Data on Emissions of Nitrogen Oxides from Stationary Sources," pp. 7–8, Air Pollution Control District, April 8, 1959, box 3 (Air Pollution Engineering Board correspondence), series 36, record group 90 (records of the U.S. Public Health Service), National Archives and Records Administration, College Park, Md., hereafter cited as "records of the U.S. Public Health Service"; D. H. Barnhart and E. K. Diehl, "Control of Nitrogen Oxides in Boiler Flue Gases by Two-Stage Combustion," *Journal of the Air Pollution Control Association* 10 (1960): 397–406; Harold M. Smith, "Composition of United States Crude Oils," *Industrial and Engineering Chemistry* 44 (1952): 2577–85.

29. Lee A. Dubridge, "Summation of Conference," in *Proceedings of the Southern California Conference,* 130–44; Wolfgang Saxon, "Lee Alvin DuBridge, 92, Ex-President of Caltech," *New York Times,* January 25, 1994.

30. U.S. Public Health Service, "National Conference on Air Pollution, November 20, 1958: Report and Recommendation of Discussion Groups," *Journal of the Air*

Pollution Control Association 9 (1959): 44–50; James Longhurst, "1 to 100: Creating an Air Quality Index in Pittsburgh," *Environmental Monitoring and Assessment* 106 (2005): 27–42.

31. Hugh S. Gorman, *Redefining Efficiency: Pollution Concerns, Regulatory Mechanisms, and Technological Change in the U.S. Petroleum Industry* (Akron, Ohio: University of Akron Press, 2001), 215–46.

32. Coordination of research by U.S. Public Health Service reflected in series 11 ("Division of Air Pollution Control, Correspondence 1965–1966"), record group 90 (records of the Public Health Service); Arthur C. Stern, letter to Jerome Wilkenfeld, March 6, 1959, and attachment, folder "Research studies," box 3 (Air Pollution Engineering Board correspondence), series 36, record group 90 (records of the U.S. Public Health Service).

33. "Pittsburgh Conference on Analytical Chemistry," *Journal of Air Pollution Control Association* 25 (1953): 358–61; Anthony S. Travis, "Instrumentation in Environmental Analysis, 1935–1975," in *From Classical to Modern Chemistry: The Instrumental Revolution,* ed. Peter J. T. Morris, 285–308 (Cambridge: Royal Society of Chemistry, 2002).

34. Edgar R. Stephens et al., "Reactions of Nitrogen Oxide and Organic Compounds in Air," *Industrial and Engineering Chemistry* 48 (1956): 1498–1504.

35. Lewis H. Rogers, Nicholas A. Renzetti, and Morris Nieburger, "Smog Effects and the Chemical Analysis of the Los Angeles Atmosphere," *Journal of the Air Pollution Control Association* 6 (1956): 165–70.

36. U.S. Public Health Service, "National Conference on Air Pollution," 44–50; August T. Rossano, Jr., "The Joint City, County, State, and Federal Study of Air Pollution in Louisville," *Journal of the Air Pollution Control Association* 6 (1956): 176–79; Charles E. Zimmer and George A. Jutze, "An Evaluation of Continuous Air Quality Data," *Journal of the Air Pollution Control Association* 14 (1962): 262–66.

37. M. D. Thomas et al., "Automatic Apparatus for Determining of Nitric Oxide and Nitrogen Dioxide in the Atmosphere," *Analytical Chemistry* 28 (1956): 1810–19; G. E. Moore and Morris Katz, "The Concurrent Determination of Sulfur Dioxide and Nitrogen Dioxide in the Atmosphere," *Journal of the Air Pollution Control Association* 7 (1957): 25–28.

38. U.S. Public Health Service, Division of Air Pollution, *Air Pollution Measurements of the National Air Sampling Network,* (Washington, D.C.: U.S. Department of Health, Education, and Welfare, 1958).

39. Thad Godish, *Air Quality* (Boca Raton, Fla.: CRC, 2004), 283–84.

40. Arnold W. Reitze, Jr., *Stationary Source Air Pollution Law* (Washington, D.C.: Environmental Law Institute, 2005), 8–10; U.S. Environmental Protection Agency, *Air Quality Criteria.*

41. U.S. Environmental Protection Agency, *Air Quality Criteria,* 6.1–33.

42. Ibid., 6.32–38.

43. Ibid., 5.1–8, 6.36–37.

44. G. B. Morgan, "New and Improved Procedures for Gas Sampling and Analysis in the National Air Sampling Network," *Journal of the Air Pollution Control Association* 17 (1967): 300–334; U.S. Environmental Protection Agency, *Air Quality Criteria,* 5.1–8, 6.36–37.

45. U.S. Environmental Protection Agency, *Air Quality Criteria,* 8.1–12, 9.1–14.

46. Ibid., 9.14–32.

47. Carl M. Shy et al., "The Chattanooga Schoolchildren Study: I. Methods, Description of Pollutant Exposure and Results of Ventilatory Functions Testing," *Journal of the Air Pollution Control Association* 20 (1970): 539–45; Carl M. Shy et al., "The Chattanooga Schoolchildren Study: II. Incidence of Acute Respiratory Illness," *Journal of the Air Pollution Control Association* 20 (1970): 582–88; U.S. Environmental Protection Agency, *Air Quality Criteria*, 10.1–9.

48. U.S. Environmental Protection Agency, *Air Quality Criteria*, 11.1–13; J. M. Heuss, G. J. Nebel, and J. M. Colucci, "National Air Quality Standards for Automotive Pollutants: A Critical Review," *Journal of the Air Pollution Control Association* 21 (1971): 535–43.

CHAPTER 10   N IN THE LAW

1. Joel A. Tarr, *The Search for the Ultimate Sink: Urban Pollution in Historical Perspective* (Akron, Ohio: University of Akron Press, 1996).

2. Martin V. Melosi, *The Sanitary City: Urban Infrastructure in America from Colonial Times to the Present* (Baltimore: Johns Hopkins University Press, 2000); Melanie DuPuis, ed., *Smoke and Mirrors: The Politics and Culture of Air Pollution* (New York: New York University Press, 2004); John T. Cumbler, "The Early Making of an Environmental Consciousness: Fish, Fishery Commissioners, and the Connecticut River," *Environmental Review* 15 (1991): 73–91.

3. J. Clarence Davies and Jan Mazurek, *Pollution Control in the United States: Evaluating the System* (Washington, D.C.: Resources for the Future, 1999), 11–16.

4. "Union's $200 Million Refinery Coming on Stream This Summer" [news release], Union Oil, Public Relations Department, May 1970, Lemont Refinery files, Illinois Environmental Protection Agency, Springfield, hereafter cited as "Lemont Refinery files."

5. Libby Hill, *The Chicago River: A Natural and Unnatural History* (Chicago: Lake Claremont, 2000); Ann Durkin Keating, *Chicago Neighborhoods and Suburbs: A Historical Guide* (Chicago: University of Chicago Press, 2008), 191.

6. The following documents appear in Lemont Refinery files: J. N. West, letter to Clarence W. Klassen, May 31, 1967; "Union's $200 Million Refinery"; E. L. Marek and Benn J. Leland, meeting notes, March 7, 1967; "Union Oil Plan for Big Lemont Refinery Told," *Chicago Tribune*, May 23, 1967, D13.

7. The following documents appear in Lemont Refinery files: Sanitary Water Board, letter to Robert Kingery, October 5, 1933; Robert Kingery, letter to Clarence W. Klassen, May 3, 1938; James W. Mulroy, letter to C. H. Broughton, May 25, 1951. Also see John Lamb, *The I&M Canal: A Corridor in Time* (Romeoville, Ill.: Lewisville University, 1987), 28.

8. The following documents appear in Lemont Refinery files: Clarence W. Klassen, letter to J. M. Lawson, May 26, 1954; J. M. Lawson, letter to Clarence W. Klassen, August 12, 1954.

9. J. M. Lawson, letter to Clarence W. Klassen, May 31, 1956, and subsequent data reports, Lemont Refinery files.

10. The following documents appear in folder "Chicago Sanitary and Ship Canal Correspondence," box 32 "Office of Enforcement and General Counsel, Records Pertaining to the Regulation of Interstate Bodies of Water, 1948–1975," record group

412 (records of the U.S. Environmental Protection Agency), National Archives and Records Administration, College Park, Md.: C. W. Klassen, letter to H. W. Poston, May 21, 1964; H. W. Poston, letter to C. W. Klassen, May 22, 1964. Also see Terrence Kehoe, *Cleaning Up the Great Lakes: From Cooperation to Confrontation* (DeKalb: Northern Illinois University Press, 1997).

11. The following documents appear in Lemont Refinery files: "Union Oil Plan"; J. N. West, letter to Clarence W. Klassen, May 31, 1967; "Union's $200 Million Refinery."

12. Joseph J. Bernosky, *Overview of Environmental Laws and Regulations: Navigating the Green Maze* (Denver, Colo.: American Water Works Association, 2011); U.S. Environmental Protection Agency, *NPDES Permit Writers' Manual*, EPA-833-B-96-003 (Washington, D.C.: U.S. Environmental Protection Agency, 1996), 1–28.

13. The following documents appear in Lemont Refinery files: State of Illinois, "Notice in the Matter of the Petition for Variance of Union Oil Company of California Chicago Refinery," December 22, 1972; Illinois Pollution Control Board, "Final Order in the Matter of Proposal of Union Oil of California to Amend the Water Pollution Regulations," March 19, 1987.

14. Hugh S. Gorman, *Redefining Efficiency: Pollution Concerns, Regulatory Mechanisms, and Technological Change in the U.S. Petroleum Industry* (Akron, Ohio: University of Akron Press, 2001), 301–22.

15. Kristoffer Whitney, "Living Lawns, Dying Waters: The Suburban Boom, Nitrogenous Fertilizers, and the Nonpoint Source Pollution Dilemma," *Technology and Culture* 51 (2010): 652–74.

16. U.S. Environmental Protection Agency, *Air Quality Criteria for Nitrogen Oxides*, Air Pollution Control Office Publication AP-84 (Washington, D.C.: Government Printing Office, 1971); U.S. Environmental Protection Agency, *Air Quality Criteria for Oxides of Nitrogen*, EPA/600/8–91/049aF (Research Triangle Park, N.C.: U.S. Environmental Protection Agency, 1993), 1:i–iii.

17. Arnold W. Reitze, *Air Pollution Control Law: Compliance and Enforcement* (Washington, D.C.: Environmental Law Institute, 2001), 79.

18. David Gerard and Lester B. Lave, "Implementing Technology-Forcing Policies: The 1970 Clean Air Act Amendments and the Introduction of Advanced Automotive Emissions Controls in the United States," *Technological Forecasting and Social Change* 72 (2004): 761–78.

19. Comments of Charles M. Heinen in "Report on the First APCA Government Affairs Seminar: The Clean Air Act," *Journal of Air Pollution Control Association* 23 (1973): 475–81.

20. Jim Motavalli, *Forward Drive: The Race to Build "Clean" Cars for the Future* (San Francisco: Sierra Club Books, 2001), 41.

21. "U.S. Charges Auto Makers Plot to Delay Fume Curbs," *New York Times*, January 11, 1969, A1; Joseph C. Robert, *Ethyl: A History of a Corporation and the People Who Made It* (Charlottesville: University of Virginia Press, 1983), 211–21.

22. Ying Zhu, Akira Takeishi, and Seiichiro Yonekura, "The Timing of Technological Innovation: The Case of Automotive Emission Control in the 1970s" (2006), Hitotsubashi University, Institute of Innovation Research, http://www.iir.hit-u.ac.jp/iir-w3/file/WP06–05takeishi.pdf; U.S. Environmental Protection Agency, "National Emission Inventory Air Pollution Emissions Trends Data," http://www.epa.gov/ttnchie1/trends.

23. Roy S. Belden, *Clean Air Act* (Chicago: American Bar Association, 2001), 55–62.

24. James Longhurst, "1 to 100: Creating an Air Quality Index in Pittsburgh," *Environmental Monitoring and Assessment* 106 (2005): 27–42.

25. Belden, *Clean Air Act*, 93–106; Hugh S. Gorman and Barry D. Solomon, "The Origins and Practice of Emissions Trading," *Journal of Policy History* 14 (2002): 293–320; Richard A. Liroff, *Reforming Air Pollution Regulation: The Toil and Trouble of EPA's Bubble* (Washington, D.C.: Conservation Foundation, 1986).

26. Mark Z. Jacobson, *Atmospheric Pollution: History, Science, and Regulation* (Cambridge: Cambridge University Press, 2002), 98, 166–67; Kenneth L. Hirsch and Steven Abramovitz, "Clearing the Air: Some Legal Aspects of Interstate Air Pollution Problems," *Duquesne Law Review* 18 (1979–1980): 53–102.

27. Edward Parson, *Protecting the Ozone Layer: Science and Strategy* (New York: Oxford University Press, 2003), 14–36.

28. Erik M. Conway, *High-Speed Dreams: NASA and the Technopolitics of Supersonic Transportation* (Baltimore: Johns Hopkins University Press, 2005); Parson, *Protecting the Ozone Layer*, 26–51; James C. White, William R. Wagner, and Carole N. Beal, eds., *Global Climate Change Linkages. Acid Rain, Air Quality, and Stratospheric Ozone* (New York: Elsevier, 1989), 70–71.

29. Morton Lippman, "The 1997 U.S. EPA Standards for Particulate Matter and Ozone," in *Air Pollution and Health*, ed. Ronald E. Hester and Roy M. Harrison, 75–100 (Cambridge: Royal Society of Chemistry, 1998); Keith Smith, ed., *Nitrous Oxide and Climate Change* (Washington, D.C.: Earthscan, 2010); T. J. Blasing, "Recent Greenhouse Gas Concentrations," Carbon Dioxide Information Analysis Center, http://cdiac.ornl.gov/pns/current_ghg.html.

30. Randy D. Down and Jay H. Lehr, eds., *Environmental Instrumentation and Analysis Handbook* (Hoboken, N.J.: Wiley, 2005); Alexander E. Farrell, "Learning to See the Invisible: Discovery and Measurement of Ozone," *Environmental Monitoring and Assessment* 106 (2005): 59–80.

31. Charles O'Jones, *Clean Air: The Policy and Politics of Pollution Control* (Pittsburgh: University of Pittsburgh Press, 1975).

32. Edward S. Rubin, Sonia Yeh, and David Hounshell, "Technology Innovations and Experience Curves for Nitrogen Oxides Control Technologies," *Journal of Air and Waste Management Association* 55 (2005): 1827–38.

33. Sanitary District of Chicago, "Memorandum Concerning the Drainage and Sewage Conditions in Chicago and the Diversion of 10,000 C.F.S. from Lake Michigan at Chicago," December 1923, Municipal Collection, Harold Washington Public Library, Chicago.

34. Joel A. Tarr and Terry F. Yosie, "Critical Decisions in Pittsburgh Water and Wastewater Treatment," in *Devastation and Renewal: An Environmental History of Pittsburgh and Its Region*, ed. Joel A. Tarr (Pittsburgh: University of Pittsburgh Press, 2003) , 64–88; Mark Tranel, *St. Louis Plans: the Ideal and the Real St. Louis* (Saint Louis: Missouri Historical Society, 2007), 61–69; Arthur D. Caster, "Metropolitan Sewer District of Greater Cincinnati Program," *Journal of the Water Pollution Control Federation* 43 (1971): 372–80.

35. Carmen F. Guarino, "Sludge Digestion Experiences in Philadelphia," *Journal of the Water Pollution Control Federation* 35 (1963): 626–35.

36. Harold E. Babbitt, *Sewerage and Sewage Treatment* (New York: Wiley, 1949), 486–87; Ernest W. Steel, *Water Supply and Sewerage* (New York: McGraw-Hill, 1960), 595; Guarino, "Sludge Digestion," 626–35.

37. C. F. Guarino, M. D. Nelson, and S. Townsend, "Philadelphia Sludge Disposal in Coastal Waters," *Journal of the Water Pollution Control Federation* 49 (1977): 737–44; M. D. Nelson and C. F. Guarino, "New Philadelphia Story Being Written by Pollution-Control Division," *Water and Wastes Engineering* 14 (1977): 22; William E. Toffey, "The Lessons of Twenty-two Years of Biosolids Recycling by the City of Philadelphia Water Department: Diversification and Continual Improvement" (unpublished presentation, March 5, 2002).

38. Edward D. Wetzel and Scott B. Murphy, *Treating Industrial Waste Interferences at Publicly-Owned Treatment Works* (Park Ridge, N.J.: Noyes Data Corporation, 1991).

39. Caroline Snyder, "The Dirty Work of Promoting 'Recycling' of America's Sewage Sludge," *International Journal of Occupational and Environmental Health* 11 (205): 415–27.

40. Robert Bastian et al., "Regulatory Issues," in *Municipal Sewage Sludge Management: Processing, Utilization, and Disposal,* ed. Cecil Lue-Hing, David R. Zenz, and Richard Kuchenrither (Lancaster, Pa.: Technomic, 1992) , 3–68

41. Alice B. Outwater and Berrin Tansel, *Reuse of Sludge and Minor Wastewater Residuals* (Boca Raton, Fla.: Lewis, 1994), 163–68; Toffey, "Lessons of Twenty-two Years."

42. John C. Stauber and Sheldon Rampton, *Toxic Sludge Is Good For You: Lies, Damn Lies, and the Public Relations Industry* (Monroe, Me.: Common Courage, 1995), 99–122; Snyder, "America's Sewage Sludge," 415–427.

43. William Toffey, "25 Year Total of Biosolid Use" [personal communication], Philadelphia Water Department, April 11, 2008.

CHAPTER 11   N AND THE SEEDS OF AN ECOLOGICAL ECONOMY

1. For examples of works in this period that examine the entanglement of nature and culture, see Bill McKibben, *The End of Nature* (New York: Random House, 1989); William Cronon, *Nature's Metropolis: Chicago and the Great West* (New York: Norton, 1991); and Richard White, *The Organic Machine: The Remaking of the Columbia River* (New York: Hill and Wang, 1996).

2. Irving M. Mintzer and J. Amber Leonard, eds., *Negotiating Climate Change: The Inside Story of the Rio Convention* (New York: Cambridge University Press, 1994); David C. Korten, *When Corporations Rule the World* (West Hartford, Conn.: Kumarian, 1995); Thomas Friedman, *The Lexus and the Olive Tree* (New York: Farrar, Straus, and Giroux, 1999); Paul S. Fischbeck and R. Scott Farrow, eds., *Improving Regulation* (Washington, D.C.: Resources for the Future, 2001).

3. Robert Costanza et al., "The Value of the World's Ecosystem Services and Natural Capital," *Nature* 387 (1997): 253–60.

4. William E. Rees, "How Should a Parasite Value Its Host?" *Ecological Economics* 25 (1998): 49–52; Donald Ludwig, "Limitations of Economic Valuation of Ecosystems," *Ecosystems* 3 (2000): 31–35; Lawrence H. Goulder and Donald Kennedy, "Valuing Ecosystem Services: Philosophical Bases and Empirical Methods," in *Nature's Services: Societal Dependence on Natural Ecosystems,* ed. Gretchen C. Daily (Washington, D.C.: Island, 1997), 23–48.

5. Oliver A. Houck, *The Clean Water Act TMDL Program: Law, Policy, and Implementation* (Washington, D.C.: Environmental Law Institute, 1999).

6. Delaware Tributary Action Team, "The Broadkill River and Watershed Public Forum to Discuss: Your Challenge, Your Choice!" (2006), http://broadkill.ocean.udel.edu/BKBooklet_bw.pdf.

7. Delaware Department of Natural Resources and Environmental Controls [prepared by Hydroqual], "Broadkill River Watershed Proposed TMDLs, Delaware" (August 2006), htpp:// www.dnrec.delaware.gov/swc/wa.

8. R. Eugene Turner and Nancy N. Rabalais, "Changes in Mississippi River Water Quality this Century," *Bioscience* 41 (1991): 140–47; Tomotoshi Okaichi et al., eds., *Red Tides: Biology, Environmental Science, and Toxicology* (New York: Elsevier, 1989).

9. Maurice L. Renard, "Annotated Bibliography on Hypoxia and Its Effects on Marine Life, with Emphasis on the Gulf of Mexico," NOAA Technical Report NMFS 21 (February 1985); Robert E. Randall and Lynn Pokryfki, "Nearshore Hypoxia in the Bottom Water of the Northwestern Gulf of Mexico from 1981–1984," *Marine Environmental Research* 22 (1987): 75–90; R. E. Turner et al., "Summer Hypoxia in the Northern Gulf of Mexico and Its Prediction from 1978 to 1995," *Marine Environmental Research* 59 (2005): 65–77.

10. U.S. Harmful Algal Bloom and Hypoxia Research and Control Act of 1998, Public Law 108–456, Title 6, November 13, 1998.

11. National Science and Technology Council, Committee on Environment and Natural Resources, *An Integrated Assessment of Hypoxia in the Northern Gulf of Mexico* (May 2000), http://oceanservice.noaa.gov/.

12. Ibid.

13. Ibid.; Robert H. Meade, ed., *Contaminants in the Mississippi River*, U.S. Geological Survey Circular 1133 (Reston, Va., 1995); Mississippi River/Gulf of Mexico Watershed Nutrient Task Force, "Action Plan for Reducing, Mitigating, and Controlling Hypoxia in the Northern Gulf of Mexico and Improving Water Quality in the Mississippi River Basin" (January 2001), pp. 6–8, http://www.epa.gov/owow/msbasin/pdf/actionplan2001.pdf.

14. Nutrient Task Force, "Action Plan, 2001," 20–23; Virginia Dale et al., *Hypoxia in the Northern Gulf of Mexico* (New York: Springer, 2010).

15. C. S. Holling, ed., *Adaptive Environmental Assessment and Management* (New York: Wiley, 1978).

16. Dale H. Besterfield et al., *Total Quality Management* (Englewood Cliffs, N.J.: Prentice Hall, 1995); W. Edwards Deming, *Out of the Crisis* (Cambridge, Mass.: MIT Center for Advanced Educational Services, 1986).

17. Craig Cochran, *ISO 9001 in Plain English* (Chico, Calif.: Paton Professional, 2008); Aseem Prakash and Matthew Potoski, *The Voluntary Environmentalists: Green Clubs, ISO 14001, and Voluntary Environmental Regulations* (New York: Cambridge University Press, 2006).

18. Ohio River Sanitation Commission, "Nutrient Reduction Activities" (2011), http://www.orsanco.org/nutrient-reduction-activities; Mohammad N. Almasri, "Nitrate Contamination of Groundwater: A Conceptual Management Framework," *Environmental Impact Assessment Review* 27 (2007): 220–42; World Wildlife Fund, *Statewide Wetlands Strategies: A Guide to Protecting and Managing the Resource* (Washington, D.C.: Island, 1992).

19. Mississippi River/Gulf of Mexico Watershed Nutrient Task Force, "Gulf Hypoxia Action Plan 2008 for Reducing, Mitigating, and Controlling Hypoxia in the Northern Gulf of Mexico and Improving Water Quality in the Mississippi River Basin" (June 2008), p. 10, http://water.epa.gov/type/watersheds/named/msbasin/action plan.cfm.

20. Peter C. Scharf and John A. Lory, "Best Management Practices for Nitrogen Fertilizer in Missouri," pub. IPM1027 (Columbia: University of Missouri Extension Service, 2006); Richard A. Cooke, Gary R. Sands, and Larry C. Brown, "Drainage Water Management: A Practice for Reducing Nitrate Loads from Subsurface Drainage Systems" (paper presented at the Gulf Hypoxia and Local Water Quality Concerns Workshop, Ames, Iowa, September 26–28, 2005).

21. Nutrient Task Force, "Action Plan, 2008," 18; Terence J. Centner, "Governmental Oversight of Discharges from Concentrated Animal Feeding Operations," *Environmental Management* 37 (2006): 745–52

22. Nutrient Task Force, "Action Plan, 2008," 23.

23. Dale et al., *Hypoxia in the Northern Gulf of Mexico.*

24. Thomas S. Bianchi et al., "The Science of Hypoxia in the Northern Gulf of Mexico: A Review," *Science of the Total Environment* 408 (2010): 1471–84; National Science Foundation, "Gulf Oil Spill: NSF Awards Rapid Response Grant to Study Impact of Oil and Methane on Microbes" [press release], June 2, 2010, http://www.nsf.gov.

25. Nutrient Task Force, "Action Plan, 2008," 8.

26. Ibid., 11.

27. Dallas Burtraw and Karen Palmer, "So2 Cap-and-Trade Program in the United States: A Living Legend of Market Effectiveness," in *Choosing Environmental Policy: Comparing Instruments and Outcomes in the United States and Europe*, ed. Winston Harrington, Richard D. Morgenstern, and Thomas Sterner (Washington, D.C.: Resources for the Future, 2004), 41–66.

28. Dallas Burtraw, "Innovation under the Tradable Sulfur Dioxide Emissions Permits Program in the U.S. Electricity Sector," Resources for the Future Discussion Paper 00–38 (June 2000), http://www.rff.org/documents/RFF-DP-00-38.pdf.

29. Michael C. Naughton, "Establishing Interstate Markets for Emissions Trading of Ozone Precursors: The Case of the Northeast Ozone Transport Commission and the Northeast States for Coordinated Air Use Management Emissions Trading Proposals," *New York University Environmental Law Journal* 3 (1994–95): 195–228.

30. Dallas Burtraw and Sarah Jo Szambelan, "U.S. Emissions Trading Markets for SO_2 and NO_x," Resources for the Future Discussion Paper 09–40 (October 2009), http://www.rff.org/rff/Documents/RFF-DP-09-40.pdf.

31. Hugh S. Gorman and Barry D. Solomon, "The Origins and Practice of Emissions Trading," *Journal of Policy History* 14 (2002): 293–320.

32. Robert N. Stavins, "Experience with Market-Based Environmental Policy Instruments," in *Handbook of Environmental Economics*, vol. 1, *Environmental Degradation and Institutional Responses*, ed. Karl-Göran Mäler and Jeffrey R. Vincent (Amsterdam: Elsevier, 2003), 355–436; S. Pagiola et al., eds., *Selling Forest Environmental Services: Market-Based Mechanisms for Conservation* (Sterling, Va.: Earthscan, 2002).

33. For an example of a work that downplays the need to integrate environmental objectives into the market, see Julian Simon, *The Ultimate Resource II* (Princeton, N.J.: Princeton University Press, 1996). For an examination of the integration

challenge, see J. B. Ruhl, Steven E. Kraft, and C. L. Lant, *The Law and Policy of Ecosystem Services* (Washington: D.C.: Island, 2007); James K. Boyce, *The Political Economy of the Environment* (Northampton, Mass.: Elgar, 2002).

34. Rodrigo P. Tarté, *Picnic con Hormigas: Reflexiones Sobre Gestión del Conocimiento y Desarrollo (Sostenible)* (Panama City: Fundación Cidudad del Saber, 2006), 191–206.

35. Personal communication with William Toffey, biosolids program manager at Philadelphia Waste Treatment Plant, August 2008.

36. National Science and Technology Council, *Integrated Assessment of Hypoxia,* 40.

37. U.S. Geological Service, "Sparrow, Surface Water Quality Modeling," http://water.usgs.gov/nawqa/sparrow.

CONCLUSION

1. Nicolas Gruber and James N. Galloway, "An Earth-System Perspective of the Global Nitrogen Cycle," *Nature* 451 (2008): 293–96.

2. Warren J. Samuels, *Erasing the Visible Hand: Essays on an Elusive and Misused Concept in Economics* (New York: Cambridge University Press, 2011).

BIBLIOGRAPHY

Abelshauser, Werner, Wolfgang von Hippel, Jeffrey Allan Johnson, and Raymond G. Stokes. *German Industry and Global Enterprise, BASF: The History of a Company.* New York: Cambridge University Press, 2004.

Acot, Pascal, ed. *The European Origins of Scientific Ecology, 1800–1901.* Amsterdam: Gordon and Breach, 1998.

Adas, Michael, ed. *Agricultural and Pastoral Societies in Ancient and Classical History.* Philadelphia: Temple University Press, 2001.

Addiscott, T. M. *Nitrate, Agriculture, and the Environment.* Cambridge, Mass.: CABI, 2005.

Ágoston, Gábor. *Guns for the Sultan: Military Power and the Weapons Industry in the Ottoman Empire.* New York: Cambridge University Press, 2005.

Ahrens, C. Donald. *Meteorology Today: An Introduction to Weather, Climate, and the Environment.* Belmont, Calif: Thompson Brooks/Cole, 2006.

Aikman, Charles M. *Manures and Principles of Manuring.* London: Blackwood, 1894.

Allen, A. B., and R. L. Allen. *The American Agriculturalist.* Vol. 9. New York: Saxton, 1850.

Allen, Robert C. "The Nitrogen Hypothesis and the English Agricultural Revolution: A Biological Analysis." *Journal of Economic History* 68 (2008): 182–210.

Allison, F. E. "The Enigma of Soil Nitrogen Balance Sheets." *Advances in Agronomy* 7 (1955): 213–50.

Almasri, Mohammad N. "Nitrate Contamination of Groundwater: A Conceptual Management Framework." *Environmental Impact Assessment Review* 27 (2007): 220–42.

Almqvist, Ebbe. *History of Industrial Gases.* New York: Kluwer /Plenum, 2003.

Altieri, V. J. *Gas Analysis and Testing of Gaseous Materials.* New York: American Gas Association, 1945.

Altschul, Aaron M. *Proteins: Their Chemistry and Politics.* New York: Basic Books, 1965.

American Public Health Association. *Standard Methods for the Examination of Water and Sewage.* New York: American Public Health Association, 1920.

Anderson, J. L. *Industrializing the Corn Belt: Agriculture, Technology, and Environment, 1945–1972.* Dekalb: Northern Illinois University Press, 2009.

Andrews, J. E., P. Brimblecombe, T. D. Jickells, and P. S. Liss. *An Introduction to Environmental Chemistry.* Oxford: Blackwell, 1996.

Ardern, E., and W. T. Lockett. "Experiments on the Oxidation of Sewage without the Aid of Filters." *Journal of the Society of Chemical Industry* 33 (1914): 523–39.

Arias, Jamie. "On the Origin of Saltpeter, Northern Chile Coast." Paper presented at the twenty-sixth annual INQUA Congress, Reno, Nevada, July 24–30, 2003.

Ashton, Basil, Kenneth Hill, Alan Piazza, and Robin Zeitz. "Famine in China, 1958–61." *Population and Development Review* 10 (1984): 613–45.

Astill, Grenville, and John Langdon, eds. *Medieval Farming and Technology: The Impact of Agricultural Change in Northwest Europe.* New York: Brill, 1997.

Aulie, Richard P. "Boussingault and the Nitrogen Cycle." *Proceedings of the American Philosophical Society* 114 (1970): 435–79.

Babbitt, Harold E. *Sewage and Sewerage Treatment.* New York: Wiley, 1922, 1949.

Bacon, Francis. *The New Atlantis.* 1627. Reprint. Minneapolis: Filiquarian, 2007.

Baldani, J. I., and V.L.D. Baldani. "History of the Biological Nitrogen Fixation Research in Gramineous Plants: Special Emphasis on the Brazilian Experience." *Annals of the Brazilian Academy of Sciences* 77 (2005): 549–79.

Balfour, Lady Eve. *The Living Soil.* London: Faber and Faber, 1943.

———. "Towards a Sustainable Agriculture–The Living Soil." Speech to the conference of the International Federation of Organic Agriculture Movements, Sissach, Switzerland, October 1977.

Baly, E.C.C. *Spectroscopy.* London: Longmans, Green, 1905.

Barker, Randolf, and Robert Herdt. *The Rice Economy of Asia.* Washington, D.C.: Resources for the Future, 1985.

Barnard, Alan, ed. *Hunter-Gatherers in History, Archaeology, and Anthropology.* New York: Berg, 2004.

Barnhart, D. H., and E. K. Diehl. "Control of Nitrogen Oxides in Boiler Flue Gases by Two-Stage Combustion." *Journal of the Air Pollution Control Association* 10 (1960): 397–406.

Barnum, Dennis W. "Some History of Nitrates." *Journal of Chemical Education* 80 (2003): 1393–96.

Barr, Robert. "Within an Ace of the End of the World, being some account of the fearful disaster which overtook the inhabitants of this earth through scientific miscalculation in the year 1904." *Windsor Magazine* 13 (1901): 17–26.

Beder, Sharon. "From Sewage Farms to Septic Tanks: Trials and Tribulations in Sydney." *Journal of the Royal Australian Historical Society* 79 (1993): 72–95.

Befu, Harumi. *Japan: An Anthropological Introduction.* New York: Harper and Row, 1971.

Belden, Roy S. *Clean Air Act.* Chicago: American Bar Association, 2001.

Bellwood, Peter. *The First Farmers: The Origins of Agricultural Societies.* Malden, Mass.: Blackwell, 2005.

Benzenberg, G. H. "The Sewerage System of the Milwaukee and the Milwaukee River Flushing Systems." *Transactions of the American Society of Civil Engineers* 30 (1893): 367–85.

Bernosky, Joseph J. *Overview of Environmental Laws and Regulations: Navigating the Green Maze.* Denver, Colo.: American Water Works Association, 2011.

Besterfield, Dale H., Carol Besterfield-Michna, and Glen H. Besterfield. *Total Quality Management.* Englewood Cliffs, N.J.: Prentice Hall, 1995.

Bettinger, Robert L. *Hunter-Gatherers: Archaeological and Evolutionary Theory.* New York: Plenum, 1991.

Biagioli, Mario. *Galileo, Courtier: The Practice of Science in the Culture of Absolutism.* Chicago: University of Chicago Press, 1994.

Bianchi, Thomas S., S. F. DiMarco, J. H. Cowan, Jr., R. D. Hetland, P. Chapman, J. W. Day, and M. A. Allison. "The Science of Hypoxia in the Northern Gulf of Mexico: A Review." *Science of the Total Environment* 408 (2010): 1471–84.

Bidwell, Percy Wells and John I. Falconer. *History of Agriculture in the Northern United States, 1620–1860.* New York: Smith, 1941.

Blacet, F. E. "Photochemistry in the Lower Atmosphere." *Industrial Engineering Chemistry* 44 (1952): 1339–42.

Blase, Melvin G., ed. *Institutions in Agricultural Development.* Ames: Iowa State University Press, 1971.

Blumler, Mark A. "Modelling the Origins of Legume Domestication and Cultivation." *Economic Botany* 45 (1991): 243–50.

Blute, Marion. "The Evolutionary Socioecology of Gestural Communication." *Gesture* 6 (2006): 177–88.

Böhlke, J. K., G. E. Ericksen, and K. Revesz. "Stable Isotope Evidence for an Atmospheric Origin of Desert Nitrate Deposits in Northern Chile and Southern California, U.S.A." *Chemical Geology* 136 (1997): 135–52.

Boussingault, J. B. *Rural Economy, in Its Relations with Chemistry, Physics, and Meterology.* Translated by George Law. London: Bailliere, 1845.

Bown, Stephen R. *A Most Damnable Invention: Dynamite, Nitrates, and the Making of the Modern World.* New York: Dunne, 2005.

Boyce, James K. *The Political Economy of the Environment.* Northampton, Mass.: Elgar, 2002.

Boyd, Robert, and Peter J. Richerson. *The Origins and Evolution of Culture.* New York: Oxford University Press, 2005.

Boyer, Elizabeth W., and Robert W. Howarth, eds. *The Nitrogen Cycle at Regional to Global Scales.* Boston: Kluwer, 2002.

Boyle, Robert. *The Sceptical Chymist; or: Chymico-Physical Doubts & Paradoxes, Touching the Spagyrist's Principles Commonly Call'd Hypostatical.* 1661. Reprint. Boston: Elibron, 2006.

Brace, C. Loring. *The Stages of Human Evolution.* Englewood Cliffs, N.J.: Prentice Hall, 1995.

Brace, D. B., ed. *The Laws of Radiation and Absorption: Memoirs by Prévost, Steward, Kirchhoff, and Kirchhoff and Bunsen* New York: American Book Company, 1901.

Bradley, W. B., H. F. Eppson, and O. A. Beath. *Livestock Poisoning by Oat, Hay, and Other Plants Containing Nitrate.* Bulletin 241. Laramie: Wyoming Agricultural Experimental Station, 1940.

Brand, John C. D. *Lines of Light: The Sources of Dispersive Spectroscopy, 1800–1930.* Amsterdam: Gordon and Breach, 1995.

Braudel, Fernand. *Civilization and Capitalism, 15th–18th Centuries.* 3 vols. New York: Harper and Row, 1982–84.

Bray, James O., and Patricia Watkins. "Technical Change in Corn Production in the United States, 1870–1960." *Journal of Farm Economics* 46 (1964): 751–65.

Brienes, Marvin. "The Fight against Smog in Los Angeles, 1943–1957." Ph.D. diss., University of California, Davis, 1975.

Brock, Thomas D. *Milestones in Microbiology: 1546 to 1940.* Englewood Cliffs, N.J.: Prentice Hall, 1961.

———. *Robert Koch: A Life in Medicine and Bacteriology.* Washington, D.C.: ASM, 1988.

Brock, William H. *Justus Von Liebig: The Chemical Gatekeeper.* New York: Cambridge University Press, 1997.

———. *William Crookes (1832–1919) and the Commercialization of Science.* Burlington, Vt.: Ashgate, 2008.

Brown, Kenneth D. Britain and Japan: A Comparative Economic and Social History Since 1900. New York: Manchester University Press, 1998.

Browne, Daniel J. *The American Muck Book.* New York: Saxton, 1851.

Bryant, Lynwood. "The Role of Thermodynamics in the Evolution of Heat Engines." *Technology and Culture* 14 (1973): 152–65

Buchanan, Brenda J., ed. *Gunpowder, Explosives, and the State: A Technological History.* Burlington, Vt.: Ashgate, 2006.

Burger, Richard L. *Chavin and the Origins of Andean Civilization.* New York: Thames and Hudson, 1992.

Burtraw, Dallas. "Innovation under the Tradable Sulfur Dioxide Emissions Permits Program in the U.S. Electricity Sector." Resources for the Future Discussion Paper 00–38. June 2000. http://www.rff.org/documents/RFF-DP-00–38.pdf.

Burtraw, Dallas, and Sarah Jo Szambelan. "U.S. Emissions Trading Markets for SO_2 and NO_x." Resources for the Future Discussion Paper 09–40. October 2009. http://www.rff.org/rff/Documents/RFF-DP-09–40.pdf.

Butcher, Samuel S., Robert J. Charlson, Gordon H. Orians, and Gordon V. Wolfe, eds. *Global Biogeochemical Cycles.* New York: Academic Press, 1992.

Cajori, Florian. *A History of Physics in Its Elementary Branches: Including the Evolution of Physical Laboratories.* London: Macmillan, 1899.

California Air Resources Board. Clearing California Skies [video]. http://www.arb.ca .gov/videos/clskies.htm.

California State Chamber of Commerce. *Proceedings of the Southern California Conference on Elimination of Air Pollution: What Has Been Done, What Is Now Being Done, What Will Be Done to Eliminate Air Pollution, November 10, 1955.* Los Angeles: California State Chamber of Commerce, 1955.

Cameron, David W., and Colin P. Groves. *Bones, Stones, and Molecules: "Out of Africa" and Human Origins.* Burlington, Mass.: Elsevier, 2004.

Cameron, Donald. "A Year's Experience with the Septic Tank System of Sewage Disposal at Exeter." *Journal of the Sanitary Institute* 43 (1897): 563–70.

Cameron, Frank T. *Cottrell, Samaritan of Science.* New York: Doubleday, 1952.

Campbell, Donald T. "Evolutionary Epistemology." In Schilpp, Paul A., ed. *The Philosophy of Karl Popper, The Library of Living Philosophers.* La Salle, Ill.: Open Court, 1974.

Canfield, Donald E., Alexander N. Glazer, and Paul G. Falkowski. "The Evolution and Future of Earth's Nitrogen Cycle." *Science* 8 (2010): 192–94.

Canter, Larry W., and Robert C. Knox. *Septic Tank System Effects on Ground Water Quality.* Chelsea, Mich.: Lewis, 1985.

Carr-Saunders, A. M. *World Population: Past Growth and Present Trends.* London: Cass, 1964.

Carson, Rachel. *Silent Spring.* Boston: Houghton Mifflin, 1962.

Casey, Hugh J. "Muscle Shoals." *Kansas Engineer* 10 (1925): 5–10, 20.

Caster, Arthur D. "Metropolitan Sewer District of Greater Cincinnati Program." *Journal of the Water Pollution Control Federation* 43 (1971): 372–80.

Centner, Terence J. "Governmental Oversight of Discharges from Concentrated Animal Feeding Operations." *Environmental Management* 37 (2006): 745–52.

Chandler, Tertius. *Four Thousand Years of Urban Growth: An Historical Census.* Lewiston, Me.: Mellen, 1987.

Chant, Colin, and David Goodman. *Pre-industrial Cities and Technology.* New York: Routledge, 1999.

Christian, David. *Maps of Time: An Introduction to Big History.* Berkeley: University of California Press, 2004.

Cipolla, Carlo. *Guns, Sails, and Empires: Technological Innovation and the Early Phases of European Expansion, 1400–1700.* New York: Pantheon, 1966.

Clark, William, Jan Golinski, and Simon Schaffer, eds. *The Sciences in Enlightened Europe.* Chicago: University of Chicago Press, 1999.

Clay, C.G.A. *Economic Expansion and Social Change: England, 1500–1700.* 3 vols. New York: Cambridge University Press, 1985.

Clay, Jason W. *World Agriculture and the Environment.* Washington, D.C.: Island, 2004.

Cochran, Craig. *ISO 9001 in Plain English.* Chico, Calif.: Paton Professional, 2008.

Cochrane, Willard W. *The Development of American Agriculture: A Historical Analysis.* Minneapolis: University of Minnesota Press, 1993.

Codispoti, L. A., J. A. Brandes, J. P. Christensen, A. H. Devol, S. W. A Naqvi, H. W. Paerl, and T. Yoshinari. "The Oceanic Fixed Nitrogen and Nitrous Oxide Budgets: Moving Targets As We Enter the Anthropocene?" *Scientia Marina* 65 (2001): 85–105.

Cohen, Mark Nathan. *The Food Crisis in Prehistory: Overpopulation and the Origins of Agriculture.* New Haven: Yale University Press, 1977.

Comly, Hunter H. "Cyanosis in Infants Caused by Nitrates in Well Water." *Journal of the American Medical Association* 129 (1945): 112–16.

Committee on the Economics of Fertilizer Use. *Status and Methods of Research in Economic and Agronomic Aspects of Fertilizer Response and Use.* Publication 918. Washington, D.C.: National Academy of Sciences/National Research Council, 1961.

Committee on the Medical and Biological Effects of Environmental Pollution. *Nitrogen Oxides.* Washington, D.C.: National Academy of Sciences, 1977.

Committee on Nitrate Accumulation. *Accumulation of Nitrate.* Washington, D.C.: National Academy of Sciences, 1972.

Commoner, Barry. *The Closing Circle.* New York: Knopf, 1971.

———. "Threats to the Integrity of the Nitrogen Cycle: Nitrogen Compounds in Soil, Water, Atmosphere, and Precipitation." Paper presented at the annual conference of the American Association for the Advancement of Science, Dallas, December 1968.

Conford, Philip. *The Origins of the Organic Movement.* Edinburgh: Foris, 2001.

Conway, Erik M. *High-Speed Dreams: NASA and the Technopolitics of Supersonic Transportation.* Baltimore: Johns Hopkins University Press, 2005.

Cook, Stanley A. *The Laws of Moses and the Code of Hammurabi.* London: Black, 1903.

Cooke, Richard A., Gary R. Sands, and Larry C. Brown. "Drainage Water Management: A Practice for Reducing Nitrate Loads from Subsurface Drainage Systems." Paper presented at the Gulf Hypoxia and Local Water Quality Concerns Workshop, Ames, Iowa, September 26–28, 2005.

Costanza, Robert, et al. "The Value of the World's Ecosystem Services and Natural Capital." *Nature* 387 (1997): 253–60.

Cottrell, Allin. *The Manufacture of Nitric Acid and Nitrates.* London: Gurney and Jackson, 1923.

Cottrell, F. G. "Fixed Nitrogen Research Laboratory." *Transactions of the American Institute of Chemical Engineers* 15 (1923): 209–20.

Cronon, William. *Nature's Metropolis: Chicago and the Great West.* New York: Norton, 1991.

Crookes, Sir William, and Sir Robert Henry Rew. *The Wheat Problem: Based on Remarks Made in the Presidential Address to the British Association at Bristol in 1898.* New York: Longmans, Green, 1917.

Crouzet, Francois. *A History of the European Economy, 1000–2000.* Charlottesville: University of Virginia Press, 2001.

Cumbler, John T. "The Early Making of an Environmental Consciousness: Fish, Fishery Commissioners, and the Connecticut River." *Environmental Review* 15 (1991): 73–91.

Cummins, Joseph. *History's Great Untold Stories: Obscure and Fascinating Accounts with Important Lessons for the World*. London: Pier 9, 2006.

Curtis, Harry, ed. *Fixed Nitrogen*. New York: Chemical Catalog Company, 1932.

Cushman, Gregory Todd. "The Lords of Guano: Science and Management of of Peru's Marine Environment, 1800–1973." Ph.D. diss.: University of Texas at Austin, 2003.

Cziko, Gary. *Without Miracles: Universal Selection Theory and the Second Darwinian Revolution*. Cambridge, Mass.: MIT Press, 1995.

Daily, Gretchen C., ed. *Nature's Services: Societal Dependence on Natural Ecosystems*. Washington, D.C.: Island, 1997.

Dale, Virginia, et al. *Hypoxia in the Northern Gulf of Mexico*. New York: Springer, 2010.

Dalton, John. *A New System of Chemical Philosophy*. London: Strand, 1808.

Danbom, David B. *The Resisted Revolution: Urban America and the Industrialization of Agriculture, 1900–1930*. Ames: Iowa State Press, 1979.

Darley, Gillian. *John Evelyn, Living for Ingenuity*. New Haven: Yale University Press, 2006.

Davidson, W. B., J. L. Doughty, and J. L. Boughton. "Nitrate Poisoning of Livestock." *Canadian Journal of Comparative Medicine and Veterinary Science* 5 (1941): 303–13.

Davies, J. Clarence, and Jan Mazurek. *Pollution Control in the United States: Evaluating the System*. Washington, D.C.: Resources for the Future, 1999.

Davy, Humphry. *Researches, Chemical and Philosophical: Chiefly Concerning Nitrous Oxide, or Dephlogisticated Nitrous Air, and Its Respiration*. London: Johnson, 1800.

Davy, John, ed. *The Collected Works of Sir Humphry Davy*. London: Smith, Elder, 1840.

Dawkins, Richard. *The Selfish Gene*. New York: Oxford University Press, 1976.

Debré, Patrice. *Louis Pasteur*. Translated by Elborg Foster. Baltimore: Johns Hopkins University Press, 2003.

Delaware Department of Natural Resources and Environmental Controls [prepared by Hydroqual]. "Broadkill River Watershed Proposed TMDLs, Delaware." August 2006. htpp://www.dnrec.delaware.gov/swc/wa.

Delaware Tributary Action Team. "The Broadkill River and Watershed Public Forum to Discuss: Your Challenge, Your Choice!" 2006. http://broadkill.ocean.udel.edu/BKBooklet_bw.pdf.

Delwiche, C. C., ed. *Denitrification, Nitrification, and Atmospheric Nitrous Oxide*. New York: Wiley, 1981.

———. "The Nitrogen Cycle." *Scientific American* 223 (1970): 137–46

Deming, W. Edwards. *Out of the Crisis*. Cambridge, Mass.: MIT Center for Advanced Educational Services, 1986.

Denemark, Robert Allen, Jonathan Friedman, Barry K. Gills, and George Modelski, eds. *World System History: The Social Science of Long-Term Change*. New York: Routledge, 2000.

Denham, Tim, and Peter White. *The Emergence of Agriculture: A Global View*. New York: Routledge, 2007.

Denny, Mark. *How the Ocean Works: An Introduction to Oceanography*. Princeton, N.J.: Princeton University Press, 2008.

DeWalt, Billie R. "Appropriate Technology in Rural Mexico: Antecedents and Consequences of an Indigenous Peasant Innovation." *Technology and Culture* 19 (1978): 32–52

Dewey, Scott Hamilton. *Don't Breathe the Air: Air Pollution and U.S. Environmental Politics, 1945–1970*. College Station: Texas A&M University Press, 2000.

Diamond, Jared M. *Guns, Germs, and Steel: The Fates of Human Societies*. New York: Norton, 1997.

Diaz, Robert J., and Rutger Rosenberg. "Spreading Dead Zones and Consequences for Marine Ecosystems," *Science* 321 (2008): 926–29.

Dobbs, Betty Jo Teeter. *The Janus Faces of Genius: The Role of Alchemy in Newton's Thought.* New York: Cambridge University Press, 1991.

Donovan, Arthur. *Antoine Lavoisier: Science, Administration, and Revolution.* New York: Cambridge University Press, 1993.

Dott, Robert H., and Roger L. Batten. *Evolution of the Earth.* New York: McGraw-Hill, 1976.

Dow, Gregory K., Nancy Olewiler, and Clyde G. Reed. "The Transition to Agriculture: Climate Reversals, Population Density, and Technical Change." 2005. Research Papers in Economics. http://repec.org.

Down, Randy D., and Jay H. Lehr, eds. *Environmental Instrumentation and Analysis Handbook.* Hoboken, N.J.: Wiley, 2005.

Dunbar, William Phillips. *Principles of Sewage Treatment.* Translated by H. T. Calvert. London: Griffin, 1908.

DuPuis, E. Melanie, ed. *Smoke and Mirrors: The Politics and Culture of Air Pollution.* New York: New York University Press, 2004.

Durrenberger, Paul E., and Judith E. Martí, eds. *Labor in Cross-Cultural Perspective.* Lanham, Md.: AltaMira, 2005.

Dyson, Freeman. *Origins of Life.* New York: Cambridge University Press, 1985.

Ebrey, Patricia Buckley. *The Cambridge Illustrated History of China.* New York: Cambridge University Press, 1999.

Eddy, Harrison P. "A Comparison of the Activated Sludge and Imhoff Tank-Trickling Filter Processes of Sewage Treatment." *Journal of the Western Society of Engineers* 21 (1916): 816–52.

Ehrlich, Paul. *The Population Bomb.* New York: Ballantine, 1968.

Eigen, Manfred, W. Gardiner, P. Schuster, and R. Winkler-Oswatitsch. "The Origin of Genetic Information." *Scientific American* 244 (1993): 88–92.

Eigen, Manfred. *The Hypercycle: A Principle of Natural Self-Organization.* New York: Springer Verlag, 1979.

Eisenstein, Elizabeth L. *The Printing Press As an Agent of Change: Communications and Cultural Transformations in Early-Modern Europe.* 2 vols. New York: Cambridge University Press, 1979.

Ellis, Carleton, and Alfred Wells. *The Chemical Action of Ultraviolet Rays.* New York: Chemical Catalog Company, 1925.

Ellis, Carleton, Alfred Wells, and Francis F. Heyroth. *The Chemical Action of Ultraviolet Rays,* rev. ed. New York: Reinhold, 1941.

Elser, James J. "A World Awash with Nitrogen." *Science* 334 (2011): 1504–5.

Emiliani, Cesare. *Planet Earth: Cosmology, Geology, and the Evolution of Life and the Environment.* New York: Cambridge University Press, 1992.

Entrikin, J. Nicholas. "Carl O. Sauer, Philosopher in Spite of Himself." *Geographical Review* 74 (1984): 387–408.

Erdkamp, Paul. *The Grain Market in the Roman Empire: A Social, Political, and Economic Study.* New York: Cambridge University Press, 2005.

Ernst, Frank A. *The Fixation of Atospheric Nitrogen.* New York: Van Nostrand, 1928.

Evans, Gillian R. *Philosophy and Theology in the Middle Ages.* New York: Routledge, 1993.

Evelyn, John. A Philosophical Discourse of Earth, Relating to the Culture and Improvement of It for Vegetation, and the Propagation of Plants As It Was Presented to the Royal Society, April 29, 1675. London: Royal Society, 1676.

Fageria, N. K. *Maximizing Crop Yields.* New York: Dekker, 1992.

Falkowski, Paul G. "Evolution of the Nitrogen Cycle and Its Influence on the Biological Sequestration of CO_2 in the Ocean." *Nature* 387 (1997): 272–75.

Falkowski, Paul G., and Linda V. Godfrey. "Electrons, Life, and the Evolution of the World's Oxygen Cycle." *Philosophical Transaction of the Royal Society, Series B, Biological Sciences* 363 (2008): 2705–16.

Farcau, Bruce W. *The Ten Cents War: Chile, Peru, and Bolivia in the War of the Pacific, 1879–1884.* Westport, Conn.: Praeger, 2000.

Farquhar, James, Aubrey L. Zerkle, and Andrey Bekker. "Geological Constraints on the Origin of Oxygenic Photosynthesis." *Photosynthesis Research* 107 (2011): 11–36.

Farrell, Alexander E. "Learning to See the Invisible: Discovery and Measurement of Ozone." *Environmental Monitoring and Assessment* 106 (2005): 59–80.

Fermi, Laura, and Gilberto Bernardini. *Galileo and the Scientific Revolution.* New York: Basic Books, 1961.

Finlay, Mark R. "The German Agricultural Experiment Stations and the Beginnings of American Agricultural Research." *Agricultural History* 62 (1988): 41–50.

———. "The Nitrogen Crisis and Its Miraculous Solution: The Legume Inoculation Industry in the United States." Paper presented to the American Society for Environmental History, Tallahassee, Florida, February 25–March 1, 2009.

Fischbeck, Paul S., and R. Scott Farrow, eds. *Improving Regulation.* Washington, D.C.: Resources for the Future, 2001.

Fosdick, Raymond B. *The Story of the Rockefeller Foundation.* New York: Harper, 1952.

Foss-Mollan, Kate. *Hard Water: Politics and Water Supply in Milwaukee, 1870–1995.* West Lafayette, Ind.: Purdue University Press, 2001.

Fowler, Gilbert J. *An Introduction to the Biochemistry of Nitrogen Conservation.* London: Arnold, 1934.

———. *Sewage Works Analyses.* New York: Wiley, 1902.

Fox, Sidney W., and Klaus Dose. *Molecular Evolution and the Origin of Life.* San Francisco: Freeman, 1972.

Francis, Christopher A., J. Michael Beman, and Marcel M. M. Kuypers. "New Processes and Players in the Nitrogen Cycle: The Microbial Ecology of Anaerobic and Archaeal Ammonia Oxidation." ISME Journal 1 (2007): 19–27.

Friedman, Thomas. *The Lexus and the Olive Tree.* New York: Farrar, Straus, and Giroux, 1999.

Fuller, George W., and James R. McClintock. *Solving Sewage Problems.* New York: McGraw-Hill, 1926.

Fullmer, June Z. *Young Humphry Davy: The Making of an Experimental Chemist.* Philadelphia: America Philosophical Society, 2000.

Fulton, John F. "Sir Kenelm Digby, F.R.S. (1603–1665)." *Notes and Records of the Royal Society of London* 15 (1960): 199–210.

Gagarin, Michael, and David Cohen. *The Cambridge Companion to Ancient Greek Law.* New York: Cambridge University Press, 2005.

Gale, Hoyt S. *Nitrate Deposits.* U.S. Geological Survey Bulletin 523. Washington, D.C.: Government Printing Office, 1912.

Galilei, Galileo. *Dialogues Concerning Two New Sciences.* 1638. Translated by Henry Crew and Alfonso de Salvio. New York: Macmillan, 1914.

Galloway, James N., and Ellis B. Cowling. "Reactive Nitrogen and the World: 200 Years of Change." *Ambio* 31 (2002): 64–71.

Galloway, James N., et al. "Nitrogen Cycles: Past, Present, and Future." *Biogeochemistry* 70 (2004): 153–226.

Galloway, James N., John D. Aber, Jan Willem Erisman, Sybil P. Seitzinger, Robert W. Howarth, Ellis B. Cowling, and B. Jack Cosby. "The Nitrogen Cascade." *Bioscience* 53 (2002): 341–56.

Garvin, Jessica, Roger Buick, Ariel D. Anbar, Gail L. Arnold, and Alan J. Kaufman. "Isotopic Evidence for an Aerobic Nitrogen Cycle in the Latest Archean." *Science* 323 (2009): 1045–48.

Gaukroger, Stephen. *Francis Bacon and the Transformation of Early-Modern Philosophy.* New York: Cambridge University Press, 2001.

Gaus, John M., Leon O. Wolcott, and Verne B. Lewis. *Public Administration and the United States Department of Agriculture.* Chicago: Social Science Research Council, Committee on Public Administration, 1940.

George, Anne. *This One and Magic Life: A Novel of a Southern Family.* New York: Avon, 1999.

Gerard, David, and Lester B. Lave. "Implementing Technology-Forcing Policies: The 1970 Clean Air Act Amendments and the Introduction of Advanced Automotive Emissions Controls in the United States." *Technological Forecasting and Social Change* 72 (2004): 761–78.

Gillispie, Charles C., ed. Dictionary of Scientific Biography. Vol. 5. New York: Scribner, 1970–80.

Gingerich, Owen. "Copernicus and the Impact of Printing." *Vistas in Astronomy* 17 (1975): 201–20.

Glover, Richard. *Peninsular Preparation: The Reform of the British Army, 1795–1809.* New York: Cambridge University Press, 1963.

Godish, Thad. *Air Quality.* Boca Raton, Fla.: CRC, 2004.

Gorman, Hugh S. *Redefining Efficiency: Pollution Concerns, Regulatory Mechanisms, and Technological Change in the U.S. Petroleum Industry.* Akron: University of Akron Press, 2001.

Gorman, Hugh S., and Barry D. Solomon. "The Origins and Practice of Emissions Trading." *Journal of Policy History* 14 (2002): 293–320.

Gower, Barry. *Scientific Method: A Historical and Philosophical Introduction.* New York: Routledge, 1997.

Gray, Chester H. "Nitrogen at Muscle Shoals." *Annals of the American Academy of Political and Social Science* 135 (1928): 166–71.

Greenspan, Frank P., and Paul E. Spoerri. "A Study of Gas Fading of Acetate Dyes." *American Dyestuff Reporter* 30 (1941): 645–50.

Gribben, John. *In Search of the Big Bang: The Life and Death of the Universe.* New York: Penguin, 1998.

Griffin, Keith. *The Political Economy of Agrarian Change: An Essay on the Green Revolution.* New York: Macmillan, 1974.

Griffith, R. O., and A. McKeown. *Photo-Processes in Gaseous and Liquid Systems.* New York: Longmans, Green, 1929.

Grigg, D. B. *The Agricultural Systems of the World: An Evolutionary Approach.* New York: Cambridge University Press, 1974.

Grist, Donald H. *Rice.* London: Longmans, 1953.

Gruber, Nicolas, and James N. Galloway. "An Earth-System Perspective of the Global Nitrogen Cycle." *Nature* 451 (2008): 293–96.

Grula, John W. "Evolution of Photosynthesis and Biospheric Oxygenation Contingent upon Nitrogen Fixation?" *International Journal of Astrobiology* 4 (2005): 251–57.

Guarino, Carmen F. "Sludge Digestion Experiences in Philadelphia." *Journal of the Water Pollution Control Federation* 35 (1963): 626–35.

Guarino, Carmen F., M. D. Nelson, and S. Townsend. "Philadelphia Sludge Disposal in Coastal Waters." *Journal of the Water Pollution Control Federation* 49 (1977): 737–44.

Haagen-Smit, A. J. "Air Conservation." *Science* 128 (1958): 869–78.

———. "Chemistry and Physiology of Los Angeles Smog." *Industrial and Engineering Chemistry* 44 (1952): 1342–46.

Haagen-Smit, A. J., C. E. Bradley, and M. M. Fox. "Ozone Formation in Photochemical Oxidation of Organic Substances." *Industrial and Engineering Chemistry* 45 (1953): 2086–89.

Hackett, Jeremiah, ed. *Medieval Philosophers*. Detroit: Gale, 1992.

Hagen, Joel B. *An Entangled Bank: The Origins of Ecosystem Ecology*. New Brunswick, N.J.: Rutgers University Press, 1992.

Haldane, John, R. H. Makgill, and A. E. Mavrogordato. "The Action As Poisons of Nitrites and Other Physiologically Related Substances." *Journal of Physiology* 21 (1897): 160–89.

Hall, Joan Houston, and Frederic G. Cassidy, eds. *Dictionary of American Regional English*. Vol. I–O. Cambridge, Mass.: Belknap, 1996.

Hallam, H. E., ed. *The Agrarian History of England and Wales*. Vol. 2, *1042–1350*. New York: Cambridge University Press, 1988.

Hammarsten, Olof. *A Text-Book of Physiological Chemistry*. New York: Scientific Press, 1914.

Harrington, Winston, Richard D. Morgenstern, and Thomas Sterner, eds. *Choosing Environmental Policy: Comparing Instruments and Outcomes in the United States and Europe*. Washington, D.C.: Resources for the Future, 2004.

Harris, David Russell, ed. *The Origins and Spread of Agriculture and Pastoralism in Eurasia*. Washington, D.C.: Smithsonian Institution Press, 1996.

Harrison, Fairfax. *Roman Farm Management: The Treatises of Cato and Varro*. New York: Macmillan, 1918.

Hartmann, Alexis F., Anne M. Perley, and Henry L. Barnett. "A Study of Some of the Physiological Effects of Sulfanilamide: II. Methemoglobin Formation and Its Control." *Journal of Clinical Investigation* 17 (1938): 699–710.

Hassan, Fekri A. *Demographic Archaeology*. New York: Academic Press, 1981.

———. "On Mechanisms of Population Growth during the Neolithic." *Current Anthropology* 14 (1973): 535–42.

Hawking, Stephen. *A Brief History of Time: From the Big Bang to Black Holes*. New York: Bantam, 1990.

Hawkins, Jeff, and Sandra Blakeslee. *On Intelligence*. New York: Times Books, 2004.

Haynes, Williams. *American Chemical Industry: A History*. Vol. 2, *1912–1922*. New York: Van Nostrand, 1945.

Hays, Samuel P. *Conservation and the Gospel of Efficiency: The Progressive Conservation Movement, 1890–1920*. Cambridge, Mass.: Harvard University Press, 1959.

———. *The Response to Industrialism, 1885–1914*. Chicago: University of Chicago Press, 1957.

Headrick, Daniel R. *Technology: A World History*. New York: Oxford University Press, 2009.

Heather, Peter J. *The Fall of the Roman Empire: A New History of Rome and the Barbarians*. New York: Oxford University Press, 2005.

Heilbroner, Robert L., and William Milberg. *The Making of Economic Society*. Upper Saddle River, N.J.: Prentice Hall, 2002.

Helferich, Gerard. *Humboldt's Cosmos: Alexander Von Humboldt and the Latin American Journey That Changed the Way We See the World*. New York: Gotham, 2004.

Hermann, Armin. *The Genesis of the Quantum Theory, 1899–1913.* Cambridge, Mass.: MIT Press, 1971.

Herrero, Antonia, and Enrique Flores, eds. *The Cyanobacteria: Microbiology, Genetics, and Evolution.* San Diego: Caister, 2007.

Hester, Ronald E., and Roy M. Harrison, eds. *Air Pollution and Health.* Cambridge: Royal Society of Chemistry, 1998.

Heuss, J. M., G. J. Nebel, and J. M. Colucci, "National Air Quality Standards for Automotive Pollutants: A Critical Review." *Journal of the Air Pollution Control Association* 21 (1971): 535–43.

Heyes, Cecilia, and David L. Hull, eds. *Selection Theory and Social Construction: The Evolutionary Naturalistic Epistemology of Donald T. Campbell.* Albany: State University of New York Press, 2001.

Hicks, Joe, and Grahame Allen. "A Century of Change: Trends in UK Statistics Since 1900." Research paper 99/111. London: House of Commons Library, December 21, 1999.

Hill, Libby. *The Chicago River: A Natural and Unnatural History.* Chicago: Lake Claremont, 2000.

Hill, Michael J. "Nitrate Toxicity: Myth or Reality." *British Journal of Nutrition* 81 (1999): 343–44.

Hilliard, Sam B. "The Dynamics of Power: Recent Trends in Mechanization on the American Farm." *Technology and Culture* 13 (1972): 1–24.

Hirsch, Kenneth L., and Steven Abramovitz. "Clearing the Air: Some Legal Aspects of Interstate Air Pollution Problems." *Duquesne Law Review* 18 (1979–1980): 53–102.

Hoagland, Ralph. "Coloring Matter of Raw and Cooked Salted Meats." *Journal of Agricultural Research* 43 (1914): 211–26.

Holland, H. D. "Geochemistry—Evidence for Life on Earth More Than 3850 Years Ago." *Science* 275 (1997): 38–39.

Holling, C. S., ed. *Adaptive Environmental Assessment and Management.* New York: Wiley, 1978.

Houck, Oliver A. *The Clean Water Act TMDL Program: Law, Policy, and Implementation.* Washington, D.C.: Environmental Law Institute, 1999.

Howard, Sir Albert. *An Agricultural Testament.* New York: Oxford University Press, 1940.

———. *The Soil and Health: A Study of Organic Agriculture.* 1947. Reprint. Lexington: University Press of Kentucky, 2006.

Howard, Sir Albert, and Yeshwant D. Wad. *The Waste Products of Agriculture: Their Utilization As Humus.* New York: Oxford University Press, 1931.

Howard, Louise E. *Sir Albert Howard in India.* London: Faber and Faber, 1953.

Howarth, Robert W., and Roxanne Marino. "Nitrogen As the Limiting Nutrient for Eutrophication in Coastal Marine Systems: Evolving Views over Three Decades." *Limnology and Oceanography* 51 (2006): 364–76.

Hubbard, Preston J. *Origins of the TVA: The Muscle Shoals Controversy, 1920–1932.* New York: Norton, 1961.

Hughes, J. Donald. *Ecology in Ancient Civilizations.* Albuquerque: University of New Mexico Press, 1975.

Husselman, Elinor M. "The Granaries of Karanis." *Transactions and Proceedings of the American Philological Association* 83 (1952): 56–73.

Hutchinson, G. Evelyn. *A Treatise on Limnology.* Vol. 1, *Geography, Physics and Chemistry.* New York: Wiley, 1957.

———. *A Treatise on Limnology.* Vol. 2, *Introduction to Lake Biology and the Limnoplankton.* New York: Wiley, 1967.

Hutton, R. F. *An Appraisal of Research on the Economics of Fertilizer Use.* Report T 55–1. Knoxville: Tennessee Valley Authority, 1955.

Ihde, Aaron John. *The Development of Modern Chemistry.* New York: Dover, 1984.

Jacobson, Mark Z. *Atmospheric Pollution: History, Science, and Regulation.* New York: Cambridge University Press, 2002.

Jarrett, H., ed. *Environmental Quality in a Growing Economy.* Baltimore: Johns Hopkins University Press, 1966.

Johnson, Adam P., H. James Cleaves, Jason P. Dworkin, Daniel P. Glavin, Antonio Lazcano, and Jeffrey L. Bada. "The Miller Volcanic Spark Discharge Experiment." *Science* 17 (2008): 404.

Johnson, Harold S. "Photochemical Oxidation of Hydrocarbons." *Industrial and Engineering Chemistry* 48 (1956): 1489–91.

Johnson, Steven. *The Ghost Map: The Story of London's Most Terrifying Epidemic—and How It Changed Science, Cities, and the Modern World.* New York: Riverhead, 2006.

Jorgensen, Sven Erik, ed. *Global Ecology.* Amsterdam: Elsevier, 2010.

Kagay, Donald J., and L. J. Andrew Villalon, eds. *Crusaders, Condottieri, and Cannon: Medieval Warfare in Societies around the Mediterranean.* Boston: Brill, 2002.

Kannaiyan, Sadasivam, ed. *Biotechnology of Biofertilizers.* Boston: Kluwer, 2002.

Kauffman, Stuart A. *The Origins of Order: Self-Organization and Selection in Evolution.* New York: Oxford University Press, 1993.

Keating, Ann Durkin. *Chicago Neighborhoods and Suburbs: A Historical Guide.* Chicago: University of Chicago Press, 2008.

Keating, Ann Durkin, Eugene P. Moehring, and Joel Tarr. *Infrastructure and Urban Growth in the Nineteenth Century.* Chicago: Public Works Historical Society, 1985.

Kehoe, Terrence. *Cleaning Up the Great Lakes: From Cooperation to Confrontation.* DeKalb: Northern Illinois University, 1997.

Kelly, Jack. *Gunpowder: Alchemy, Bombards, and Pyrotechnic: The History of the Explosive That Changed the World.* New York: Basic Books, 2004.

Kinnicutt, Leonard P., C.E.A. Winslow, and R. Winthrop Pratt. *Sewage Disposal.* Boston: Gilson, 1919.

Kirsch, Peter. *The Galleon: The Great Ships of the Armada Era.* London: Conway Maritime, 1990.

Kistiakowsky, George B. *Photochemical Processes.* New York: American Chemical Society, 1928.

Kitsikopoulos, Harry. "Convertible Husbandry vs. Regular Common Fields: A Model on the Relative Efficiency of Medieval Field Systems." *Journal of Economic History* 64 (2004): 462–99.

Klein, Richard M., Sue Adamowicz, Timothy D. Perkins, and Heiko Liedeker. "Precipitation As a Source of Assimilable Nitrogen: A Historical Survey." *American Journal of Botany* 75 (1988): 928–37.

Klotz, Martin G. "Nitrifier Genomics and the Evolution of the Nitrogen Cycle." *FEMS Microbiology Letters* 278 (2008): 146–56.

Knight, David. *Humphry Davy: Science and Power.* New York: Cambridge University Press, 1998.

Knud-Hansen, Chris. "Historical Perspective of the Phosphate Detergent Conflict." Working paper 94–54. Boulder, Colo.: Conflict Research Consortium, February 1994.

Koeve, W., and P. Kahler. "Heterotrophic Denitrification vs. Autotrophic Anammox— Quantifying Collateral Effects on the Oceanic Carbon Cycle." *Biogeosciences Discussions* 7 (2010): 1813–37.

Konhauser, Kurt O., Stefan V. Lalonde, Larry Amskold, and Heinrich D. Holland. "Was There Really an Archean Phosphate Crisis?" *Science* 2 (2007): 1234.

Korten, David C. *When Corporations Rule the World.* West Hartford, Conn.: Kumarian, 1995.

Krier, James E., and Edmund Ursin. *Pollution and Policy: A Case Essay on California and Federal Experience with Motor Vehicle Air Pollution, 1940–1975.* Berkeley: University of California Press, 1977.

Kuhn, Thomas S. *The Copernican Revolution: Planetary Astronomy in the Development of Western Thought.* Cambridge, Mass.: Harvard University Press, 1957.

Kuiper, G. P., ed. *The Solar System.* Vol. 3, *The Earth As a Planet.* Chicago: University of Chicago Press, 1954.

Kyōka, Kokusai Shokuryō Nōgyō. *Agriculture in Japan.* Tokyo: Japan FAO Association, 1958.

Lal, Deepak. *Unintended Consequences: The Impact of Factor Endowments, Culture, and Politics on Long-Run Economic Performance.* Cambridge, Mass.: MIT Press, 2001.

Lamb, John. *The I&M Canal: A Corridor in Time.* Romeoville, Ill.: Lewisville University, 1987.

Lamer, Mirko. *The World Fertilizer Economy.* Stanford, Calif.: Stanford University Press, 1957.

Lawes, John Bennet. *The Rothamsted Memoirs on Agricultural Chemistry and Physiology.* Vol. 1, *Containing Reports of Field Experiments on Vegetation, Published 1847–1863 Inclusive.* London: Clowes, 1893.

Layton, Edwin. "Mirror-Image Twins: The Communities of Science and Technology in 19th- Century America." *Technology and Culture* 12 (1971): 562–80.

LeConte, Joseph. *Instruction for the Manufacture of Saltpetre.* Columbia: South Carolina Executive Council, 1862.

Lee, Richard B., and Richard Daly, eds. *The Cambridge Encyclopedia of Hunters and Gatherers.* New York: Cambridge University Press, 1999.

Leicester, Henry M. *The Historical Background of Chemistry.* New York: Wiley, 1956.

Leigh, G. J. *The World's Greatest Fix: A History of Nitrogen and Agriculture.* New York: Oxford University Press, 2004.

Leighton, Philip A. *Photochemistry of Air Pollution.* New York: Academic Press, 1961.

Levere, Trevor H. *Transforming Matter: A History of Chemistry from Alchemy to the Buckyball.* Baltimore: Johns Hopkins University Press, 2001.

L'hirondel, J., and J. L. L'hirondel. *Nitrate and Man: Toxic, Harmless, or Beneficial.* New York: CABI, 2002.

Liebig, Justus [von]. *Chemistry in Its Application to Agriculture and Physiology.* Edited by Lyon Playfair. Cambridge: Owen, 1842.

Likens, Gene E., ed. *Some Perspectives of the Major Biogeochemical Cycles.* New York: SCOPE, 1981.

Limburg, Karin E. "The Biogeochemistry of Strontium: A Review of H. T. Odum's Contributions." *Ecological Modelling* 178 (2004): 31–33.

Linden, Stanton J., ed. *The Alchemy Reader: From Hermes Trismegistus to Isaac Newton.* New York: Cambridge University Press, 2003.

Liroff, Richard A. *Reforming Air Pollution Regulation: The Toil and Trouble of EPA's Bubble.* Washington, D.C.: Conservation Foundation, 1986.

Littman, F. E., H. W. Ford, and N. Endow. "Formation of Ozone in the Los Angeles Atmo-
    sphere." *Industrial and Engineering Chemistry* 48 (1956): 1492–97.
Long, Pamela O. *Openness, Secrecy, Authorship: Technical Arts and the Culture of Knowledge
    from Antiquity to the Renaissance.* Baltimore: Johns Hopkins University Press, 2001.
Longhurst, James. "1 to 100: Creating an Air Quality Index in Pittsburgh." *Environmental
    Monitoring and Assessment* 106 (2005): 27–42.
Loomis, R. S., and D. J. Conner. *Crop Ecology: Productivity and Management in Agricultural
    Systems.* New York: Cambridge University Press, 2011.
Lopez-Garcia, D. M., E. Douzery, P. Forterre, M. Van Zuilen, P. Claeys, and D. Prieur.
    "Ancient Fossil Record and Early Evolution (ca. 3.8 to 0.5 Ga)." *Earth, Moon, and
    Planets* 98 (2006): 247–90.
Ludwig, Donald. "Limitations of Economic Valuation of Ecosystems." *Ecosystems* 3
    (2000): 31–35.
Lue-Hing, Cecil, David R. Zenz, and Richard Kuchenrither, eds. *Municipal Sewage Sludge
    Management: Processing, Utilization, and Disposal.* Lancaster, Pa.: Technomic, 1992.
Lurquin, Paul F. *The Origins of Life and the Universe.* New York: Columbia University
    Press, 2003.
Luscombe, David, and Jonathan Riley-Smith, eds. *The New Cambridge Medieval History,*
    Vol. 4, part 2, *c. 1024–c. 1198.* New York: Cambridge University Press, 2004.
Lynn Hopcroft, Rosemary. *Regions, Institutions, and Agrarian Change in European History.*
    Ann Arbor: University of Michigan Press, 1999.
Mäler, Karl-Göran, and Jeffrey R. Vincent, eds. *Handbook of Environmental Economics.* Vol.
    1, *Environmental Degradation and Institutional Responses.* Amsterdam: Elsevier, 2003.
Malthus, Thomas R. *An Essay on the Principle of Population.* 1798. Reprint. New York:
    Penguin, 1986.
Man, John. *Genghis Khan: Life, Death, and Resurrection.* New York: St. Martin's, 2005.
Mancinelli, R. L., and C. P. McKay. "The Evolution of Nitrogen Cycling." *Origins of Life
    and Evolution of the Biosphere* 18 (1988): 311–25.
Margolies, Daniel Stuart. "Guano and the State in British and American Foreign Policy,
    1840–1860." Ph.D. diss., University of Wisconsin–Madison, 1993.
Marsh, George Perkins. *Man and Nature; or, Physical Geography As Modified by Human
    Action.* New York: Scribner, 1865.
Martin, R. S., T. A. Mather, and D. M. Pyle. "Volcanic Emissions and the Early Earth
    Atmosphere." *Geochimicae et Cosmochimica Acta* 71 (2007): 3673–85.
Martin, William H. "Public Policy and Increased Competition in the Synthetic Ammonia
    Industry." *Quarterly Journal of Economics* 73 (1959): 373–92.
Marx, Karl. *Capital: A Critique of Political Economy.* Translated by Samuel Moore and
    Edward Aveling. New York: Cerf, 1906.
Matchett, Karin. "At Odds over Inbreeding: An Abandoned Attempt at Mexico/United
    States Collaboration to 'Improve' Mexican Corn, 1940–1950." *Journal of the History
    of Biology* 39 (2006): 345–72.
Mathew, W. M. "Peru and the British Guano Market, 1840–1870." *Economic History
    Review* 23 (1970): 112–28.
Matossian, Mary Allerton Kilbourne. *Shaping World History: Breakthroughs in Ecology,
    Technology, Science, and Politics.* New York: Sharp, 1997.
Mauskopf, Seymour H. "Gunpowder and the Chemical Revolution." *Osiris* 4 (1988):
    93–118.
McCosh, Frederick W. J. *Boussingault: Chemist and Agriculturist.* Boston: Kluwer, 1984.

McDonald, James M., Michael E. Ollinger, Kenneth E. Nelson, and Charles R. Handy. *Consolidation in U.S. Meatpacking.* Agricultural Economic Report 785. Washington, D.C.: U.S. Department of Agriculture, 2000.

McEvedy, Colin, and Richard Jones. *Atlas of World Population History.* New York: Penguin, 1978.

McIsaac, Gregory, and Mark B. David. "On the Need for Consistent and Comprehensive Treatment of the N Cycle." *Science of the Total Environment* 305 (2003): 249–55.

McKibben, Bill. *The End of Nature.* New York: Random House, 1989.

McNeill, William H. *The Age of Gunpowder Empires, 1450–1800.* Washington, D.C.: American Historical Association, 1989.

Meade, Robert H., ed. *Contaminants in the Mississippi River.* U.S. Geological Survey Circular 1133. Reston, Va., 1995.

Meek, Ronald L. *Marx and Engels on Malthus.* London: Lawrence and Wishart, 1953.

Melillo, Edward D. "Strangers on Familiar Soil: Chile and the Making of California, 1848–1940." Ph.D. diss., Yale University, 2006.

Melosi, Martin V. *The Sanitary City: Urban Infrastructure in America from Colonial Times to the Present.* Baltimore: Johns Hopkins University Press, 2000.

Merchant, Carolyn. *The Death of Nature: Women, Ecology, and the Scientific Revolution.* New York: Harper and Row, 1980.

Merriman, Mansfield. *Elements of Sanitary Engineering.* New York: Mansfield Merriman, 1918.

Meskell, Lynn. *Private Life in New Kingdom Egypt.* Princeton, N.J.: Princeton University Press, 2004.

Metcalf, Leonard, and Harrison P. Eddy. *Sewerage and Sewage Disposal.* New York: McGraw-Hill, 1922.

Metzler, Dwight F., and Howard A. Stoltenberg. "The Public Health Significance of High Nitrate Waters As a Cause of Infant Cyanosis and Methods of Control." *Transactions of the Kansas Academy of Science* 53 (1950): 194–211.

Meyer, Milton W. *A Concise History of China.* Lanham, Md.: Rowman and Littlefield, 1994.

Meyer, R. D., R. A. Olson, and H. F. Rhoades. "Ammonia Losses from Fertilized Nebraska Soils." *Agronomy Journal* 53 (1961): 241–44.

Milburn, William. *Oriental Commerce: Containing a Geographic Description of the Principle Places in the East Indies, China, and Japan with the Produce, Manufacture and Trade.* Vol. 1. London: Black, Parry, 1813.

Miller, Edward, ed. *The Agrarian History of England and Wales.* Vol. 3, 1348–1500. New York: Cambridge University Press, 1991.

Miller, S. L. "A Production of Amino Acids under Possible Primitive Earth Conditions." *Science* 117 (1953): 528.

Mintzer, Irving M., and J. Amber Leonard, eds. *Negotiating Climate Change: The Inside Story of the Rio Convention.* New York: Cambridge University Press, 1994.

Mississippi River/Gulf of Mexico Watershed Nutrient Task Force. "Action Plan for Reducing, Mitigating, and Controlling Hypoxia in the Northern Gulf of Mexico and Improving Water Quality in the Mississippi River Basin." January 2001. http://www.epa.gov/owow/msbasin/pdf/actionplan2001.pdf.

Mississippi River/Gulf of Mexico Watershed Nutrient Task Force. "Gulf Hypoxia Action Plan 2008 for Reducing, Mitigating, and Controlling Hypoxia in the Northern Gulf of Mexico and Improving Water Quality in the Mississippi River Basin." June 2008. http://water.epa.gov/type/watersheds/named/msbasin/actionplan.cfm.

Moore, G. E., and Morris Katz. "The Concurrent Determination of Sulfur Dioxide and Nitrogen Dioxide in the Atmosphere." *Journal of the Air Pollution Control Association* 7 (1957): 25–28.

Morgan, G. B. "New and Improved Procedures for Gas Sampling and Analysis in the National Air Sampling Network." *Journal of the Air Pollution Control Association* 17 (1967): 300–34.

Morris, Peter J. T., ed. *From Classical to Modern Chemistry: The Instrumental Revolution.* Cambridge: Royal Society of Chemistry, 2002.

Morris, R. J. *Cholera, 1832: The Social Response to an Epidemic.* New York: Holmes and Meier, 1976.

Mosier, Arvin R., J. Keith Syers, and John R. Freney, eds. *Agriculture and the Nitrogen Cycle: Assessing the Impacts of Fertilizer Use on Food Production and the Environment.* Washington, D.C.: Island, 2004.

Motavalli, Jim. *Forward Drive: The Race to Build "Clean" Cars for the Future.* San Francisco: Sierra Club Books, 2001.

Mulder, A. A., A. A. van de Graaf, L. A. Robertson, and J. G. Kuenen. "Anaerobic Ammonium Oxidation Discovered in a Denitrifying Fluidized Bed Reactor." *FEMS Microbiology Ecology* 16 (1995): 177–184.

Multhauf, Robert P. "The French Crash Program for Saltpeter Production, 1776–94." *Technology and Culture* 12 (1971): 163–81.

———. "Sal Ammoniac: A Case History in Industrialization." *Technology and Culture* 6 (1965): 569–86.

Murowchick, Robert E. *China: Ancient Culture, Modern Land.* Norman: University of Oklahoma Press, 1994.

Naoum, Phokion. *Nitroglycerine and Nitroglycerine Explosives.* Translated by E. M. Symmes. Las Vegas: Angriff, 1928.

National Academy of Sciences. *Eutrophication: Causes, Consequences, Correctives.* Washington, D.C.: National Academy of Sciences, 1969.

———. *Proceedings of the Seventh Annual Meeting of the Agricultural Research Institute, Oct. 13–14, 1958.* Publication 644. Washington, D.C.: National Academy of Sciences/National Research Council, 1958.

National Science and Technology Council, Committee on Environment and Natural Resources. *An Integrated Assessment of Hypoxia in the Northern Gulf of Mexico.* May 2000. http://oceanservice.noaa.gov/.

Naughton, Michael C. "Establishing Interstate Markets for Emissions Trading of Ozone Precursors: The Case of the Northeast Ozone Transport Commission and the Northeast States for Coordinated Air Use Management Emissions Trading Proposals." *New York University Environmental Law Journal* 3 (1994–95): 195–228.

Navarro-González, Rafael, Christopher P. McKay, and Delphine N. Mvondo. "A Possible Nitrogen Crisis for Archaean Life Due to Reduced Nitrogen Fixation by Lightning." *Nature* 412 (2001): 61–64.

Needham, Joseph. *Science and Civilisation in China.* Vol. 4, *Physics and Physical Technology.* Part 2, *Mechanical Engineering.* New York: Cambridge University Press, 1985.

Needham, Joseph, and Francesca Bray. *Science and Civilisation in China.* Vol. 6, *Biology and Biological Technology.* Part 2, *Agriculture.* New York: Cambridge University Press, 1984.

Needham, Joseph, and Peter Golas. *Science and Civilisation in China.* Vol. 5, *Chemistry and Chemical Technology.* Part 13, *Chemistry and Chemical Technology, Mining.* New York: Cambridge University Press, 1999.

Needham, Joseph, Ho Ping-Yu, Lu Gwei-djen, and Wang Ling. *Science and Civilisation in China*. Vol. 5, *Military Technology*. Part 7, *The Gunpowder Epic*. New York: Cambridge University Press, 1986.

Nei, Masatoshi, and Richard K. Koehn, eds. *Evolution of Genes and Proteins*. Sunderland, Mass.: Sinauer Associates, 1983.

Nelson, L. B., and R. E. Uhland. "Factors That Influence Loss of Fall Applied Fertilizers and Their Probable Importance in Different Parts of the United States." *Soil Science Society of America Proceeding* 19 (1955): 492–96.

Nelson, M. D., and C. F. Guarino, "New Philadelphia Story Being Written by Pollution-Control Division." *Water and Wastes Engineering* 14 (1977): 22.

Nesbit, J .C. *On Agricultural Chemistry and the Nature and Properties of Peruvian Guano*. London: Longman, 1856.

Newman, William R., and Anthony Grafton, eds. *Secrets of Nature: Astrology and Alchemy in Early Modern Europe*. Cambridge, Mass.: MIT Press, 2006.

Newman, William R., and Lawrence M. Principe. *Alchemy Tried in the Fire: Starkey, Boyle, and the Fate of Helmontian Chymistry*. Chicago: University of Chicago Press, 2002.

Newton, W., and C. J. Nyman, eds. *Proceedings of the First International Symposium on Nitrogen Fixation*. Vol. 2. Pullman: University of Washington Press, 1975.

Nicholson, Paul, and Ian Shaw, eds. *Ancient Egyptian Material and Technologies*. New York: Cambridge University Press, 2000.

Niklas, Karl J. *The Evolutionary Biology of Plants*. Chicago: University of Chicago Press, 1997.

Nisbet, Euan, and C. Mary R. Fowler. "The Evolution of the Atmosphere in the Archaean and Early Proterozoic." *Chinese Society Bulletin* 56 (2011): 4–13

Nitecki, Matthew H., and Doris V. Nitecki, eds. *Origins of Anatomically Modern Humans*. New York: Plenum, 1994.

Nordenskiold, Erik. *The History of Biology*. New York: Tutor, 1928.

Noyes, William A., Jr., and Philip A. Leighton. *The Photochemistry of Gases*. New York: Reinhold, 1941.

Odum, Eugene P. *Fundamentals of Ecology*. Philadelphia: Saunders, 1953.

Ogilvie, Sheilagh C., and Markus Cerman, eds. *European Proto-Industrialization: An Introductory Handbook*. New York: Cambridge University Press, 1996.

O'Jones, Charles. *Clean Air: The Policy and Politics of Pollution Control*. Pittsburgh: University of Pittsburgh Press, 1975.

Okaichi, Tomotoshi, Donald M Anderson, and Takahisa Nemoto, eds. *Red Tides: Biology, Environmental Science, and Toxicology*. New York: Elsevier, 1989.

O'Keefe, M. Timothy. *Seasonal Guide to the Natural Year—Florida, with Georgia and Alabama Coasts: A Month by Month Guide to Natural Events*. Golden, Colo.: Fulcrum, 1996.

Outwater, Alice B., and Berrin Tansel. *Reuse of Sludge and Minor Wastewater Residuals*. Boca Raton, Fla.: Lewis, 1994.

Overton, Mark. *Agricultural Revolution in England: The Transformation of the Agrarian Economy, 1500–1850*. New York: Cambridge University Press, 1996.

Padmanabhan, Thanu. *After the First Three Minutes: The Story of Our Universe*. New York: Cambridge University Press, 1998.

Page, Denys Lionel. *The Santorini Volcano and the Desolation of Minoan Crete*. London: Society for the Promotion of Greek Studies, 1970.

Pagiola, Stefano, Joshua Bishop, and Natasha Landell-Mills, eds. *Selling Forest Environmental Services: Market-Based Mechanisms for Conservation*. Sterling, Va.: Earthscan, 2002.

Parker, Geoffrey. *The Military Revolution: Military Innovation and the Rise of the West.* New York: Cambridge University Press, 1988)

Parson, Edward. *Protecting the Ozone Layer: Science and Strategy.* New York: Oxford University Press, 2003.

Partington, J. R. *A History of Greek Fire and Gunpowder.* 1960. Reprint. Baltimore: Johns Hopkins University Press, 1999.

Pearse, Langdon, ed. *Modern Sewage Disposal.* New York: Federation of Sewer Works Associations, 1938.

Perkins, John H. *Geopolitics and the Green Revolution: Wheat, Genes, and the Cold War.* New York: Oxford University Press, 1997.

———. "The Rockefeller Foundation and the Green Revolution, 1941–1956." *Agriculture and Human Values* 7 (1990): 6–18.

Pelouze, Jules, and Edmond Fremy. *General Notions of Chemistry.* Translated by Edmund C. Evans. Philadelphia: Lippincott, 1854.

Planning Committee on Eutrophication. *Report of the Planning Committee on Eutrophication.* Washington, D.C.: National Academy of Sciences/National Research Council, 1965.

Pollan, Michael. *The Omnivore's Dilemma: A Natural History of Four Meals.* New York: Penguin, 2006.

Pomeranz, Kenneth. *The Great Divergence: China, Europe, and the Making of Modern World Economy.* Princeton, N.J.: Princeton University Press, 2000.

Ponting, Clive. *A Green History of the World: The Environment and the Collapse of Great Civilizations.* New York: St. Martin's, 1991.

Poole, Anthony M., and David Penny. "Evaluating Hypotheses for the Origin of Eukaryotes." *BioEssays* 29 (2007): 74–84.

Postan, M. M., ed. The Cambridge Economic History of Europe from the Decline of the Roman Empire. Vol. 1, Agrarian Life of the Middle Ages. New York: Cambridge University Press, 1966.

Postgate, John. *Nitrogen Fixation.* New York: Cambridge University Press, 1998.

Powlson, David S., Tom M. Addiscott, Nigel Benjamin, Ken G. Cassman, Theo M. de Kok, Hans van Grinsven, Jean-Louis L'hirondel, Alex A. Avery, and Chris van Kessel. "When Does Nitrate Become a Risk for Humans?" *Journal of Environmental Quality* 37 (2008): 291–95.

Prakash, Aseem, and Matthew Potoski. *The Voluntary Environmentalists: Green Clubs, ISO 14001, and Voluntary Environmental Regulations.* New York: Cambridge University Press, 2006.

Preston, Thomas. *The Theory of Light.* London: Macmillan, 1901.

Rahman, Mustafizur, Azit Kumar Podder, Charles van Hove, Z. N. Tahmida Begum, Thierry Heulin, and Anton Hartmann, eds. *Biological Nitrogen Fixation Associated with Rice Production.* Boston: Kluwer, 1996.

Randall, Robert E., and Lynn Pokryfki. "Nearshore Hypoxia in the Bottom Water of the Northwestern Gulf of Mexico from 1981–1984." *Marine Environmental Research* 22 (1987): 75–90.

Raymond, Jason, Janet L. Siefert, Christopher R. Staples, and Robert E. Blankenship. "The Natural History of Nitrogen Fixation." *Molecular Biology and Evolution* 21 (2004): 541–54.

Read, John. *Explosives.* Harmondsworth, Eng.: Penguin, 1943.

———. *From Alchemy to Chemistry.* 1955. Reprint. Mineola, N.Y.: Dover, 1995.

Rees, William E. "How Should a Parasite Value Its Host?" *Ecological Economics* 25 (1998): 49–52.

Reitze, Arnold W., Jr. *Air Pollution Control Law: Compliance and Enforcement.* Washington, D.C.: Environmental Law Institute, 2001.

———. *Stationary Source Air Pollution Law.* Washington, D.C.: Environmental Law Institute, 2005.

Renard, Maurice L. "Annotated Bibliography on Hypoxia and Its Effects on Marine Life, with Emphasis on the Gulf of Mexico." NOAA Technical Report NMFS 21. February 1985.

Reynolds, Terry. *Stronger Than a Hundred Men: A History of the Vertical Water Wheel.* Baltimore: Johns Hopkins University Press, 1983.

Richter, Daniel D., Jr., and Daniel Markewitz. *Understanding Soil Change: Soil Sustainability over Millennia, Centuries, and Decades.* New York: Cambridge University Press, 2001.

Riley-Smith, Jonathan. *The Crusades: A History.* New Haven: Yale University Press, 2005.

Rindos, David. *The Origins of Agriculture: An Evolutionary Perspective.* Orlando, Fla.: Academic Press, 1984.

Rindt, D. W., G. M. Blouin, and J. G. Getsinger. "Sulfur Coating on Nitrogen Fertilizer to Reduce Dissolution Rate." *Journal of Agricultural Food Chemistry* 16 (1968): 773–78.

Robinson, Elmer, and Robert C. Robbins. "Gaseous Nitrogen Compounds from Urban and Natural Sources." *Journal of the Air Pollution Control Association* 20 (1970): 303–6.

Robert, Joseph C. *Ethyl: A History of a Corporation and the People Who Made It.* Charlottesville: University of Virginia Press, 1983.

Robertson, H. E., and W. A. Riddell. "Cyanosis of Infants Produced by High Nitrate Concentration in Rural Waters of Saskatchewan." *Canadian Journal of Public Health* 40 (1949): 72–77.

Rodale, Robert. "Who Pays for Agricultural Research?" *Organic Gardening and Farming* 1 (1954): 16–20.

Rogers, Lewis H., Nicholas A. Renzetti, and Morris Nieburger. "Smog Effects and the Chemical Analysis of the Los Angeles Atmosphere." *Journal of the Air Pollution Control Association* 6 (1956): 165–70.

Rome, Adam W. *The Bulldozer in the Countryside: Suburban Sprawl and the Rise of American Environmentalism.* New York: Cambridge University Press, 2001.

Roscoe, Henry E. *John Dalton and the Rise of Modern Chemistry.* New York: Macmillan, 1895.

Rossano, August T., Jr. "The Joint City, County, State, and Federal Study of Air Pollution in Louisville." *Journal of the Air Pollution Control Association* 6 (1956): 176–79.

Rossi, Paolo. *Francis Bacon: From Magic to Science.* Translated by Sacha Rabinovitch. Chicago: University of Chicago Press, 1978.

Rowe, F. M., and K.A.J. Chamberlain. "The Fading of Dyeings on Cellulose Acetate Rayon." *Journal of the Society of Dyers and Colourists* 53 (1937): 268–378.

Rowe, Gilbert T., C. Hovey Clifford, and K. L. Smith. "Benthic Nutrient Regeneration and Its Coupling to Primary Productivity in Coastal Waters." *Nature* 255 (1975): 215–17.

Rubin, Edward S., Sonia Yeh, and David Hounshell. "Technology Innovations and Experience Curves for Nitrogen Oxides Control Technologies." *Journal of Air and Waste Management Association* 55 (2005): 1827–38.

Ruhl, J. B., Steven E. Kraft, and C. L. Lant. *The Law and Policy of Ecosystem Services.* Washington: D.C.: Island, 2007.

Russell, Edward John. *Soil Conditions and Plant Growth*. London: Longmans, Green, 1917.

Russell, W.M.S. "Population, Swidden Farming and the Tropical Environment." *Population and Environment* 10 (1988): 77–94.

Rutherford, William, Arthur Gamgee, and Thomas Fraser. "Report on the Progress of Physiology." *Journal of Anatomy and Physiology* 2 (1868): 177–93.

Ruttan, Vernon W., and Yujiro Hayami. "Technology Transfer and Agricultural Development." *Technology and Culture* 14 (1973): 119–51.

Sachs, Julius. *History of Botany, 1530–1860*. Oxford: Clarendon, 1890.

Salvin, V. S., W. D. Paist, and W. J. Myles. "Advances in Theoretical and Practical Studies of Gas Fading." *American Dyestuff Reporter* 41 (1952): 297–302.

Samuels, Warren J. *Erasing the Visible Hand: Essays on an Elusive and Misused Concept in Economics*. New York: Cambridge University Press, 2011.

Sargent, Rose-Mary. *The Diffident Naturalist: Robert Boyle and the Philosophy of Experiment*. Chicago: University of Chicago Press, 1995.

Scharf, Peter C., and John A. Lory. "Best Management Practices for Nitrogen Fertilizer in Missouri." Publication IPM1027. Columbia: University of Missouri Extension Service, 2006.

Schellen, Heinrich. *Spectrum Analysis in Its Application to Terrestrial Substances*. New York: Appleton, 1872.

Schepers, J. S., and W. R. Raun, eds. *Nitrogen in Agricultural Systems*. Madison, Wisc.: American Society of Agronomy, 2008.

Schrader-Frechette, Kristin, and Laura Westra, eds. *Technology and Values*. Lanham, Md.: Rowman and Littlefield, 1977.

Schumacher, E. F. *Small Is Beautiful: Economics As If People Mattered*. New York: Perennial, 1973.

Schwartz, A. S. "Methemoglobinemia of Unknown Origin in a Two-Week-Old Infant." *American Journal of Diseases of Children* 60 (1940): 652–59.

Seccombe, Wally. *A Millennium of Family Change: Feudalism to Capitalism in Northwestern Europe*. New York: Verso, 1992.

Seckbach, Joseph, ed. *Symbiosis: Mechanisms and Model Systems*. Dordrecht, the Netherlands: Kluwer, 2002.

Selznick, Philip. *TVA and the Grass Roots: A Study in the Sociology of Formal Organizations*. Berkeley: University of California Press, 1949.

Service, Elman R. *Profiles in Ethnology: A Revision of a Profile of Primitive Culture*. New York: Harper and Row, 1963.

Shy, Carl M., J. P. Creason, M. E. Pearlman, K. E. McClain, F. B. Benson, and M. M. Young. "The Chattanooga Schoolchildren Study: I. Methods, Description of Pollutant Exposure and Results of Ventilatory Functions Testing." *Journal of the Air Pollution Control Association* 20 (1970): 539–45

Shy, Carl M., J. P. Creason, M. E. Pearlman, K. E. McClain, F. B. Benson, and M. M. Young. "The Chattanooga Schoolchildren Study: II. Incidence of Acute Respiratory Illness." *Journal of the Air Pollution Control Association* 20 (1970): 582–88

Simon, Julian. *The Ultimate Resource II*. Princeton, N.J.: Princeton University Press, 1996.

Skinner, G. William. *The City in Late Imperial China*. Stanford, Calif.: Stanford University Press, 1977.

Slater, J. W. *Sewage Treatment, Purification, and Utilization*. London: Whittaker, 1888.

Smil, Vaclav. "Eating Meat: Evolution, Patterns, and Consequences." *Population and Development Review* 28 (2002): 599–639.

———. *Energy in Nature and Society: General Energetics of Complex Systems.* Cambridge, Mass.: MIT Press, 2008.

———. *Enriching the Earth: Fritz Haber, Carl Bosch, and the Transformation of World Food Production.* Cambridge, Mass: MIT Press, 2001.

Smith, Bruce. *The Emergence of Agriculture.* New York: Scientific American Library, 1995.

Smith, G. Carlton. *TNT: Trinitrotoluenes and Mono- and Dinitrotoluenes, Their Manufacture and Properties.* New York: Van Nostrand, 1918.

Smith, Harold M. "Composition of United States Crude Oils." *Industrial and Engineering Chemistry* 44 (1952): 2577–85.

Smith, J. Maynard. *The Theory of Evolution.* Harmondsworth: Penguin, 1966.

Smith, Keith, ed. *Nitrous Oxide and Climate Change.* Washington, D.C.: Earthscan, 2010.

Snow, John. "On the Mode of Communication of Cholera." 1854. Excerpted and adapted as *Snow on Cholera.* New York: Hafner, 1965.

Snyder, Caroline. "The Dirty Work of Promoting 'Recycling' of America's Sewage Sludge." *International Journal of Occupational and Environmental Health* 11 (205): 415–27.

Sprent, Janet I. *The Ecology of the Nitrogen Cycle.* New York: Cambridge University Press, 1987.

Stanford Research Institute. *The Smog Problem in Los Angeles County: Report on the First Twelve Months of Research.* Los Angeles: Western Oil and Gas Association, 1948.

———. *The Smog Problem in Los Angeles County: A Report on Studies to Determine the Nature and Causes of Smog.* Los Angeles: Western Oil and Gas Association, 1954.

———. *The Smog Problem in Los Angeles County: Second Interim Report on Studies to Determine the Nature and Sources of the Smog.* Los Angeles: Western Oil and Gas Association, 1949.

Stauber, John C., and Sheldon Rampton. *Toxic Sludge Is Good For You: Lies, Damn Lies, and the Public Relations Industry.* Monroe, Me.: Common Courage, 1995.

Stearns, Peter N. *The Industrial Revolution in World History.* Boulder, Colo.: Westview, 1993.

Steel, Ernest W. *Water Supply and Sewerage.* New York: McGraw-Hill, 1960.

Stephens, Hugh W. *The Texas City Disaster.* Austin: University of Texas Press, 1997.

Stephens, Edgar R., Philip L. Hanst, Robert C. Doerr, and William E. Scott. "Reactions of Nitrogen Oxide and Organic Compounds in Air." *Industrial and Engineering Chemistry* 48 (1956): 1498–1504.

Stewart, W.D.P. "Biological and Ecological Aspects of Nitrogen Fixation by Free-Living Micro-Organisms." *Proceedings of the Royal Society of London, Series B, Biological Sciences* 172 (1969): 367–88.

Stoltzenberg, Dietrich. *Fritz Haber: Chemist, Nobel Laureate, German, Jew.* Philadelphia: Chemical Heritage Press, 2005.

Strack, Hermann L., and Gunter Stemberger. *Introduction to the Talmud and Midrash.* New York: Meridian, 1959.

Stradling, David. *Smokestacks and Progressives: Environmentalists, Engineers, and Air Quality in America, 1881–1951.* Baltimore: Johns Hopkins University Press, 1999.

Steuart, William Mott. *Manufacturers, 1905.* Part 4, *Special Report on Selected Industries.* Washington, D.C.: U.S. Bureau of the Census, 1908.

Style, D.W.G. *Photochemistry.* New York: Dutton, 1930.

Surovell, T. A. "Early Paleoindian Women, Children, Mobility, and Fertility." *American Antiquity* 65 (2000): 493–508.

Szabadváry, Ferenc. *History of Analytical Chemistry.* Translated by Gyula Svehla. Langhorn, Pa.: Gordon and Breach, 1992.

Takekoshi, Yosaburō. *The Economic Aspects of the History of the Civilization of Japan.* Vol. 3. New York: Routledge, 2004.

Tarling, Nicholas, ed. *The Cambridge History of Southeast Asia.* Vol. 1, *From Early Times to c.1500.* New York: Cambridge University Press, 1993.

Tarr, Joel A., ed. *Devastation and Renewal: An Environmental History of Pittsburgh and Its Region.* Pittsburgh: University of Pittsburgh Press, 2005.

———. *The Search for the Ultimate Sink: Urban Pollution in Historical Perspective.* Akron, Ohio: University of Akron Press, 1996.

Tarté, Rodrigo P. *Picnic con Hormigas: Reflexiones Sobre Gestión del Conocimiento y Desarrollo (Sostenible).* Panama City: Fundación Cidudad del Saber, 2006.

Tattersall, Ian. *The World from Beginnings to 4000 b.c.e.* New York: Oxford University Press, 2008.

Taylor, Peter J. "Technocratic Optimism, H. T. Odum, and the Partial Transformation of Ecological Metaphor after World War II." *Journal of the History of Biology* 21 (1988): 213–44.

Teich, Albert, ed. *Technology and the Future.* New York: St. Martin's, 2008.

Thatcher, Oliver J., and Edgar Holmes McNeal, eds. *A Source Book for Medieval History.* New York: Scribner, 1905.

Thirsk, Joan, ed., *The Agrarian History of England and Wales.* Vol. 5, *1500–1750.* New York: Cambridge University Press, 1991.

Thomas, M. D., J. A. MacLeod, R. C. Robbins, R. C. Goettelman, R. W. Eldridge, and L. H. Rogers. "Automatic Apparatus for Determining of Nitric Oxide and Nitrogen Dioxide in the Atmosphere." *Analytical Chemistry* 28 (1956): 1810–19.

Thompson, F.M.L. "The Second Agricultural Revolution, 1815–1880." *Economic History Review* 21 (1968): 62–77.

Tidy, C. M. "The Process for Determining the Organic Purity of Potable Waters." *Journal of the Chemical Society* 35 (1879): 46–106.

Tranel, Mark. *St. Louis Plans: The Ideal and the Real St. Louis.* Saint Louis: Missouri Historical Society, 2007.

Trigger, Bruce G. *Understanding Early Civilizations.* New York: Cambridge University Press, 2003.

Troeh, Frederick R., and Louis M. Thompson. *Soils and Soil Fertility.* New York: Blackwell, 2005.

Tuan, Yi-Fu. *A Historical Geography of China.* Piscataway, N.J.: Aldine Transaction, 2008.

Turner, M. E., J. V. Beckett, and B. Afton, *Agricultural Rent in England, 1690–1914.* New York: Cambridge University Press, 2004.

Turner, R. Eugene, and Nancy N. Rabalais. "Changes in Mississippi River Water Quality This Century." *Bioscience* 41 (1991): 140–47.

Turner, R. Eugene, Nancy N. Rabalais, E. M. Swenson, M. Kasprzak, and T. Romaire. "Summer Hypoxia in the Northern Gulf of Mexico and Its Prediction from 1978 to 1995." Marine Environmental Research 59 (2005): 65–77.

Tyndall, John. *New Fragments.* London: Longmans, Green, 1892.

Uekoetter, Frank. "The Strange Career of the Ringelmann Smoke Chart." *Environmental Monitoring and Assessment* 106 (2005): 11–26.

U.S. Congress, Joint Committee on Muscle Shoals. *Leasing of Muscle Shoals.* 69th Cong, 1st sess., 1926.

U.S. Department of Agriculture. *Land: The 1958 Yearbook of Agriculture.* Washington, D.C.: Government Printing Office, 1958.

———. *Soil: 1957 Yearbook of Agriculture*. Washington, D.C.: Government Printing Office: 1957.

———. *Yearbook of the U.S. Department of Agriculture*. Washington, D.C.: Government Printing Office, 1914.

———. *Yearbook of the U.S. Department of Agriculture*. Washington, D.C.: Government Printing Office, 1915.

U.S. Environmental Protection Agency. *Air Quality Criteria for Nitrogen Oxides*. Air Pollution Control Office Publication AP-84. Washington, D.C.: Government Printing Office, 1971.

———. *Air Quality Criteria for Oxides of Nitrogen*. Report EPA600/8–91/049aF. Washington, D.C.: Government Printing Office, 1993.

———. *NPDES Permit Writers' Manual*. EPA-833-B-96-003. Washington, D.C.: U.S. Environmental Protection Agency, 1996.

U.S. Public Health Service. *Drinking Water Standards*. Washington, D.C.: U.S. Department of Health, Education, and Welfare, 1962.

———. "National Conference on Air Pollution, November 20, 1958: Report and Recommendation of Discussion Groups." *Journal of the Air Pollution Control Association* 9 (1959): 44–50.

U.S. Public Health Service, Division of Air Pollution. *Air Pollution Measurements of the National Air Sampling Network*. Washington, D.C.: U.S. Department of Health Education and Welfare, 1958.

U.S. House of Representatives, Committee on Military Affairs. *Muscle Shoals Propositions*. 67th Cong., 2nd sess., 1922.

U.S. House of Representatives, Subcommittee on National Security Policy and Scientific Developments. *The Green Revolution: Symposium on Science and Foreign Policy*. 91st Cong., 2nd sess., 1969.

Van Slyke, Donald D., and Erik Vollmund. "Studies of Methemoglobin Formation." *Journal of Biological Chemistry* 66 (1925): 415–24.

Van Zanden, J. L. "The First Green Revolution: The Growth of Production and Productivity in European Agriculture, 1870–1914." *Economic History Review* 44 (1991): 215–39.

Veblen, Thomas T., Kenneth R. Young, and A. R. Orme. *The Physical Geography of South America*. New York: Oxford University Press, 2007.

Vernadsky, Vladimir I. *The Biosphere*. Translated by David B. Langmuir. Revised and annotated by Mark A. S. McMenamin. New York: Copernicus, 1998.

Vinten-Johansen, Peter. *Cholera, Chloroform, and the Science of Medicine: A Life of John Snow*. New York: Oxford University Press, 2003.

Vitousek, Peter M., John D. Aber, Robert W. Howarth, Gene E. Likens, Pamela A. Matson, David W. Schindler, William H. Schlesinger, and David G. Tilman. "Human Alteration of the Global Nitrogen Cycle: Sources and Consequences." *Ecological Applications* 7 (1997): 737–50.

Vogel, Hermann. *The Chemistry of Light and Photography*. New York: Appleton, 1889.

Vogt, William. *Road to Survival: A Discussion of Food in Relation to the Problem of Growing Population*. New York: Sloane Associates, 1948.

Von Martels, Z.R.W.M, ed. *Alchemy Revisited: Proceedings of the International Conference on the History of Alchemy*. Leiden, the Netherlands: Brill, 1990.

Waeser, Bruno. *The Atmospheric Nitrogen Industry*. Translated by Ernest Fyleman. Philadelphia: Blakiston's Sons, 1936.

Wagner, John A. *Encyclopedia of the Hundred Years War*. Westport, Conn.: Greenwood, 2006.

Wallace, Henry A. "The Engineering-Scientific Approach." Paper delivered before the American Association for the Advancement of Science, Boston, December 29, 1933.

Waller, Philip J. *Town, City, and Nation: England, 1850–1914*. New York: Oxford University Press, 1983.

Wallerstein, Immanuel. The Modern World-System. Vol. 1, Capitalist Agriculture and the Origins of the European World-Economy in the Sixteenth Century. New York: Academic Press, 1974.

———. The Modern World-System. Vol. 2, Mercantilism and the Consolidation of the European World-Economy, 1600–1750. New York: Academic Press, 1980.

Walton, Graham. "Survey of Literature Relating to Infant Methemoglobinemia Due to Nitrate-Contaminated Water." *American Journal of Public Health* 41 (1951): 986–95.

Watt, B., and A. Merill. *Composition of Foods*. Agricultural Handbook 8. Washington, D.C.: U.S. Department of Agriculture, 1975.

Weart, Spencer R. *The Discovery of Global Warming*. Cambridge, Mass.: Harvard University Press, 2003.

Weinberg, Steven. *The First Three Minutes: A Modern View of the Origin of the Universe*. New York: Basic Books, 1993.

Wendel, William B. "The Control of Methemoglobinemia with Methylene Blue." *Journal of Clinical Investigation* 18 (1939): 179–85.

Wetzel, Edward D., and Scott B. Murphy. *Treating Industrial Waste Interferences at Publicly-Owned Treatment Works*. Park Ridge, N.J.: Noyes Data Corporation, 1991.

White, James C., William R. Wagner, and Carole N. Beal, eds. *Global Climate Change Linkages: Acid Rain, Air Quality, and Stratospheric Ozone*. New York: Elsevier, 1989.

White, Leslie A. *The Evolution of Culture: The Development of Civilization to the Fall of Rome*. New York: McGraw-Hill, 1959.

White, Lynn, Jr. *Medieval Technology and Social Change*. Oxford: Clarendon, 1962.

White, Richard. *The Organic Machine: The Remaking of the Columbia River*. New York: Hill and Wang, 1996.

Whitney, Kristoffer. "Living Lawns, Dying Waters: The Suburban Boom, Nitrogenous Fertilizers, and the Nonpoint Source Pollution Dilemma." *Technology and Culture* 51 (2010): 652–74.

Whitton, Brian, and Malcolm Potts, eds. *The Ecology of Cyanobacteria*. Boston: Kluwer, 2000.

Wigelsworth, Jeffrey R. *Science and Technology in Medieval European Life*. Westport, Conn.: Greenwood, 2006.

Wiley, Harvey W. *Principles and Practice of Agricultural Analysis*. Vol. 2, *Fertilizers*. Easton, Pa.: Chemical Publishing Company, 1895.

Willoughby, Pamela R. *The Evolution of Modern Humans in Africa: A Comprehensive Guide*. New York: AltaMira, 2007.

Winiwarter, Verena. "Saltpeter: An Explosive Environmental History in Early Modern Europe." Paper delivered at the American Society of Environmental History's annual conference, Saint Paul, Minn., 2006.

Winslow, C.E.A. "The Scientific Disposal of City Sewage: Historical Development and the Present Status of the Problem." *Technological Quarterly* 28 (1905): 317–32.

Wise, William. *Killer Smog: The World's Worst Air Pollution Disaster*. Chicago: Rand McNally, 1968.

Woodworth, John M. *Cholera Epidemic of 1873 in the United States: The Introduction of Epidemic Cholera through the Agency of the Mercantile Marine: Suggestions of Measures of Prevention.* Washington, D.C.: Government Printing Office, 1875.

World Health Organization, *International Standards for Drinking Water.* Geneva: World Health Organization, 1958.

World Wildlife Fund. *Statewide Wetlands Strategies: A Guide to Protecting and Managing the Resource.* Washington, D.C.: Island, 1992.

Wright, Lawrence. *Clean and Decent: The Fascinating History of the Bathroom and the Water Closet.* New York: Viking, 1960.

Wrigley, Edward A. *Population and History.* New York: McGraw-Hill, 1969.

Wrigley, Edward A., and Roger Schofield. *The Population History of England, 1541–1871: A Reconstruction.* New York: Cambridge University Press, 2002.

Xu, Hui-lian, James F. Parr, and Hiroshi Umemura, eds. *Nature Farming and Microbial Applications.* Binghamton, N.Y: Food Products Press, 2000.

Youngblood, Norman. *The Development of Mine Warfare: A Most Murderous and Barbarous Conduct.* Westport, Conn.: Greenwood, 2006.

Yung, Y. L., and M.C. McElroy. "Fixation of Nitrogen in the Prebiotic Atmosphere." *Science* 203 (1979): 1002–4.

Zaehle, Sonke, Pierre Friedlingstein, and Andrew D. Friend. "Terrestrial Nitrogen Feedbacks May Accelerate Future Climate Change." L01401. *Geophysical Research Letters* 37 (2010): L01401: 1–5.

Zalasiewicz, Jan, et al., "Are We Now Living in the Anthropocene?" *GSA Today* 18 (2008): 4–8.

Zanetti, J. Enrique. *The Significance of Nitrogen.* New York: Chemical Foundation, 1932.

Zhu, Ying, Akira Takeishi, and Seiichiro Yonekura. "The Timing of Technological Innovation: The Case of Automotive Emission Control in the 1970s." 2006. Hitotsubashi University, Institute of Innovation Research. http://www.iir.hit-u.ac.jp/iir-w3/file/WP06–05takeishi.pdf.

Ziman, John, ed. *Technological Innovation As an Evolutionary Process.* New York: Cambridge University Press, 2000.

Zimmer, Charles E., and George A. Jutze. "An Evaluation of Continuous Air Quality Data." *Journal of the Air Pollution Control Association* 14 (1962): 262–66.

Zobell, C. E. "Factors Influencing the Reduction of Nitrates and Nitrites by Bacteria in Semisolid Media." *Journal of Bacteriology* 24 (1932): 273–81.

INDEX

ABOUT THE AUTHOR

HUGH S. GORMAN studies the historical interaction between technological innovation, changes in human uses of the environment, and policy choices, with the goal of informing current policy discussions about sustainability. He is the author of *Redefining Efficiency: Pollution Concerns, Regulatory Mechanisms, and Technological Change in the U.S. Petroleum Industry* and teaches in the energy and environmental policy graduate program at Michigan Technological University. He has a Ph.D. in History and Policy from Carnegie Mellon University.